FEMINIST
CHALLENGES

FEMINIST CHALLENGES

Social and Political Theory

Edited by
Carole Pateman and Elizabeth Gross

The Northeastern Series in Feminist Theory
Northeastern University Press
BOSTON

Published in North America by Northeastern University
Press, 1987
Published in Australia by Allen & Unwin Australia,
1986

Library of Congress Cataloging in Publication Data
Feminist Challenges.
  (The Northeastern series in feminist theory)
  Bibliography: p.
  1. Feminism—Philosophy. 2. Feminism.
I. Pateman, Carole. II. Gross, Elizabeth. III. Series.
HQ1154.F4455   1986   305.4'2'01
86—8512
ISBN 1—55553—003—6
ISBN 1—55553—004—4 (pbk.)

Composed in Sabon by Graphicraft Typesetters Ltd,
Hong Kong
Printed in Hong Kong

91 90 89 88 87 86   5 4 3 2 1

Contents

Acknowledgements

This book was conceived in part as a response to an absence of feminist analyses of conventional or 'male-stream' political and social theory; in part as a response to a call for feminist writing made by a newly formed feminist publishing and book-packaging collective, Redress Press. While this book was in preparation, because of the usual financial problems that confront cooperative projects, Redress Press was forced to scale down its commitments and to concentrate mainly on literature.

We would like to acknowledge here the enthusiasm and cooperation of the Redress Press collective. Thanks must also go to John Iremonger for his encouragement and support, and to Venetia Nelson for carefully checking all manuscripts and making useful suggestions. Our greatest appreciation must go to our contributors, who have all been both efficient in their work and gracious in persevering with the usual delays. Last but not least our thanks go to our families and friends who put up with us during the book's production.

Contributors

JUDITH ALLEN is a historian who does research on the history of feminist and masculinist thought, and women's social history. She completed her PhD on Women, Crimes and Policing in New South Wales 1880–1939 in 1983, and has published widely on this subject. At present she is working on a book on the history of Australian government and politics from a feminist perspective, and on a history of feminist thought, 1875–1925. She teaches women's studies in the School of Humanities at Griffith University.

ROSI BRAIDOTTI has a BA from the Australian National University and a PhD from the Sorbonne. She lives in Paris and teaches philosophy in the Paris Programme of the University of Columbia as well as at the Collège International de Philosophie. She has published on issues related to feminism and philosophy and is the author of a forthcoming book on the subject. She is a member of the editorial board of the feminist journal *Les Cahiers du Grif*.

LENORE COLTHEART has a BA from the University of Queensland and a PhD from Griffith University. She was a lecturer in politics at the University of New England from 1981 to 1984 and has been the principal of Mary White College at the university since 1983. She is at present a consultant to the Public Works Department, New South Wales. She has seven children, aged fourteen to twenty-three.

MOIRA GATENS is a tutor in the Department of General Philosophy at Sydney University. She is at present completing a PhD on the gendering of the mind and body, reason and passion, culture and nature, in modern philosophy from Descartes to Sartre. Her current interests include philosophy of the body and emotions and contemporary feminist theory.

ELIZABETH GROSS is a lecturer in the Department of General Philosophy at Sydney University, where she completed a PhD in 1980. She teaches in the areas of feminism, psychoanalytic theory, semiotics, and recent French philosophy, and is at present translating and writing about Luce Irigaray (with C. Sheaffer-Jones and P. Barker), to be published as *Body-to-Body Against the Mother*, and editing a volume called *Futur* Fall: Excursions into Post-Modernity* (with T. Threadgold and D. Kelly), and doing research in the areas of feminist philosophy, deconstruction and Michel Foucault.

GENEVIEVE LLOYD is a graduate of Sydney University, with postgraduate degrees from the University of Oxford. She is a senior lecturer in philosophy at the Australian National University. She is the author of *The Man of Reason: 'Male' and 'Female' in Western Philosophy* (London: Methuen, 1984 and Minneapolis: University of Minnesota Press, 1985). She has articles in *Australasian Journal of Philosophy*, *Metaphilosophy*, *Mind*, *Philosophy*, *Philosophy and Literature*, *Social Research*, and *Critical Philosophy*.

CATRIONA MACKENZIE is a PhD candidate in the Department of Philosophy at the Australian National University. Her philosophical areas of interest include Hegel, contemporary French philosophy, and methodological issues concerning feminism and philosophy. She is also interested in feminist literary theory.

CAROLE PATEMAN is a reader in government at Sydney University and a fellow of the Academy of Social Sciences in Australia. In 1984–85 she was a fellow at the Center for Advanced Study in the Behavioral Sciences, Stanford, and in 1985–86 is visiting professor of politics at Princeton University. She is author of *Participation and Democratic Theory* (Cambridge University Press, 1970) and *The Problem of Political Obligation* (Cambridge: Polity Press, 1985) and has contributed to politics and philosophy journals. In 1985 she presented the Jefferson Memorial Lectures at the University of California, Berkeley, on the subject of Women and Democratic Citizenship.

BEVERLY THIELE is a senior tutor at Murdoch University. She graduated in sociology from Flinders University in 1976, then moved to Western Australia to work in women's studies, both as tutor and research assistant. She is now writing her PhD thesis on Reproduction in Socialist Accounts of the Woman Question, Britain 1880–1900.

JANNA THOMPSON is a senior lecturer in the Philosophy Department, Latrobe University, where she lectures on feminism, political theory and marxism, among other materials. She has published widely on feminist issues and is editing a special issue of the *Australasian Journal of Philosophy* on the theme of Women and Philosophy.

MERLE THORNTON taught politics and philosophy for several years at the University of Queensland, and began the teaching of women's studies there at a time when it had not been previously taught in Australia. She has been active in the women's movement and was especially associated with the successful campaigns to remove the marriage bar for women in the Commonwealth public service and to end the outlawing of women's bar drinking in Queensland. She has published numerous articles, on the social and political theory of gender, on Marx and on education. She is at present a full-time writer of fiction, including original work for film and television. She is a member of the committee appointed to advise the government on the future of the National Film and Sound Archive.

ANNA YEATMAN is a senior lecturer in Sociology at the Flinders University of South Australia, and is also involved in the Master's of Policy and Administration program at Flinders. Current research interests include: the history of 'personhood' with reference to processes of women's admission to modern structures of citizenship; children and social policy; and changing models of state bureaucracy and administration.

CAROLE PATEMAN

1 Introduction
The theoretical subversiveness of feminism

Over the past decade an impressive and original body of feminist criticism of social and political theory has been created. The essays in the present volume illustrate the work of Australian feminist scholars in this field, and they have been specially written for *Feminist Challenges*.* The contributors come from various academic disciplines —philosophy, politics, sociology, and history—and both young and established scholars are represented. Not all have tenured positions, and a glance at the biographical sketches reveals a pattern of institutional affiliation typical of women's relationship to academia. The essays provide an excellent illustration of some of the major issues and approaches in feminist theory in the past few years. The editors issued only the most general guidelines, so that it is striking how common themes and concerns have surfaced, notably the very difficult and complex questions of the theoretical and practical significance of sexual difference, and what it means to be a woman and a feminist engaged in theoretical inquiry.

The most important feature of the book is that all the contributors raise some extremely far-reaching questions about the conventional assumptions and methods of contemporary social and political theory. They show very clearly how feminist theorists are now challenging the most fundamental presuppositions and categories of what Mary O'Brien (1981) has aptly called male-stream theory. Virtually all the

---

* An early version of Moira Gatens' chapter was given as a paper to the Women and Philosophy Conference in Adelaide, August 1983; Beverly Thiele's chapter was presented at the Australasian Political Studies Association and Conference in Adelaide, August 1985.

social and political theory that is enshrined in the classic works and contemporary textbooks, radical as well as conservative, is male-stream thought. This means that feminist theorists are in an exposed position. Their arguments are as potentially subversive of conventionally radical theory, including marxism, as of other theories, and those radicals who might be expected to be the allies of feminist scholars are as often as not hostile or, at best, indifferent. To ask embarrassing questions about the relation between women and men, and to argue that sexual domination is central to, though unacknowledged in, modern social and political theory, is to touch on some emotions, interests, and privileges very different from those disturbed by arguments about class.

Feminist theory has taken a variety of forms during its long history, and there are many continuities in the arguments of present-day feminists and their predecessors of the past three centuries. The new development in feminism is that contemporary work is distinguished by a radical challenge to the most fundamental aspects of existing social and political theory. One of the first undertakings of the present generation of feminist theorists was to reread and reinterpret the classic texts (largely political theory texts) to establish what the great writers had said about women, and what place was allotted to them in their theories (see especially Moller-Okin, 1979b; Clark and Lange, 1979; Elshtain, 1981; Pitkin, 1984; Lloyd, 1984). Such work is essential because the standard commentaries and textbooks usually either pass over the (often very lengthy) discussions of women and the relation between the sexes in the classic texts as peripheral to the real concerns of the authors, or offer an exposition of patriarchal arguments that assumes their validity is self-evident. Nor do the standard works show any awareness of the way in which classic theories are bound up with a defence of masculinity against the dangers of femininity (Pitkin, 1984). Feminist scholars have succeeded in throwing a great deal of new light onto the theoretical fathers and the manner in which their theories are constructed, and have thus illuminated the basic presuppositions of the conventional understanding of 'political', 'social' and 'historical' inquiry. For many of us at least, the classics can no longer be read as we were taught to read them.

The manner in which the theorists and the works included in the 'Western Tradition' of social and political thought are chosen has also been questioned: why do standard discussions ignore J.S. Mill's 'The Subjection of Women'? Why is Paine's reply to Burke's polemic against the French revolution studied, but not Mary Wollstonecraft's earlier reply? Why have the early socialists, who were concerned with relations between the sexes and new modes of household organisation, been dismissed as 'utopian'? why, more generally, are none of the feminist theorists' writing from the seventeenth century onward discussed, when the most minor male figures are given their due? Classic writers are discussed in this book in the chapters by Genevieve Lloyd, Merle Thornton, Lenore Coltheart, and Janna Thompson, and Beverly Thiele analyses the strategies by which women have been rendered invisible in social and political theory.

Some of the central concepts of social and political theory have come under feminist scrutiny too, and a wide range of traditional problems have been discussed, such as consent, power, equality of opportunity, and justice. The revival of the organised feminist movement has also led to the appearance of new problems on the theoretical agenda, such as sexuality, abortion, motherhood and housework. Some of these new problems, notably abortion, have been much discussed in conventional theoretical circles, and the way in which certain problems, but not others, have been carried into the male-stream, together with the manner in which they have been defined and discussed, raises a larger and difficult question. The question is also highlighted by recent attempts by some scholars to look at the history of political thought from a specifically feminist perspective (see especially O'Brien, 1981; Hartsock, 1983; Eisenstein, 1981), and is suggested by the phrase 'male-stream' thought. The question is: what is, and should be, the relationship of feminist theorists to the classics and to conventional theoretical methods?

When contemporary feminists first began to discover the full extent and the outspokenness of the misogyny in many of the texts, and began to appreciate fully that the classic theorists were patriarchalists, almost to a man, one immediate response was to declare that the whole tainted heritage must be rejected and that feminist theorists must make a new start. Similarly, when faced with numerous recent philosophical examples of methodologically impeccable discussions of abortion that conspicuously fail to acknowledge that only women can become pregnant, there is a strong temptation to insist that feminism and philosophy should go their separate ways. However, it is impossible completely to turn our backs on the classics or on contemporary methodology, because all modes of discourse reflect and are implicated in the past to a greater or lesser degree. Moreover, there are valuable insights to be gained and lessons to be learned from male-stream theory. This is not to say that the task is to put women on an equal theoretical footing with men in existing theory. Okin's pathbreaking study showed that such a goal was illusory. More recent investigations have been uncovering further how the understanding of 'theory' is dependent on an opposition to women and all that is symbolised by the feminine and women's bodies, and why, traditionally, women's intuition and deficiency in rationality have been presented as the antithesis of the logic, order and reason required of theorists.

The question, then, is not how feminists are to create theory *ab initio*, but how we are to develop the most appropriate forms of criticism and our own, distinctive approaches, in order to dismantle and transform social and political theory.

A variety of responses to the problem of the relationship of feminism to theory are presented below, and various suggestions are made about the ways in which feminists can make (cautious) use of the theories and methods carried along in the male-stream. The opening chapter by Moira Gatens presents a clear, general discussion of three major approaches to the relationship of feminism to orthodox philosophical theory, and Rosi Braidotti looks at the relationship of feminists to ethical theory. Catriona Mackenzie's analysis of Simone de Beauvoir provides a specific case study of the problems arising when a feminist makes direct use of a male-stream theory, in this instance, existentialism. The chapter by Elizabeth Gross shows how two French feminists, Kristeva and Irigaray working in a very different tradition from the Anglo-American theory familiar to most Australian students of social and political theory, are confronting the problem. 'History', too, rests on the same dichotomies and divisons as the 'social' and the 'political', and so feminist historians, as Judith Allen demonstrates, are faced with many of the same theoretical problems. In the final chapter, Elizabeth Gross tackles the question head-on: what is feminist theory?

More generally, the discussions also show that although feminist scholarship deals with the social position of women, not all theoretical work that discusses women and women's problems is feminist. This is not to say that feminist theorists all argue in the same way or agree with each other; quite the contrary, as the contributions to this book illustrate. To appreciate the difference between discussions of 'women's issues' and distinctively feminist argument, it is necessary to distinguish two forms of inquiry. On the one hand, there is work which draws on the rich source of new topics for theoretical discussion provided by the women's movement, but which treats these merely as additional problems to be investigated through existing analytical techniques and theoretical perspectives. On the other hand, there is work which proceeds from a distinctive feminist theoretical standpoint, and so asks specific kinds of questions and uses particular forms of argument.

It is perhaps an indication of the impact that feminism—and work falling into the second category—has already made on social and political theory, that several recent discussions have insisted that feminist theory is nothing more than the inclusion of women and the relation between the sexes into existing theories. Feminist criticism is thus blunted and feminism made safe for academic theory. Two recent examples of such domestication of feminism can be found in Richards

(1982) and Charvet (1982). Richards incorporates feminism into individualist liberalism and argues that feminism is not a movement of women or for women, but is about a type of injustice, the injustice suffered by women because of their sex. Thus, there is nothing distinctive about feminism; it is merely one type of response to injustice that, in this case, happens to concern women. This allows Richards to bring feminism within the boundaries of John Rawls's influential, and patriarchal, theory of justice (see Kearns, 1983; Moller-Okin, 1984). Similarly, Charvet claims that feminism is the application of a general theory of freedom to relations between men and women, and he incorporates feminism into a conservative theory that is little more than a restatement of Hegel's claim that the subordination of women within the family is rational.

Domesticated feminism seems neither to be theoretically innovative nor to be raising questions that have not already been asked, albeit in different contexts, by conventional social and political theorists. This is inevitable, because domesticated feminism denies that sexual domination is at issue, or that feminism raises a problem, the problem of patriarchy, that is repressed in other theories. From ancient times, theorists have struggled over the question of how the rule of some people over others could be justified, but in all the long controversy over rule by slave-masters, by kings, by lords, by elites, by representatives, by the ruling class, by the vanguard party, sexual domination has remained virtually unquestioned. Men's domination of women has formed the taken-for-granted natural basis for social and political life, even in the visions of the most revolutionary theorists. If domesticated versions of feminism recognise sexual power, it is taken to pose no special problems or to have no special status, since it is assumed that relations between men and women can be analysed in the same way, using the same categories, as relations between any other superiors and subordinates.

Feminists reject this assumption, and this not only sets them apart from theorists busily domesticating feminism, but also brings them into direct conflict with liberals and socialists. The conflict with liberalism began as soon as feminist arguments appeared in the seventeenth century, when the fundamental assumptions and categories of modern social and political theory were first developed. Strictly, it is anachronistic to refer to these early writings as feminist; the term 'feminism' (coined in France) did not come into general use until the end of the nineteenth century (Offen, 1985). However, the arguments of seventeenth- (see Goreau, 1985) and eighteenth-century writers, such as Mary Astell (1668–1731) and the much better known Mary Wollstonecraft, establish a long tradition of argument, still relevant and heard today, that is unequivocally 'feminist' (see Goreau, 1985). Moreover, anachronism notwithstanding, if this tradition is not named, it can all too easily disappear from view once again.

Feminist theory has always led a subterranean existence, never acknowledged by academic theorists (or by most of the theoretical leaders of social and political movements). Nor is the neglect mere oversight. If the full history of 300 years of feminist theory is ever written, it will reveal how feminists have persistently criticised a body of radical thought, liberal and socialist, that has not just happened to exclude women—an omission that could be remedied within the theories as they stand—but which is constructed from within a division between the public (the social, the political, history) and the private (the personal, the domestic, the familial), which is also a division between the sexes. The classic theorists, as Genevieve Lloyd's chapter shows, are explicit enough about women's lack of the capacities required by the free and equal 'individuals' who can take their place in the public realm (see also Brennan and Pateman, 1979; Pateman, 1980b; 1983b). The masculine, public world, the universal world of individualism, rights, contract, reason, freedom, equality, impartial law, and citizenship, is taken to be the proper concern of social and political theory. 'Theory' has been constructed within the sexual division between the private and public spheres, and theorists look to the latter sphere. But they cannot acknowledge that the public sphere gains its meaning and significance only in contrast with, and in opposition to, the private world of particularity, natural subjection, inequality, emotion, love, partiality—and women and femininity; if they did so, they would have to question their conception of theoretical inquiry. The patriarchal separation of the two spheres and the sexes is therefore repressed in contemporary theory, and the private sphere is treated as the natural foundation of civil life that requires no critical theoretical scrutiny. In this volume, Anna Yeatman shows how theoretical rejection of the private, womanly world has impoverished sociological theory, and Judith Allen shows how this has truncated the study of history. The ultimate irony is that feminists are now accused of introducing an irrelevant and harmful separation between women and men into theoretical inquiry.

There are few problems about the relationship of feminism and conservatism, which is a theory of inequality and subjection. The difficulties arise with liberalism and socialism. The latter, like feminism, are specifically modern doctrines, sharing common origins in the proclamation of the natural freedom and equality of individuals. Liberalism and socialism are presented as theories of individual freedom and equality—interpreted very differently, of course, by liberals and socialists—that are universal in their scope. It is all too easy to take the claim of universalism at face value, and so suppose that feminism is no more than a generalisation of liberal or socialist assumptions and arguments to women. Appearances are misleading here. Both theories are patriarchal, which means that their apparently universal categories, such as the 'individual', the 'worker', the 'social', or the 'political', are sexually particular, constructed on the basis of male attributes, capacities and modes of activity. Despite the long history of leftist criticism of liberalism, the critics rarely questioned its patriarchalism. It is therefore not surprising that the problem of men's domination of women is absent from modern social and political theory; if it is admitted, fundamental theoretical principles are thrown into question.

One of the most important and complex legacies of the past for feminism is the construction of the ostensibly universal 'individual' within the division between private and public. The sexually particular character of the individual is at the heart of the problem of equality and sexual difference, which is a major concern of contributors to this book. The 'individual' is masculine, but, because he appears universal and because the categories of liberalism and socialism appear to hold out a universal promise, it seems either (for liberals) that the task of feminism is to make good this promise and incorporate women into existing institutions as equals, or (for socialists) to carry out the class revolution which will bring true universalism into being. The difficulty, in both cases, is that feminism is seen as a matter of fitting women into a unitary, undifferentiated framework that assumes that there is only one—universal—sex. Or, to put this another way, it is easy to suppose, in the face of the long history of assertion that women's capacities necessitate our exclusion from public life, that the only appropriate response is to insist that sexual difference is irrelevant. However, this line of argument leaves intact the sexually particular characterisation of the public world, the individual and his capacities.

Since the seventeenth century, one of the major feminist arguments has been that women possess the same capacities and abilities as men, and, if only educated properly, can do everything that men can do. The argument is admirable, as far as it goes. What it glosses over is that there is a womanly capacity that men do not possess, and thus it implicitly denies that birth, women's bodies and the feminine passions inseparable from their bodies and bodily processes have any political relevance. Mary O'Brien (1981) has explored some of the reasons why our theoretical heritage lacks 'a philosophy of birth', and other feminist scholars have drawn attention to the manner in which the conventional understanding of the 'political' is built upon the rejection of physical birth in favour of the masculine creation of (giving birth to) social and political order (see also Hartsock, 1983; Pitkin, 1984; Pateman, 1984). It is thus hardly surprising that much current feminist theory, including that represented in this book, is concerned with women's bodies.

When feminism is taken to be about nothing more than equality in the sense of women attaining the same status as individuals, workers or citizens as men, it is difficult to find a convincing defence against the longstanding anti-feminist charge that feminists want to turn women into men. The 'universal' standing that is to be won is that of a being with masculine characteristics engaging in masculine activities. Existing patriarchal theory has no place for women *as women*; at best, women can be incorporated as pale reflections of men. In this collection the problem of equality is addressed directly by Merle Thornton and Janna Thompson and, more indirectly, by several other contributors. In the final chapter, Elizabeth Gross sets out some reasons why feminists should be more concerned with autonomy than equality. The formal, liberal civil and political equalities are important, of course, and now that women have attained a large measure of formal equality with men, and legal reforms to promote equality of opportunity are being enacted, the contradictions in taking individualism and universalism at face value are being revealed; equality of opportunity and 'gender-neutral' laws, policies and language all too frequently result in absurdities, or work against women. In the USA, where these trends are most developed, maternity benefits, for example, have been defended as 'provided to help the existence of the human race ... If a man could bear children he would be under the same law'. On the other hand, the exclusion of pregnancy from California disability insurance was declared constitutional in 1974 because it was based on a disability, namely pregnancy, not upon sex; the programme, it was said, 'divides potential recipients into two groups—pregnant women and non-pregnant persons ... The fiscal and actuarial benefits thus accrue to members of both sexes' (quotations are from Midgley and Hughes, 1983:160–61). The very difficult question is where, theoretically, do we go from these kinds of absurdities?

There have been many famous critiques of the abstract character of liberal individualism, but none has ever questioned the most fundamental abstraction of all: the abstraction of the 'individual' from the body. In order for the individual to appear in liberal theory as a universal figure, who represents anyone and everyone, the individual must be disembodied. That is to say, a natural fact of human existence, that humankind has two bodies, female and male, must be disregarded. The theorists who recognised this fact, whether radical like Rousseau or conservative like Hegel, invariably assumed that women's bodies had no place in the public world. The public 'individual' was masculine, yet, at the same time, this figure was presented as universal, which means that, for universalism to be maintained, the attributes of the individual are implicitly abstracted from the body. If they were not so abstracted it would become clear that 'the' individual has the body of one sex. Feminists are thus bringing women's bodies to the centre of theoretical argument, but current discussions are very different from those of the classic writers. Nor should they be confused with the recent revival of patriarchal argument by McMillan (1982), who assumes that a critique of abstract individualism and recognition of the social relevance of sexual difference leads necessarily to a complete identification of women with the private sphere, maternity and childcare, and who rejects 'artificial' birth control, abortion and pain relief in childbirth. The discussions that follow are also different again from the recent work by American feminists on motherhood and maternal thinking, which, so far, has few counterparts in Britain or Australia (see, for example, Ruddick, 1982; Trebilcot, 1984).

Feminist theory, for the first time, opens up the possibility of new approaches that reject what, until now, have been seen as the only alternatives; either 'gender-neutral' abstract individualism, or a social individualism that prescribes that women's bodies, bodily processes and passions entail our submission to men's will and judgments. This collection provides some examples of these new perspectives. The chapter by Anna Yeatman represents one feminist response to the general problem of sexual difference. Yeatman argues for a de-gendered conception of individual personality and the domestic sphere, the site where personality is developed, so that we would no longer talk in terms of the familiar categories of 'women' and 'men' (see also Levine, 1984). Janna Thompson's discussion points in the same direction. A very different approach underlies Catriona Mac-kenzie's analysis of de Beauvoir and Lenore Coltheart's and Judith Allen's chapters. Some of the implications of moving in this direction are made explicit by Rosi Braidotti and Elizabeth Gross. They draw on the work of French feminists, who have been greatly influenced by, but are also critical of, psychoanalytic theory and recent French philoso-phy, which reaches back to Nietzsche in its deconstruction of the idea of a unified individual or self. Braidotti also draws on the work of Foucault who sees the body, and the multiplicty of disciplines imposed on it, as central to the modern political order. French feminist theory begins from women's bodies and their social meanings; it is, first and foremost, embodied theory. However, it is still far from clear exactly what form a feminist theory of the (feminine) body and the body politic will take.

It is, however, very apparent that distinctively feminist theory begins from the recognition that individuals are feminine and mascu-line, that individuality is not a unitary abstraction but an embodied and sexually differentiated expression of the unity of humankind. To develop a theory in which women and femininity have an autonomous place means that the private and the public, the social and the political, also have to be completely reconceptualised; in short, it

9

means an end to the long history of sexually particular theory that masquerades as universalism. Whether or not patriarchal theory is ultimately subverted, this book, along with other recent feminist theory, shows that a very rich and exciting beginning has been made.

PART I
The Challenge to Theory

2 Feminism, philosophy and riddles without answers

'Would you tell me, please, which way I ought to go from here?'

'That depends a good deal on where you want to get to,' said the Cat.

'I don't much care where—' said Alice.

'Then it doesn't matter which way you go,' said the Cat.

'—so long as I get *somewhere*,' Alice added as an explanation.

'Oh, you're sure to do that,' said the Cat, 'if only you walk long enough.'

Alice felt that this could not be denied, so she tried another question. 'What sort of people live about here?'

'In *that* direction,' the Cat said, waving its right paw around, 'lives a Hatter: and in *that* direction,' waving the other paw, 'lives a March Hare. Visit either you like: they're both mad.'

'But I don't want to go among mad people,' Alice remarked.

'Oh, you can't help that,' said the Cat: 'we're all mad here, I'm mad. You're mad.'

'How do you know I'm mad?' said Alice.

'You must be,' said the Cat, 'or you wouldn't have come here.'

(Carroll 1972:88–89)

This quotation is intended to act, thematically, as an allegorical description of the kind of argument presented in this paper concerning the relationship between feminism and theory, or more specifically, feminists working in philosophy. Some readers may recall that Alice opts for the path in the left, and thus, for the March Hare. However, regardless of her choice, she wanders into the Mad Hatter's Tea Party—she meets both the Hatter and the Hare, each in the company of the other. That the company Alice consciously seeks has little to do with the company she finds herself in is relevant to the present concern in the following way. It will be central to my argument throughout this chapter, concerning the relations between feminism and philosophy, that feminists working within the discipline of philosophy cannot *choose* to pursue and create a theory of women's subjectivity, of women's social and political existence, and so on, independently of or in spite of the Western philosophical tradition. Like the Mad Hatter, the assumptions and frameworks of traditional philosophy will crop up in the most unlikely places and in a most alarming manner. Traditional philosophy cannot, in my view, simply be ignored, particularly by those who find themselves in the Wonderland of philosophy. But perhaps I am jumping ahead here and offering solutions to the riddle before it has been posed. The riddle is 'What is the relation, if any, between feminism and philosophy?'

An overview of past and present relations between feminist theory and philosophical discourse suggests three dominant ways in which this relation could be characterised. I would like to examine, in detail, all three. Before doing so, however, a note of caution should be struck. These three approaches or attitudes to philosophy, by feminists, are not easily separated or discrete, nor necessarily in complete opposition to each other.

BELLEROPHONTIC LETTERS

The first way in which the relationship between feminist theory and philosophy has been characterised may be seen as a form of radical feminism or theoretical separatism. These feminists present two kinds of arguments. The first is that there is no relation between feminism and philosophy or more generally between feminism and *theory*. Feminism, on this view, is pure *praxis*, the very activity of theorising being somehow identified with masculinity or maleness. Perhaps the view of Solanas would be appropriate to quote here. She writes:

> The male's inability to relate to anybody or anything makes his life pointless and meaningless (the ultimate male insight is that life is absurd), so he invented philosophy ... Most men, utterly cowardly, project their inherent weaknesses onto women, label them female weaknesses and believe themselves to have female strengths; most philosophers, not quite so cowardly, face the fact that male lacks exist in men, but still can't face the fact that they exist in men only. So they label the male condition the Human Condition, pose their nothingness problem, which horrifies them, as a philosophical dilemma, thereby giving stature to their animalism, grandiloquently label their nothingness their 'Identity Problem', and proceed to prattle on pompously about the 'Crisis of the Individual', the 'Essence of Being', 'Existence preceding Essence', 'Existential Modes of Being' etc., etc. (Solanas, 1969:265)

14

These problems are described by Solanas as specifically *male* problems. The female, on her account, exhibits no such perverse relation to her being, which she grasps intuitively and without lack. Philosophy, or theory, on this view is a male enterprise, arising out of an inherent inadequacy of the male sex.

The second argument of feminists, still within this first approach, is that there is a relation between feminism and philosophy but that it is historically, and *necessarily*, an oppressive one. This group argues that philosophy is, necessarily, a masculine enterprise that owes its existence to the repression or exclusion of femininity and as such it is of no use to feminists or their projects. In fact, philosophy may be seen, on this view, as a dangerous and ensnaring trap (Daly, 1978:intro.). Political action, if it is to be effective, needs to dissociate itself from traditional theory. What is needed is not a new theory but, as d'Eaubonne argues, a mutation. She writes:

> It is essential today that the spirit of the revolution to be accomplished go beyond what has been called until now the 'revolutionary spirit', just as the latter went beyond reformism. Ultimately, it is no longer a revolution that we need, but a *mutation* ... (d'Eaubonne, 1980:66, emphasis added)

The history of philosophy is, on this view, obsolete, dead or dying; we must 'start from scratch', and as for history, she cries: 'Spit on Hegel!' In terms of the first approach then, the reply to the riddle of relation between feminism and philosophy is that the relation is disjunctive. One chooses feminism *over* philosophy. This approach to philosophy has several problems. It is dependent for its rationale on an unspoken and unexamined proposition that philosophy, as a discipline or an activity, coincides with its past. It assumes that philosophy is and will be what it was. This reification of philosophy misses the point that philosophy is, among other things, a human activity that is *ongoing*. Some philosophers may have proposed that their systems were closed, complete, and able to transcend history, but this is no reason for us to assent to their propositions. Since the objects of philosophical inquiry (that is, the human being, its cultural, political, and linguistic environment), are not static entities, the project of philosophy is, necessarily, open-ended. The conception of philosophy as a system of truths that could, in principle, be complete, true for all time, relies on the correlative claim that nature or ontology and truth or epistemology are static. In that feminists in the first approach accept the picture that philosophy likes to present of itself it allows this dominant characterisation free rein. Moreover, the first approach, if presented as a practical and viable alternative for feminism, rather than as a limited strategy, may have a lesson to learn from the story of Bellerophon.

Bellerophon, a brave warrior from Greek mythology, travels to a new land, unaware that he carries on his person, in the form of a letter, the orders for his own execution. Whether or not feminist consciousness is 'inscribed' in an analogous fashion is a matter of great debate. The response of any particular person to this question would be influenced by that person's commitment, or lack of commitment, to the psychoanalytic view of the unconscious, to various structuralist and post-structuralist claims concerning the social construction of consciousness, and so on. My own view is that one's *conscious* intentions have less to do with one's practical and theoretical behaviour than some feminists would have us think. It is the recalcitrant attitude of human beings to social change, regardless of their conscious intentions, that led many feminists, especially in the mid- and late seventies, to study the unconscious and its relation to the production and reproduction of patriarchal and class ideologies. That this analysis has been abandoned by some and continues, for those who are still working within its parameters, to prove difficult, does not mean that it is, therefore, inessential. Perhaps the study needs to be tackled from another direction, a question I will consider in the third part of this chapter. For now I shall do no more than indicate that the first approach towards the question of the relation between feminism and philosophy, if presented as a long-term programme, is utopian and runs the serious risk of reproducing, elsewhere, the very relations which it seeks to leave behind.

THE PROJECT OF EXTENSION

Whereas the first approach, in its most extreme form, sees both the method or framework of philosophy and its concrete content as antithetical to feminist aims, the second approach is characterised by seeing the *content* only as oppressive to women. In other words, feminists in the second category, a category that may be typified by, though not limited to, the stance of liberal feminists, agree that historically, philosophy has had an oppressive relation to women (of misogyny, of omission) but that this relation is not a *necessary* one. They argue or assume that philosophy as a discipline and as a method of inquiry is entirely neutral with regard to sex. Researchers adopting this approach view the history of philosophy as male-dominated, but argue that women are presently in a situation of being able to correct this bias. Here, then, the relation between feminist theory and philosophy is envisaged as a complementary one, where feminist theory adds to, or completes, traditional or existing philosophy, by filling in the 'gaps' in political, moral and social theory. By *adding* an analysis of the specific social, political and economic experience of women, this approach seeks to transform philosophy from a male-dominated enterprise into a *human* enterprise.

In its more radical form this approach may do more than merely add the lived experience of women; it may also purport to offer the means by which that experience may be altered. Philosophy may be seen, in other words, as more than a merely *descriptive* tool—it may also be seen as a transformative activity which is capable not only of analysing social relations but also of providing a means whereby one may intervene and change those relations. The answer of these feminists to our riddle is to opt for the conjunction, at least initially. I say *initially* because implicit in much of their work is the notion of the 'inbuilt obsolescence' of feminism. Eventually, they suppose, it will be unnecessary to retain a specifically feminist perspective. Once the goal of equality is reached, feminism would be redundant.

What this approach usually entails is the adoption of a particular philosophical theory (for example liberalism, existentialism, marxism), as a method of analysis which then takes 'woman' as its object, as its (philosophical) problem. Certainly, I think that this is what Wollstonecraft attempts, vis-a-vis egalitarianism, in *A Vindication of the Rights of Woman*; what de Beauvoir attempts, vis-a-vis existentialism, in *The Second Sex*; and what Mitchell attempts, vis-a-vis both psychoanalysis and marxism, in *Psychoanalysis and Feminism*. It is for this reason that I do not wish to reduce this second approach to liberal feminism alone. It is work done under the rubric of this second approach that epitomises the dominant relation between feminism and philosophy since Wollstonecraft and is, for that reason, worth examining in detail.

Consider de Beauvoir's own contention concerning the use of existentialism in understanding the situation of women:

> [I]t is regardless of sex that the existent seeks self justification through transcendence—the very submission of women is proof of that statement. What they demand today is to be recognized as existents by the same right as men and not to subordinate existence to life, the human being to its animality.
> *An existentialist perspective has enabled us, then, to understand how the biological and economic condition of the primitive horde must have led to male supremacy.* The female, to a greater extent than the male, is the prey of the species . . . in maternity woman remained closely bound to her body, like an animal. (de Beauvoir, 1975:97, emphasis added)

For the moment it is enough to note de Beauvoir's commitment to Sartre's view of the (female) body and its relation, for Sartre, to immanence. I will be picking up this point later in the section where I will consider the effect of the necessary precommitments of feminists who use existing philosophical systems to explore the existence and experience of women.

Wollstonecraft's views on the education of women reveal a similar precommitment, this time to egalitarianism. She writes:

> [T]he most perfect education, in my opinion, is such an exercise of the understanding as is best calculated to strengthen the body and form the heart. Or, in other words, to enable the individual to attain such habits of virtue as will render it independent. In fact, it is a farce to call any being virtuous whose virtues do not result from the exercise of its own reason. This was Rousseau's opinion respecting men; I *extend* it to women ... (Wollstonecraft, 1975:103, emphasis added)

So, we see that the theory, the philosophical framework employed by these feminists, is considered unproblematic. The problem, the problem of how these philosophical paradigms relate to women, is seen as a problem of *content*. The framework remains intact while the content is *extended*, sometimes altered, to include women, to account theoretically for the position of women and, possibly, to offer the means whereby that position may be transformed. Philosophy is thus employed as the *method* which takes women or feminism as its object of inquiry. It seems to me that there are several problems involved in this second approach that are connected to the nature of the critique these feminists offer. The explicit critique of Rousseau, offered by Wollstonecraft, for example, is *internal* to his philosophy. The philosophy of Rousseau per se is not a problem for Wollstonecraft; rather, it is its exclusive application to males that is, for her, the problem. The difficulties I see in this approach will be treated in turn.

The neutral framework, sexist content, claim

What I want to examine here is the claim that philosophy as a discipline, that the work of any particular philosopher, taken as a method of inquiry, is neutral and that it is the content only, that is, what a philosophical framework is 'filled' with that is sexist or inadequate in relation to women. To be clearer, I want to investigate the claim that, for example, existentialism, as a philosophy, is sex-neutral, to investigate the claim that the sexism of *Being and Nothingness* is limited to its use of misogynistic metaphors and sex-blind examples. I have no quarrel with the contention that philosophy, from Plato to the present, *is* riddled with statements that are anti-woman or anti-feminist—this has been demonstrated, by feminists, ad nauseum. Rather, I am interested in taking to task the claim that it is to this extent *only* that philosophy has denigrated women or generally been inappropriate in terms of offering an adequate analysis of women. If it were the case that the misogyny or inadequacy (in relation to women) of philosophy were merely a problem of content (that is, of the philosopher's personal attitudes or values infecting his otherwise neutral system) then the project of extension and inclusion would be viable. I am no longer convinced, however, that Sartre's metaphors, for example, are incidental or accidental to his overall thesis. It is not only a matter of the specific content, the concrete examples, offered by him being inadequate as an account of *human* being. I would argue that his philosophy is inadequate in general outline too. In other words, the project of *extending* philosophies, which may have excluded or been oppressive to women in the past, in order that they may include women, non-oppressively, in the future, is viable only on condition that the general form or framework of any particular philosophy is sex-neutral. It is to this claim that I would like to turn, again by way of existentialism.

Consider Sartre's account of the existence of others, exemplified by 'the Look'. This entire section of *Being and Nothingness* is written in terms of an individual man encountering an individual man and in terms which assume the mutual apprehension of the intersubjective reciprocity of subjecthood. He writes: 'my apprehension of the Other in the world as probably being a man refers to my permanent possibility of being-seen-by-him; that is, to the permanent possibility that a subject who sees me may be substituted for the object seen by me' (Sartre, 1977:257). Would this thesis, robbed of its apparent neutrality, convey the same meaning? Take a concrete situation, experienced by most, if not all, women at some time in their lives. The example is supplied by M. Tax.

> A young woman is walking down a city street. She is excruciatingly aware of her appearance and of the reaction to it (imagined or real) of every person she meets. She walks through a group of construction workers who are eating lunch in a line along the pavement. Her stomach tightens with terror and revulsion; her face becomes contorted into a grimace of self-control and fake unawareness; her walk and carriage become stiff and dehumanized. No matter what they say to her, it will be unbearable. She knows that they will not physically assault her or hurt her. They will only do so metaphorically. What they will do is *impinge* on her. They will demand that her thoughts be focussed on them. They will use her body with their eyes. They will evaluate her market price. They will comment on her defects, or compare them to those of other passers-by. They will make her a participant in their fantasies without asking if she is willing. They will make her feel ridiculous, or grotesquely sexual, or hideously ugly. Above all, they will make her feel like a *thing*. (Tax, 1973:28)

The question we must ask is 'Does this situation reveal to the men in it (in line with Sartre's thesis) that this woman's existence involves for them the possibility of their objectification?', that is, that the woman, as seeing subject, may be substituted for the woman, the seen object? I think not. What has happened to the purported reciprocity of 'the Look'? What, on reflection, does this situation suggest about Sartre's philosophy? It suggests that it is a philosophy about men, about free and equal subjectivities that encounter each other in a situation of struggle for mastery. It is a description that is inappropriate for some men in some situations, and, I would argue, for all women in some situations. This point is qualitatively different from the predominant feminist criticism of the sexism of philosophers throughout the history of Western thought. It is not a point directed at content, at what is said or what is *not* said about women, but rather, about what *can* and *cannot* be said about women within the terms of particular philosophical theories.

What are the limitations to what de Beauvoir can say, having adopted the existentialist method, about women, their situation, their character? What precommitments are entered into by feminists when they apply this or that philosophical view to the position of women? What factors are preselected and hence predetermined to rise to prominence? What will be excluded? Some questions are foreclosed by the method, whether it be existentialism, psychoanalysis, marxism or liberalism. For feminists employing existentialism, the problem of women's relation (or *lack* of it) to transcendence, is seen as crucial; for feminists employing psychoanalysis, the problem of the social construction of women as (symbolically) *lacking*, is seen as crucial; for feminists employing marxism, the problem of women's relation (or *lack* of it) to productive labour is seen as crucial; and so on. The point I'm making is that the history of philosophy is the history of man defining man as having a particular relation to some essential faculty or power. This faculty or power may be rationality, transcendence, productive labour, etc.; what is important is that man's relation to this power or his capacity to embody it is deemed crucial to his subjectivity. The relation of many feminists to this history is revealed in the attempt to extend this analysis of man to include woman. This involves assuming the neutrality of the essential power or faculty under consideration with regard to sex and social position and positing it instead as crucial to the *human* subject. The tendency of these feminists to extend this analysis to women is encouraged by the implicit assumption, common in philosophy, that the analysis is universally applicable.

Where does this situate feminists who work within this mode? On my view it does *not*, necessarily, imply that they are wasting their time or that their contributions to feminist theory are minimal. On the contrary, I would argue that many feminists who believe themselves to be engaged in this kind of research are, in fact, doing something quite different. However, they are doing it in such a way that they make their work, and their contributions to philosophy *invisible*. This leads me to the second point of criticism of this second way of conceptualising the relation between feminism and philosophy.

Women, philosophy and invisibility
Michele Le Doeuff (1977:10) has remarked that one area in which women have free access to philosophy, today, is in the area of

20

commentary on the 'Great Classics'. She observes, in this context, 'Who better than a woman to show fidelity, respect and remembrance? A woman can be trusted to perpetuate the words of the Great Discourse: she will add none of her own.' Le Doeuff's point is, I think, misplaced, the point being not so much that woman, as philosophical commentator, will *add* no words of her own but that she will *claim* none as her own. She will endeavour, as far as possible, to make herself, her thought, and the reconstructive work necessary to interpretation, invisible. It is in terms of the exercise of this capacity—to order without appearing to interfere; to extract and clarify what was, apparently, there all along; to extrapolate and expand; to draw out consequences and point out repercussions of the thought of the Master, *as if* these thoughts and associations lie latent in the text, expectantly awaiting the discerning eye—that women who are philosophers often render themselves invisible. It is to this invisibility of the work of women in philosophy, including women who are feminists, that I would now like to turn. In the context of the employment, by feminists, of existing philosophies to explain and/or alter the position of women, the following question arises: Is it accurate to describe the work of these feminists as merely the *extension* of the content of existing philosophies, or is it the case that they are, in fact, offering alternative frameworks that bear only a superficial or historical relation to existing philosophies? In other words, is the existentialism of de Beauvoir the same as the existentialism of Sartre? Is Mitchell's account of psychoanalysis consistent with Freud's? and so on. In what way do these women make themselves and their contribution to the theory they employ invisible?

De Beauvoir states clearly in *The Second Sex* that woman is the other, not only to man but also to herself. Her explanation of the oppression of women is partly in terms of the problem of female subjectivity, that is, that woman is perceived *and* perceives herself as *object*. This account is, already, clearly at odds with Sartre's account in *Being and Nothingness*. For Sartre, at least the Sartre of *Being and Nothingness*, the other is always a subject. His analysis of interpersonal and social relations, in 1943, has little to offer in terms of a theory of *structural* oppression. His analysis revolves around *individual* power relations and individual consciousnesses. Coupled with Sartre's conception of 'bad faith', this analysis can offer little more than an understanding of women's oppression as a form of bad faith. It is de Beauvoir, in 1949, who offers this theory of oppression, and—this is my point—in a way that obscures her contribution to the viability of existentialism as a *social* theory. The Sartre of 1952 has already picked this up. In a rare though half-hearted display of acknowledgement of the role that de Beauvoir had played in forming his philosophy, he writes: 'Genet is first an object—and an object to others . . . Simone de

Beauvoir has pointed out that ... woman is an object to the other and to herself before being a subject' (Sartre, 1964:37). I do not believe Sartre could have offered his 'biography' of Genet, nor the view we find there on freedom, were it not for de Beauvoir's contributions to existentialism. Space does not permit me to offer similar examples of Mitchell's relation to psychoanalysis, or of other feminists' relation to marxism. The examples I have chosen are those that I imagine to be the most accessible and familiar. My point is not to seek out past plagiarisms or even to demand that the work of women in the past be acknowledged—though both projects are worthy of investigation. My present concern is to make visible and analyse the mechanisms by which women's work in philosophy has been rendered negligible in order that those of us who are feminists, and who work within philosophy *as* feminists, do not duplicate this history.

The point I have made in this section concerning the process of rendering women's work invisible relates back to the first point concerning framework and content. The framework of any particular philosophy, I have argued, is not sex-neutral. Feminists who have attempted to extend or alter the content of these philosophies have done more than add and 'tidy-up'. They have also, often, modified the *framework* of the philosophy they employ, though in a way that is not always readily visible. I have tried to indicate previously that this problem of the invisibility of the contributions of feminist philo-sophers to philosophy is compounded by the alleged neutrality of the framework with regard to sex or gender, on the one hand, and its patently inadequate applicability to *both* sexes, on the other. The inadequacy of any particular philosophy that is being put to this feminist purpose reflects then, because of these factors, back onto 'woman'. That is, women's existence is not seen as problematising existentialism or psychoanalysis or marxism but rather woman herself is seen as the problem. Somehow she is characterised as defying theorisation. How many times have we heard: from marxists—'the woman question'; from psychoanalysts—'woman, the dark conti-nent'; 'woman the enigma'; and more recently from other quarters, 'Does woman exist?'. The supposed neutrality of both the framework and the particular faculty or power that is deemed essentially human in the terms of that framework contribute to a situation where the inadequacy of philosophical theory does not throw 'philosophy' into question but '*woman*'. This leads me on to the third and final point of criticism relevant to this second kind of relation between feminism and philosophy, that is, the question of legitimation.

Philosophy and legitimation
Part of the initial training of any philosopher involves grasping and being able to reproduce an appropriate philosophical style. Of course,

this style varies historically and according to the particular tradition one finds oneself within. However, a PhD thesis in geometric form or in the genre of dialogue, though both are historically prevalent in philosophy, would not, I suspect, be favourably received, at present, in any tradition. What is deemed an appropriate philosophic style by university authorities, by journal editors, and by publishing houses appears to have a consistency that is closely connected to a normative standard, decided, in part, by tradition, but also, no doubt, masking discursive power relations. What are some of the major factors that determine whether a piece of research is philosophical? Clearly it is not merely the subject matter but also the mode of presentation of that subject matter. *Nausea* is literature, *Being and Nothingness* is philosophy. *The Idiot* is not a philosophical text although it deals with issues common to the philosophy of ethics. By what processes are some texts considered legitimate, philosophically, and others not? At the present time we could say that for work to be considered philosophical it should be clear and logically ordered and argued rather than ambiguous, descriptive or merely persuasive. For work to be counted as philosophical it should be rational and objective, rather than emotive or subjective. The view presented should be evident, in principle, to all rather than relying on private knowledge or exclusive lived experience. Philosophy aims at the universal, the abstract, stressing rationality, the creation of a clear mind, whereby the universal may be apprehended. It is not concerned with the particular, with the contingent. Personal opinion is to be overcome or to be transformed, if possible, into public and authorised knowledge.

These criteria concerning the public legitimation of philosophy do not always sit comfortably with feminist research. One of the effects of this process by which work is considered legitimate is that any research that displays overt political or personal commitment or involvement is considered, for that reason, to be illegitimate, to be not-philosophy. This places most, if not all, feminist research in a difficult position apropos its philosophical credentials. One way for feminists who are also philosophers to retain both their feminism and their commitment to philosophy is to use *existing* philosophical theories in their study of women. The benefits attached to this option are obvious. First, feminists who work within this approach are able, by this means, to retain both their commitment to philosophy and their commitment to feminism by including feminist concerns in a way that does not disrupt the preset boundaries and assumptions of philosophy. Second, the accounts and findings of these feminist philosophers are more likely to be judged as legitimate by virtue of their close association with past or existing philosophies which, after all, do purport to be concerned with *human* existence. Hence, it is with this final point, the point concerning the process by which

philosophy separates itself from other modes of inquiry and legitimates this separation, that all three points that I have raised in this
section converge. The questions of framework vs. content, women's
invisibility in philosophy, and the legitimising processes of philosophy
are, it seems to me, all interconnected. The investigation of *how* they
are interconnected belongs properly to the third approach discussed in
the final section of this chapter. It should be said here, however, that
the seeds of the third approach are planted in the second. The third is
not possible without the second being logically prior.

THROUGH THE LOOKING-GLASS

> The Hatter opened his eyes very wide on hearing this; but all he *said*
> was, 'Why is a raven like a writing desk?'...
> 'Have you guessed the riddle yet?' the Hatter said, turning to Alice
> again.
> 'No, I give it up,' Alice replied, 'What's the answer?'
> 'I haven't the slightest idea,' said the Hatter.
> 'Nor I,' said the March Hare.
> Alice sighed wearily. 'I think you might do something better with the
> time,' she said, 'than wasting it in asking riddles that have no answers.'
> (Carroll, 1972:94–97)

The third way in which one could articulate the relation between
feminist theory and philosophy holds more in common with the first
approach than with the second in terms of the way in which feminists
working within this third approach see philosophy. In other words,
the view espoused by feminists who work within this third approach is
that philosophy is not neutral in character, that the problem of the
relationship between women and philosophy, of how women's
subjectivity is put into philosophical discourse, is not merely a
problem of content. The difference between the third and the first lies
not in the perception of the relation between feminism and philosophy but rather in the *response* to that situation. Whereas feminists
in the first category argue that women should ignore or avoid
philosophical tradition, feminists in the third argue that this tradition
must be confronted. These theorists have often worked in the second
approach, and have arrived at their present view because of difficulties encountered there. In a sense, feminist philosophers working in
the third approach *invert* the method of feminist philosophers
working in the second. Whereas, in the second approach, feminist
philosophers take philosophy as the method and feminism or women
as the object of study, researchers in the third category take feminist
theory or a feminist perspective as their starting point and *philosophy
itself* as the object of study. This entails the creation of a situation
where one can raise, as meaningful, questions pertaining to philoso-

phical paradigms and their commitments, the effects of women's interventions into philosophy, and the processes whereby some discourses are judged legitimate, philosophically, and others not. These questions are all put into crisis, I believe, by the presence of feminist discourses in the philosophical field. They are questions that many philosophers would prefer to be left unasked. They are questions that threaten the very fabric and constitution of contemporary philosophy.

It is at the conjuncture of the three questions I raised earlier, concerning the neutrality of philosophical frameworks, the invisibility of women both as the objects of philosophical discourse and as the subjects of philosophical discourse, and the process by which philosophy legitimates itself, that the third approach lies. And it is this third approach only that can show how all three questions interconnect. By *self-consciously* demonstrating that any philosophical paradigm is *not* neutral, these feminists make themselves, both as philosophers and as women, *visible*. By making themselves visible, they in turn throw into question the legitimacy of claims and assumptions in philosophy that have been taken as axiomatic. In so far as this approach questions the very foundation and status of philosophy it also reveals the investments and concerns of philosophy. It does this by demonstrating not only *what* is excluded from a particular philosophy but also *why* it is crucial, for the very existence of that philosophy, to exclude it. In this vein, some feminists are at present engaged in projects involving the way in which the human body and sensation are treated in philosophy and the effects of this treatment on the philosophical construction of femininity (Gross, 1983; Lloyd, 1984).

In examining the history of philosophy feminists do not necessarily duplicate that history. They endeavour, one hopes, to understand its character, to listen to its 'reason' not in order to reproduce it but in order to challenge the undertones, the silences of philosophy. Both the method or framework and the content, and the connections between them, are studied. They are studied, not always for what is said but also for what is *not* said; for what *cannot* be said; examined not only in terms of the privileging of, say, reason, but also for what is involved in the denigration of passion. Many feminists involved in projects of this kind claim that philosophy may not be able to tell us a great deal about women but it can tell us a great deal about men and male desire. The desire for objectivity, for example, is in itself a subjective drive and this subjective drive throws into question the objectivity that many philosophers claim for their accounts. The desire, which underlies the work of Descartes, for a unified and universally appropriate science, is itself in need of examination. The seventeenth-century project of subordinating ontology and metaphysics to a certain and foundational epistemology is a project that reflects social needs and desires that are a far cry from our own. The fixing of being and the mirroring conception of that being's access to the world and knowledge, so ably described by Rorty (1980), is no longer tenable or appropriate to our needs today. This shift in concern is evidenced by the stress in recent feminist philosophy, on *becoming* rather than being, on *possibilities* rather than certainty and on meaning or *significance* rather than truth.

A common reaction of some feminists and philosophers to this cultivation of a philosophy of ambiguity entailing, as it does, the rejection of universal truths, is to accuse feminists who support this developing philosophy of being the mistresses of critique, of being merely reactive to dominant traditions in philosophy and, in this sense, of being entirely negative. This kind of response is typified by the demand put to feminist theory to show what it has to offer independently of critique, that is, a demand to inspect the theory-building capabilities of feminism. Now it seems to me that this demand is based on a misconception concerning the investments, interests and character of the kind of feminist philosophy I have outlined in this section. In so far as this approach to philosophy has involved itself extensively in a critique of universal and totalising forms of knowledge it is evident that it is not going to involve itself with a repetition of theory-building which aims at the formation of unilateral predictive propositions. This isn't to say that this third approach of feminists to philosophy is anti-theoretical. Rather, it indicates a commitment to a conception of theory, practice and strategy which refutes the traditional theory/practice split. The feminist challenge to dominant philosophical pronouncements—concerning the equality of 'man', the lauding of a universal and singular rationality, and so on—is offered from an acknowledged necessary embeddedness in lived experience and is the result of the exploration of the contradictions manifest in that experience.

As recent feminist research has demonstrated (Harding and Hintikka, 1983; Finn and Miles, 1982) the predominant contemporary treatment of ontology, epistemology, ethics and politics as separate disciplines with discrete concerns is not only unable to withstand critical scrutiny but such scrutiny, additionally, exposes the political nature of maintaining these spheres as separate (Flax, 1983:248ff). It allows, for example, free rein to the notion that a writer can be entirely objective, can transcend his political, social and sexual identity and speak from utopia. Pointing out the necessary interconnections between ontological, epistemological and political commitments in philosophical discourses is akin to turning over a tapestry and examining the interconnections of the threads that from the 'right' side of the fabric give the impression of discrete figures and patterns. Understanding the nature and formation of those patterns and figures

26

and their necessary interconnectedness is crucial if feminists are to grasp the way in which philosophy has constructed, and continues to construct, femininity and masculinity, reason and nature. It is essential, in other words, that feminists do not continue to take philosophy and its overt pronouncements at face value. I have tried to explain, in the preceding section, the ways in which this prima facie approach to philosophy is inadequate. The study of the underside of philosophy is characteristic of this third kind of relation between feminist theory and philosophy. What remains to be, briefly, explored is the common resistance to following the insights of this approach through to their logical conclusion. In other words, there is still a large leap to be made in terms of the way we conceptualise political struggle and action. Many feminists who would agree with the sentiments expressed in this third section still ask 'But when do we begin to produce *real* feminist theory?'; 'What is the next step—how do we get *beyond* patriarchal theory?'. It is to these kinds of questions, so often heard at women's conferences and seminars, that I would like to turn.

It is in *The Principles of Philosophy* that Descartes (1970:211) described philosophy as being like a tree: metaphysics being the roots that are not visible but essential, physics being the trunk, and the branches being all the other aspects of philosophy, including ethics and politics. His point in using this metaphor is that the extremities of the tree, including its fruit, cannot be understood or improved without a thorough knowledge of the tree as a complete organic system. The ethico-political theory of Descartes is notoriously spare and, according to the philosopher himself, this is because ethics and politics are, necessarily, the last objects of knowledge to be reached by reason. Put another way, if we are to understand and improve human social and political existence then we must first understand the principles of human nature, initially, as a particular and then in relation to the regulative system of nature as a whole. This is the way that Hobbes, Spinoza, Hume and Rousseau all proceed. The answer to the first query 'What, essentially, is a human being?' sets determining limits to what kind of social, political and ethical organisation is thought to be suitable to it. In all these theorists' work human nature is thought to have an essentially constant and universal character that is, in differing degrees, considered to be mutable—improvable or corruptible. In other words, the kind of social and political organisation and the ethical and legal principles that are to govern that organisation are deduced from what a human being is thought to be, what its needs, desires, capabilities and limitations are. Once this ontological problem is fathomed the management of groups of such beings is largely a matter of deduction from these first principles. What must be kept in mind here, however, is that this mode of philosophising involves a *formal* conception of human nature or human essence.

27

The introduction of the notion of a socially constructed subject, which is a notion absolutely central to feminist theory, completely undermines the coherence of the traditional approach to political philosophy and the naive mechanical and organic metaphors that accompany it. To change one's conception of what a subject is changes, necessarily, the conception of what that subject can know or become. This is one of the most important insights of feminist theory, yet it is one that many feminists have not taken account of in relation to their ethico-political stance. The scant commitment that some feminists have concerning what human being is, is incompatible with the desire, of these same feminists, to have and to pursue a definite ideal future. To view human being as a social product devoid of determining universal characteristics is to view its possibilities as open-ended. This is not to say that human being is not constrained by historical context or by rudimentary biological facts but rather that these factors set the outer parameters of possibility only. Within these constraints, if they can be called that, there is an almost limitless variety of possibilities. Social, political and ethical life, in the terms of this third feminist philosophy, must be acknowledged as 'processes involved in' rather than actions that have a definite beginning and end and a clear ethos. The blueprint notion of political action is not a feminist one and is certainly not implicit in, or even consistent with, *all* feminist theory. The questions alluded to in section two of this chapter—'What is woman?' 'Does woman exist?'—are distinctive in their desire to capture and fix woman's being, woman's desire. They result in the destruction of the productive ambiguity of a present femininity that is lived out in a female body that for historical and socio-political reasons is at present an existence that is simultaneously extremely rich and painfully contradictory. To investigate how this lived femininity has been constructed involves living with and experimenting with these ambiguities. The notorious difficulty involved in capturing and defining femininity has been noted, negatively, throughout the history of Western thought, from Aristotle to Freud. What is relatively novel is that any positivity could be attached to this ambiguity and that any theoretically coherent justification could be offered for it.

The reply of the third approach then to the riddle of the relationship between feminism and philosophy would be neither disjunctive nor conjunctive. Rather, these feminists would seek to shift the terrain and say that the riddle is Being itself—and as such it has no 'answer'. Both feminism and philosophy address this riddle—each in their own way and each with their own investments at stake. The interesting point to make here, in this third section, is that it is becoming increasingly clear that neither philosophy *nor* feminism can afford to continue to ignore each other. This may involve, for philosophy, that it accepts its ruptures, its gaps. To attempt to close the ruptures created by feminist discourses in philosophy, in order to ensure that philosophy remains intact, is not only undesirable—it is futile. These ruptures should rather be widened and be welcomed *as possibilities* rather than feared as 'lacks'. Posing riddles that have no answer is something the Mad Hatter and philosophy have in common. The interrogation of philosophy, like the trial of the Mad Hatter, should be seen as providing the means to 'move beyond' some riddles but not as an end in itself—since still other riddles will pose themselves. This developing feminist philosophy involves neither the 'death' nor obsolescence of feminism or philosophy, but rather the transformation of both. The salient point here is that there cannot be an unadulterated feminist theory which would announce our arrival at a place where we could say we are 'beyond' patriarchal theory and patriarchal experience. Nor can there be *a* philosophy which would be neutral, universal or truly *human* in its character, thus rendering feminism redundant. Acknowledging this entails also acknowledging that a commitment to feminist politics *necessarily* involves a ceaseless critical engagement with and interrogation of our (theoretical/practical) existences.

BEVERLY THIELE

3 Vanishing acts in social
and political thought:
Tricks of the trade

It is common knowledge among feminists that social and political theory was, and for the most part still is, written by men, for men and about men. The classic theorists of political philosophy are all firmly within what O'Brien (1981:5) calls the 'male-stream': their subject matter reflects male concerns, deals with male activity and male ambitions and is *directed away from* issues involving, or of concern to, women. As a consequence, women themselves do not appear as actors in the realm of social and political thought. Where she is present, woman is either a partial figure engaged in activities which can easily be described by direct analogy to men (as with the Marxist worker—a sexless creature), or she is an ideological construction of the male theorist's imagination—we see 'Woman' in all her glory rather than *real* women. What is missing from social and political theory is, to use Clark and Lange's (1979:viii) phrase, Women qua women. What women are, do and can become are not the central concerns of male-stream theory nor are they considered appropriate concerns for such theory.

The legerdemain by which real women are made to disappear from theories about human society and polity deserves close attention. A skilful magician contrives to draw the eye away from whatever device enables the lovely lady to vanish from view, but a critical mind can discover these artifices and help expose magic acts for what they are—exercises in illusion.

Artemis March (1982) began an investigation into women's disappearance from male-stream scholarship by identifying the forms their invisibility takes in androcentric sociology. I want to extend this analysis to political theory and go a little further by disclosing the tricks which help theorists to eliminate women from 'the discourse' (D. Smith, 1979:147). Neither 'elimination' nor 'invisibility' are used in a purely literal sense, though there are literal examples within the male-stream. Rather the terms are intended to include the process whereby women are marginalised and their contribution to society is trivialised: they are 'eliminated' from the central focus of the theory and 'invisible' in as much as they do not appear as subjects in their own right.

The schema at the end of this chapter summarises its material. It is not intended as a classificatory schema of social and political theories but rather as a guide for sensitive feminist reading of such texts. It is, if nothing else, an early warning system for patriarchal scholarship.

Such an analysis has implications for two other debates of current interest. The first of these is the question of how subversive is the feminist critique of social and political philosophy as we know it? Can male-stream thought be redeemed by simply writing women back into the field or does corrective action necessitate a radical alteration of the nature of the discipline? The second issue concerns the nature of feminist scholarship itself. What are the implications of our critique of male-stream thought for our own practice as scholars? These concerns will be discussed towards the end of this chapter.

THE MAGIC ACTS

As noted earlier, Artemis March developed her typology of women's invisibility from a study of androcentric sociological theory, but there is little difficulty extending it to political theory and it is equally valuable for both disciplines. The three forms of invisibility she identified were exclusion, pseudo-inclusion and alienation.

Exclusion
Invisibility of this form involves women being completely ignored or neglected because the subject of such theories are explicitly male or male-dominated institutions and activities. Women are excluded by default; they become invisible by being disregarded. Typically no explanation is offered for the selection of subject matter barring the implicit presumption that these institutions and activities are important. March (1982:100) suggests that Weber, for example, structurally excludes women from his theory by setting priorities in subject matter and data which focus attention on social processes and activities in which women are only marginally involved, if at all.

There is, however, another far less subtle form of exclusion practised in political theory, and this is when women are, for no given reason, simply dropped from the discourse. Their disappearance is magical. In this second form women may in fact get mentioned but, to the extent that theoretical propositions about women bear any relation to the main thesis, they might just as well not be there at all. In such cases the theory's shortcomings are frequently all too apparent. Hobbes is an example. He assumes an initial State of Nature in which men and women are explicitly equal and in which women have natural authority over children, but he ends up with a Commonwealth entirely inhabited by men. Women's absence is so marked that Brennan and Pateman (1979:187) have described the Hobbesian family in civil society as a 'one parent family' where that parent is a father. Why women never make it into membership of the Commonwealth is never explained, and their relation to civil society has continued to plague liberal and social contract theorists ever since (Brennan and Pateman, 1979; Pateman, 1980a).

It should be stressed, though it is not clear if March also thinks so, that the exclusion of women is an active process rather than a result of passive neglect. It is not a simple case of lapsed memory; these theorists don't just forget to talk about women; rather, women are structurally excluded from the realm of discourse or, for the sake of theoretical preoccupations and coherency, they are deliberately dropped. This distinction is important to what comes later as the implications of forgetfulness for a truly universal, *human* political theory are quite different from those of active exclusion. Moreover to speak of these theorists as simply neglecting women is to describe a process they are engaged in as a forgivable mistake they make.

The illusion that their only sin is one of omission is, I think, encouraged more in commentaries on the classic texts than by the 'great men' themselves. Clark and Lange (1979:ix), to take a feminist example, state that 'most theory up to the nineteenth century explicitly excludes females', and yet, as Carole Pateman (1983c:4) pointed out, many of these pre-nineteenth-century theorists had something to say, and in some cases a good deal to say, about women. The problem is that much of this material is ignored by later commentators and, in some cases, has even been deleted by the editors of classic texts. For example, Book 5 of *Emile*, in which Rousseau draws his picture of Sophy, has proved such an embarrassment to his admirers that in several editions of the work it is simply omitted (O'Brien, 1981:95). The studied silences with which subsequent commentators have passed over passages on women is indicative of continuing efforts by our contemporaries to slam the door on whatever meagre foot we happen to have in it. That feminist scholarship should make the same presumption is more dangerous, however, as these are the very passages which, among other things, provide us with our insights into the active nature of exclusion.

Pseudo-inclusion

Pseudo-inclusion differs from exclusion in that the theory appears to take women into account but then marginalises them. Women become defined as a 'special case', as anomalies, exceptions to the rule which can be noted and then forgotten about. What is normative is male. In instances of pseudo-inclusion some excuse is usually offered for this dismissal of women as a special case, frequently, as we shall see later, taking the form of an argument from 'Nature'.

March's choice of Durkheim's *Suicide* is an excellent one, particularly given his treatment of the statistics on female suicides. This data contradicts Durkheim's thesis about why people commit suicide, but rather than change the theory or admit that it is not universally applicable, he embarks on a long explanation of the peculiarities of woman's nature. We are, to quote March (1982:103), 'too primitive to absorb the niceties of male civilisation, too dense to be deeply affected by the unweavings and reweavings of the social fabric, too self-contained to be socially vulnerable'. For these reasons we become unsuitable subjects for Durkheim's study and, as Beth Pengelly's (1981) careful analysis of *Suicide* reveals, he actually deletes the statistical data on women halfway through the text.

Rousseau provides another example. He is one of those social and political theorists who actually expends a considerable amount of effort on women but, once again, treats them quite differently from men. In this case his primary human values—freedom and equality—are not just irrelevant to women; they are, in Rousseau's ideal republic, necessarily inappropriate values for women. Men are told in *The Social Contract*, 'To renounce one's liberty is to renounce one's quality as a man, the rights and also the duties of humanity', while women, according to Book 5 of *Emile*, 'must be trained to bear the yoke from the first so that they may not feel it: to master their own caprices and submit themselves to the will of others' (C. Gould, 1980:19). As Moller-Okin (1979a:401) commented, 'Emile is educated to be his own man and Sophie to be his own woman', and it is with the Emiles of this world and the civil society they construct that Rousseau is primarily concerned.

Alienation

The third form of invisibility March describes in her typology refers to those theories which Clark and Lange (1979:ix) call 'extensionally male'. That is, they include women as subjects but they do not speak of the parameters of women's lives without distortion. Women's experience is interpreted through male categories because the methodology and values of the theorists remain androcentric. Despite any commitment these scholars have to the subject of women, their perspective interferes with their interpretation of women's experience, in particular by underwriting the selection of that part of women's lives which is deemed significant. How else can Mill see education as women's gateway to liberal equality and freedom, and fail to see that their continued responsibility for childrearing constrains both their access to education and, once they've got it, what they can do with it (for example Pateman, 1980b:31).

Some of the best examples of women's alienation in theory come from the marxist tradition, for example, Engel's description of women's oppression as *class* oppression. Similarly marxist-feminist attempts to use marxism to understand women's oppression have often resulted in this type of invisibility for their subjects: our domestic labour, once seen as non-productive, is now thought to 'produce use-values' for capitalism rather than service the need of men in a patriarchy; procreation is not race regeneration but 'reproducing the labour-force'; and our position within the family and relations with other family members are significant only as part of the 'social relations of production' not reproduction. These efforts at incorporating women into marxist theory are hardly adequate as 'each of these additions structurally locates women as adjunctive to the main focus of men's relations with men through their relations to the means of economic production' (March, 1982:105). Women's activity is still treated from an androcentric perspective and there is no effort to shift the grounding of the analysis away from male ego and experience, and onto female ego and experience. Women qua women remain both invisible and eccentric.

Not surprisingly, such theory seems strangely unable to change the conditions of women's lives. John Stuart Mill, for all his efforts on behalf of women's rights, never profoundly challenged structural aspects of women's experience; responsibility for childbearing and child-rearing, preoccupation with family domestic labour, etc. He still thought the traditional division of labour between men and women offered most women the best conditions for self-development. Only exceptional women needed to seek fulfilment elsewhere and then only by ensuring that their natural duties were not neglected. Mill never extended equal opportunity into the home; he simply gave women a choice of traditional role or a double burden: while he 'wanted women to *have* the right to enter any occupation ... he did not want, or expect, them to *exercise* that right' (Hughes, 1979:533).

TRICKS OF THE TRADE

Although March does not discuss the mutual exclusivity of each of these types it is fairly clear that they cannot be seen this way. Marx in the *German Ideology*, for example, exhibits pseudo-inclusion as well as alienation. It seems then that the best value can be gleaned from

March's work if it is treated less as a classificatory scheme for social and political theorists and more as a typology of possible approaches. This is even truer of the second series of categories, the techniques of invisibility. These are invariably used in combination with each other to bring about women's exclusion, and in some cases are consistently paired. Not only is this second list not composed of mutually exclusive items, it is also far from exhaustive. The techniques are simply the ones I and my feminist friends have come across in our forays into social and political theory so far.

Decontextualisation

By decontextualisation, I am referring to the practice in theorising of abstracting from real people, real activities and events in order to make generalisations about 'Man', 'Society' and so on. The important problem with this process is that it allows a theorist's commonsense assumptions about the world and reality to intervene between the real and ideal, the particular/concrete and the universal or general. Decontextualisation contributes to the myth of objectivity by facilitating the subtle intervention of value systems, ideology and consciousness into the process of theory construction. It is these things which determine what theorists consider important, essential and relevant to their theory, and what they do not. It determines which particular experiences are recognised as common and generalised and which are thought to be idiosyncratic and reasonable to exclude.

C. Gould (1980:9) has suggested that one of the most important deletions which takes place between the concrete and the abstract is gender: that being male or female is considered irrelevant to being human. This may be so, but what has traditionally occurred is that the abstraction from gender difference to what is truly human—to what is supposedly shared in common by both sexes—has been distorted by the intrusion of male-stream consciousness. What is *male* becomes the basis of the Abstract, the Essential and the Universal, while what is female becomes accidental, different, other.

We can see this fairly clearly in Weber's work where both sexes are decontextualised—abstracted from reality—but while abstract man is writ large in Weber's theory, abstract woman is written off. Moller-Okin (1980:10) makes a similar point about the intrusion of common-sense, value-laden assumptions when she observes that political philosophers have asked different questions of men and women: 'Philosophers who, in laying the foundations for their political theories, have asked "What are men like?" "What is man's potential?" have frequently, in turning to the female sex, asked what are women for?'

Universalisms

Decontextualisation and universalisms are closely linked because, just as the claim of objectivity obscures the value-laden nature of theorising, the claim to universality disguises the different treatment of men and women in social and political thought. Decontextualisation enables a theorist to 'take (or mistake), unreflectively and therefore uncritically, the part for the whole, the particular for the universal and essential, or the present for the external' (C. Gould, 1980:21), and in the case of male-stream thought it also enables the theorist to take (or mistake) the male for the human.

Language is a great facilitator of universalisms. Terms such as 'man' and 'mankind' are used as if they were *generic* when in effect they are *genderic*. 'He' is assumed to be the all-inclusive pronoun, even though a close examination of the text makes it all too apparent that the author literally means 'he'. As Moller-Okin (1980:5) pointed out, 'the dangerous ambiguity of such linguistic usage ... [is that] it enables philosophers to enunciate principles as if they were universally applicable, and then to proceed to exclude all women from their scope'. Sexist language disguises the omission and denies the exception being made of women.

Naturalism

Perhaps the most common and persistent of the techniques used to separate women from men and exclude the former from the central grounds of theory is the recourse to the excuse proffered by 'Nature'. Underlying this is one of the many dualisms (nature/culture) apparent in male-stream thought. The significance of dualisms will be discussed shortly, but what makes the natural/social dualism distinctive, and deserving of closer scrutiny, is its efficacy in the disappearing act.

There are two reasons for this. In the first place, what is 'natural' ceases to require a social or political explanation; it is simply given, a constant which can be taken for granted. Marx, for example, uses this ploy to eliminate reproduction from dialectical materialism. Although a necessary condition for the 'reproduction' [*sic*] of capital, the propagation of the species, he says, need not concern the capitalist as it can be safely left up to the labourer's natural instincts (Marx, 1954). When reproduction is conceptualised as 'natural' it becomes incapable of generating social change and is written out of historical materialism. Of course, eliminating reproduction from theory has ramifications beyond chucking out the baby. The bathwater—women and the sexual and social relations arising from reproduction (the family, etc.)—are largely thrown out as well. Only the faintest of grimy rings remains to remind us that these too have some relevance to human experience, society and history.

The irony in this deletion of reproduction was nicely exposed by Mary O'Brien in *The Politics of Reproduction* (1981). She points to the selectivity of such a rationale:

36

Clearly, reproduction has been regarded as quite different from other natural functions which, on the surface, seem to be equally imbued with necessity: eating, sexuality and dying, for example, share with birth the status of biological necessities. Yet it has never been suggested that these topics can be understood only in terms of natural science. They have all become the subject matter of rather impressive bodies of philosophical thought; in fact we have great modern theoretical systems firmly based upon just these biological necessities ... [Dialectical Materialism, Psychoanalysis, and Existentialism] ... The inevitability and necessity of these biological events has quite clearly not exempted them from historical force and theoretical significance. (O'Brien, 1981:20)

And yet it has, in the eyes of the male-stream, for reproduction and women.

This raises the second important feature of naturalisms in social and political thought; the considerable ambiguity in the implications and significance of what is designated 'natural'. Natural men and natural women often imply quite different things to a political theorist, and this inconsistency is very clearly related to his political intent. When Rousseau, for example,

refers to the natural man and to the natural woman, he has two distinct reference points in mind. Natural man is man of the original state of nature; he is totally independent of his fellows, devoid of selfishness, and equal to anyone else. Natural women, however, is defined in accordance with her role in the golden age of the patriarchal family; and she is, therefore, dependent, subordinate, and naturally imbued with those qualities of shame and modesty that will serve both to make her sexually appealing to her husband, and to cause her to preserve her chastity as her most precious possession. (Moller-Okin, 1979a:401–2)

Male nature is independent, active and truly human while female nature, conveniently for the status quo, fits her only for a narrow domestic role. The convenience is on man's part: his nature is such that he may transcend his animality by escaping into the human political realm of civil society, but only because women, trapped by their biology into remaining in the private sphere, oversee all the animal-like functions of mastication, defecation and copulation. He may still have to do the number one and two but she will clean the loo.

Dualisms

As noted earlier the excuse of 'Nature' is based on the opposition between what is 'natural' and what is 'social'. Such oppositions on dualisms are very common motifs in Western social and political thought—mind/body, nature/culture, emotion/reason, subject/object, public/private, individual/social, concrete/abstract, and so on. All of them should be approached with extreme caution because more often than not they line up with that fundamental dichotomy, male/female.

Women are all body and no mind, closer to nature than culture, in the private realm not the public, emotional rather than rational, etc. etc. There are two important points to recognise about dualisms. In the first place the dichotomous terms are commonly regarded as separate and opposed. Nancy Jay (1981:44) noted that instead of being viewed as mere contraries (A/B), which can recognise continuity between the terms without shattering the distinction being drawn, most dualisms are regarded as logical contradictions (A/Not A). One can be *either* subject *or* object, either rational or emotional, never both. Whereas contrary distinctions are limited as dichotomies by discourse— responsive to any need for expanded distinctions (for example man/ woman/child) or for integrative concepts (for example the subjectivity of an object or commitment to reason)—logical dichotomies limit discourse: 'Such distinctions are all-encompassing. They do not cover every possible case of the category ... to which they are applied, but they are, and logically *do*, order "the entire universe, known and knowable"' (Jay, 1981:44). The fuzzy middle ground between male and female, nature and culture, public and private is lost to view.

The second important feature of logical contradictions is that they contain an implicit value judgment. One pole (A) has positive value, the other (Not A) is negative:

> Dualism always poses an ethical choice, an either/or: one opposite is always preferable to the other. There is no room for gradations and levels, for complexities, for paradox, for multi-focusing. Dualities reinforce linear, cause-and-effect, hierarchical thinking ... Dualities have an ethical base, each pair contains two opposities, one of which is 'good' and the other 'bad'. Each pair is a binary, containing, in itself, a value judgement. (Starrett, 1976:9)

We all know which of the dualisms listed above are intended to be regarded positively.

For the feminist critic of social and political thought, dualisms provide useful ways of disclosing the male-stream nature of discourse. Their appearance in a text frequently embodies women's oppression and exclusion. When J.S. Mill outlines in *On Liberty* (1972:75) the relationships between public and private realms he reveals, for all his undoubted feminism, his male perspective. The private realm as an arena of freedom and autonomy, as compensation for the compromises of the public sphere, has meaning only for men. Women exist principally in the private sphere, an arrangement which is, for Mill, both normative and ideal. For them the private sphere expresses control not freedom, submission not autonomy; it is the realm in which they consent to be ruled by the exercise of *male* autonomy and freewill. As Mary O'Brien (1981:93) argued, the relationship between public and private spheres has the same significance for reproductive relations as class struggle has for productive relations and, in their use of dualistic concepts, Mill and other male-stream theorists are engaged in male praxis vis-a-vis women's oppression.

Appropriation and reversal
One final tool of patriarchal scholarship is what Mary Daly (1978:8) has termed 'reversals'. These are images and symbols of women-centred processes which, as part of the male method of mystification, are 'stolen, reversed, contorted and distorted by the misogynist mix-masters' (Daly, 1978:75). Reversals ensure that women's activities and contributions to society and life are denigrated and trivialised, and they do so by appropriating the imagery and symbolism of those women-centred processes for male activities. Marx's use of the term reproduction—the reproduction of daily life, the reproduction of the labour force—is an example of reversal. It is more than mere analogy because by appropriating the symbolism for male process the original activity (birth) is deprived of its meaning and significance; for Marx, men make history and themselves, women *merely* make babies.

Birth, not surprisingly, is a prime candidate for reversal in the hands of male theorists. Whatever is considered the primary male activity becomes characterised as truly creative, truly human. In Marx it is production, in Plato, rational thought: *Wisdom*, argued Plato in one of his dialogues on love, is the *true life-force*—a meeting of minds is necessary for the birth of the truly human. Since this meeting of minds is a homosexual activity the components of real reproductive activity (sexuality, women, pregnancy and parturition) are relegated to a lower and ethically inferior level of existence. Note the imagery of this passage from part of the dialogue: Plato is suggesting that the immortality of fame is superior to the immortality which comes from having children. He is talking only about men:

> so those who are pregnant in body turn to women and are enamoured in this way, and thus, by begetting children, secure for themselves, so they think, immortality and memory and happiness, 'providing all things for the time to come', but those who are pregnant in the soul, for there are some who conceive in the soul more than in the body, what is proper for souls to conceive and bear. And what is proper?—wisdom and virtue in general—to this class belong all creative poets, and those artists and craftsmen who are said to be inventive. But much of the greater wisdom . . . and the most beautiful, is that which is concerned with the ordering of cities and homes, which we call temperance and justice. (Plato, 1970:150)

Male politics wins out in the end.

FEMINIST CRITICISM AND FEMINIST SCHOLARSHIP

Let me by way of conclusion make a few observations on the implications of this critique, and thereby return to the question I raised at the beginning about whether, and how, such a bias may be corrected: How profound is the feminist critique? and what lessons does it hold for the development of feminist scholarship?

From what we have seen about the practices of male-stream theorists and the nature of their theories about women, two things are clear. First, the exclusion of women from the realm of discourse is not simply a sin of omission—a simple matter of neglect or forgetfulness which can be rectified by putting women back in—because we've seen that even when women do constitute part of the subject matter of political theory they are still rendered invisible by the orientation, techniques and methodology used by the theorists (that is, pseudo-inclusion and alienation). Presence, *being there*, is no guarantee of visibility, of accurate or appropriate treatment by the discipline.

Second, it is clear that invisibility cannot simply be a case of bias or unexplored assumptions or simple misogyny (although undoubtedly many of these theorists were misogynists). If this were the case then a commitment to overcoming bias or a feminist consciousness should be enough to write integrated political theory, and yet, it isn't. Mill, in spite of his feminism, was unable to write into liberal theory women who were, like men, free and equal individuals; and marxist-feminists still produce theory in which women are alienated from themselves.

It might be countered that what we lack is simply the right sort of corrections, that we need, as McCormack (1981) suggests, '[j]ust theory'. This claim rests on the assumption that the 'psychology of knowledge' may reflect a male power structure in science and society, but that the 'logic of knowledge' is gender-free (McCormack, 1981:4). It is doubtful, however, whether there is any real value to be gained by the abstraction of epistemology from its social context. As is clear from this analysis, and is even more clear in the closing chapters of Susan Moller-Okin's book *Women in Western Political Thought* (1980), the relationships between male-stream theories of human society and polity, and the patriarchal status quo is fairly straightforward. At the end of her book, Moller-Okin tries to do a counterfactual experiment on Aristotle, Rousseau and Mill by putting women back into their respective theories as the equal of men. She concludes that 'it is by no means a simple matter to integrate the female half of the human race into a tradition of political theory which has ... defined them and intrafamilial relationships, as outside the scope of political', and suggests that they cannot be included 'without challenging age-old assumptions about the family, its traditional sex-roles, and its relation to the wider world of political society' (Moller-Okin, 1980:286).

Here Moller-Okin is revealing two facets of traditional androcentric political theory which make the difficulties of putting women back in, and of correcting bias, particularly acute. The first is that the exclusion of women—the opposition of women, family and nature on the one hand, to men, civil society and politics on the other—is fundamental to the definition of what is political, of what is an appropriate subject for political theory. To include women requires a fundamental change of direction for the discipline. Second, social and political theory is part of the praxis of men. It is both indicative of, and an agent in the oppression of women by men. By including women alongside men the traditional generic divisions of patriarchal society are profoundly challenged. Dorothy Smith (1979:148), writing of contemporary efforts to redress the balance in sociology without changing the nature of the theory itself, noted:

> The problem is that this procedure is one which, whether it is additive or truly critical, treats the 'agenda' of the discipline as given. But this agenda ... is grounded in the working worlds and relations of men, whose experience and interests arise in the course of, and in relation to, participation in the ruling apparatus of society.

We would appear then to have grounds for scepticism about the extent to which social and political philosophy may be redeemed. The exclusion of women is a foundation stone of the discipline and must therefore have profound implications for its 'logic of knowledge'.

So what are our alternatives? It seems fairly obvious that if women's lives cannot be adequately theorised about by androcentric thought then we could in the first instance try to write theory from a gynocentric perspective, one which instead of being grounded in the experiences of men has at its centre a female ego. On the surface this would seem to beg the question of an integrated, truly universal political theory and lend credence to criticism that our reading of the tradition of Western political thought is negative, accusatory and narrow (Tenenbaum, 1982:137). Such a view, I think, is both inaccurate and misrepresents feminist ambitions. As Mary O'Brien's theorising in *The Politics of Reproduction* (1981) illustrates so well, gynocentric theory is more than a mere counterbalance. It should not be conceived of as the complement to, or the opposite of male-stream thought but, because it takes off from the insights gained from a feminist perspective on the male-stream, it can and does transform and transcend androcentric theory. As March (1982:99) suggests, 'a gynocentric perspective expands and diversifies the domain of what theorists theorise. In this sense, we can argue that a female-centered theoretical perspective can be more objective, because less is assumed and more is examined'. It is a turn of a spiral, not the flip of a coin.

More importantly for feminist scholarship, gynocentric theory not only challenges and transforms the *content* of political philosophy; it also challenges and transforms its *methodology*. In taking off from our critique of male-stream thought we are sensitised to the political uses of the male-stream's magic tricks and do not have to perform on the

Forms of invisibility*

(active) Exclusion	Pseudo-inclusion	Alienation
Disregards women	Makes women a special case	Reinterprets women's experience
Problematic assumptions	*Problematic assumptions*	*Problematic assumptions*
Data consists of external, visible acts	That male data is normative and therefore interpretations and models based on men are adequate	Same as pseudo-inclusion
Male ego is the assumed centre from which theory is spun out		*Women as objects of analysis*
Women as objects of analysis	Women don't really count, therefore can delegitimate as 'anomalous' the female data or gender differences	Incorporation of women into male categories (e.g. bourgeois)
Data on women not collected	Single set of social relations exists	Women as converted to data/roles in conceptual schema which are male-centred (e.g. reproducer of labour force)
Data on women not analysed	*Women as objects of analysis*	
Women as subjects/actors	Judge/interpret women's actions in male-centred activities/organisations by male norms	*Women as subjects/actors*
Women not conceived as political actors – acting in self-interest		Male naming of female experience, women forced to think through their experience via male categories (e.g. feminity as penis envy)
Priorities given to male activities/actors	*Women as subjects/actors*	
	Women seen only in marginal relation to male activities/spheres	
e.g. Weber, Hobbes	e.g. Durkheim, Rousseau	e.g. Marx, marxist-feminists, J.S. Mill

Tricks which bring about invisibility⁺

Decontextualisation	Universalism	Naturalism	Dualism	Appropriation/Reversal
Abstracts from reality. Ideology, consciousness determine what is important, essential, universal (male) and what is deleted as insignificant and irrelevant (female) e.g. Weber Differential treatment of men and women – what men and women are/do/can be vs what women are for	Obscures bias in decontextualisation e.g. Language which claims to be generic obscures partiality	What is 'natural' ceases to require an explanation (e.g. Marx) Ambivalence regarding 'nature' and 'natural' reflects the purpose of naturalism in theory i.e. to exclude women	Differentiate male from female and invest male pole with positive value and female with negative value viz. A-not A dichotomy They embody women's oppression and exclusion and exemplify male-stream character of social and political thought e.g. Mill	Images/symbols/descriptions which are stolen from woman-centred processes and reversed for male scholarship e.g. Marx: men make history, women make babies. Weber: men act women react

* extracted from March (1982:107)

same terms. Nancy Jay (1981) recognises that dichotomies needn't be treated as logical contradictions and Mary Daly (1978) reclaims our symbolism from the reversals and appropriations of patriarchal scholarship. More importantly, because our critique emerges from our experience of exclusion, we can consciously choose to write theory which is profoundly reflexive. With Mary O'Brien (1981:1–11) we write theory out of our experience and back into our experience. We are not only looking at a different subject: we are also doing a different type of scholarship.

ROSI BRAIDOTTI

4 Ethics revisited: Women and/in philosophy

This chapter deals with the normative power of reason within Western philosophy. One of the premises on which it rests is that philosophy, like all the so-called 'human sciences' stands for an instrumental approach to language.

The main issue I shall raise in the first section involves the status of philosophy as a discipline, that is to say as a discursive model. My aim is to point out and to question the normative style of enunciation as the dominant mode of philosophical discourse, particularly in so far as it affects the binary opposition of masculine and feminine values. Feminist theory and practice will provide the critical stand necessary to sustain my questioning of this philosophical opposition. In the second section I shall try to define the different strategies undertaken by women in philosophy and to develop an overview of the specific brand of activity known as 'feminist theory'. In the third section I shall turn to some contemporary European philosophers' reaction to the presence of and the discursive impact made by women in philosophy. In this respect I will ask whether feminism can lend itself to the formulation of non-hegemonic types of theoretical discourse.

The beginning, like all beginnings, can only be 'formless and empty'. It is not towards the hallowed monuments of the history of philosophy that I intend to draw your attention, but rather towards the least philosophical of all subject matter: women, as they are depicted in a novel called *Kinflicks* (Alther, 1975).

It is the story of a simple girl from a middle-class background who ends up in an ivy-league college in the United States of America. Struggling with the intellectual requirements of this institution, she becomes particularly interested in philosophy, which is embodied in her favourite teacher, Miss Head. The rigorous intellectual discipline of philosophy stands for order, self-control, harmony—qualities that young Ginny of *Kinflicks* sadly lacks. It is almost as a consequence of this lack that she develops an intense case of fascination for the great overachievers who have written the history of philosophy.

Taking their example much too literally, Ginny becomes a caricature of the very ideas she so passionately believes in: she talks like a Cartesian textbook, imitates the Spinozist subject and by concentrating all her energies on this game of projection, leads a life of emotional sterility.

Her passionate quest for knowledge is thus directly proportional to her feeling of fundamental intellectual and emotional inadequacy. Ginny feels she ought not to have been let into the institution of higher learning—she is a sort of impostor. And yet this feeling of illegitimacy feeds into her desire to learn; after all, she does want to become Miss Head's favourite pupil, and the desire to be a dutiful daughter spurs her on to bigger and better things.

Then, one day, Ginny meets the leftist campus radical—Eddie—but refuses to get involved, saying:

> You see, I'm apolitical. I agree with Descartes when he says that his maxim is 'to try always to conquer himself rather than fortune, and to alter his desires rather than change the order of the world, and generally accustom himself to believe that there is nothing entirely within his power, but his own thoughts'. (p. 242)

This fails to impress Eddie, whose reply is quick, clear and to the point: 'Descartes? . . . If my eyes were rotting in my skull from disuse I wouldn't read Descartes, that fascist son of a bitch!' (p. 249) Unperturbed, Ginny strikes back: 'Politics . . . is nothing but personal opinion, . . . I am not interested in opinions, I'm interested in truth.' Staring at her violently, weighing every word with soul-shattering hatred, Eddie utters the inevitable: 'And Descartes is truth? Have you read Nietzsche yet?'

This is the point of no return. Ginny rushes to read Nietzsche, particularly his demystification of rationality, and a few days later she resumes the conversation with Eddie: 'Something very definitely is wrong . . . I've just read what that bastard Nietzsche says about Descartes . . . I think it sucks.' Eddie positively beams: 'It sucks, uh? Do you know what that means—to suck?' Ginny is disconcerted and cannot see what sucking has to do with Descartes. Eddie declares triumphantly: 'Absolutely nothing . . . that's my whole point: I suck therefore I am, what do you think of that?'

This is the beginning of a great friendship between the two women, which will grow into a full love affair. Under Eddie's influence Ginny becomes the rebellious daughter; turning her back on Miss Head's set of values, which she now decries as 'moral paralysis', she decides to drop out of college altogether. The pursuit of excellence is replaced by intense experimentation in the woman's movement and eventually out of it—to become a 'new' mother in her own right.

It seems to me that this rather schematised portrait of 'women in philosophy' is very useful to raise a few key issues concerning women's involvement with philosophy as a theoretical practice. The question is: what sort of 'structures' are at work in the case of women involved in philosophical theory? By structures I mean first of all the psycho-sexual drives and the sort of human interaction they are likely to give rise to. Second, I mean social relations, mediated by money and authority; finally, linguistic structures as vehicles of communication.

WOMEN IN PHILOSOPHY

Philosophy seems to provide Ginny with an ideal outlet for her basic insecurity; she thus projects onto theoretical achievements her need for mastery and self-fulfilment. These feelings are clearly related to the fact that Ginny is a woman—but is this fact really as 'simple' as it looks? Ginny needs above all to be rescued from the confusing mess that is the female body, female sexuality and the web of social contradictions that is marked upon and carried by the idea of 'femininity'.

Becoming a good, that is to say a rational, philosopher is for Ginny a way to escape from the female condition. Miss Head—cold, cerebral and life-denying—is the ideal model to represent this desire for self-control. Ginny's libidinal economy consists in swapping her sexual/bodily existence for an idealised self-image as a masterful being. By becoming her own idealised image of herself she is, at long last, her own man!

This young woman has swallowed the misogyny of a cultural system where masculine values dominate and she reproduces it unconsciously in her attempt to be better than she is, better than a woman, that is to say—a man! This process of identification to phallocratic values raises several conceptual and ideological questions: to what an extent can any cultural system be value-free? How can sexual difference be inscribed as one of the key values in our culture? Are there any 'feminine' values and what is their 'nature'? Second, what price do women have to pay—intellectually, sexually and materially—in order to gain access to higher cultural and intellectual achievements, be it in theory, art or science? How does the total 'price' women pay for their drive towards self-fulfilment compare with the price men are asked to pay? Is there not a fundamental lack of symmetry in the libidinal as well as the material economy of the two sexes?

The fact that Ginny gains some peace of mind in the ultimate flight from womanhood can be explained with some help from psychoanalytic theories. Some obviously relevant areas of Freudian thought are: the nature of the female superego (Freud, 1932); women's relationship to the cultural and artistic activities that represent the great achievement of mankind (Freud, 1930); the question of female 'masochism' (Deutsch, 1945).

It is not my purpose here to deal with this complex problematic, but rather to stress that what binds Ginny to the lords and masters of higher learning is something akin to intense desire. Unless one is prepared to argue that women's desire is implicitly self-destructive one should re-examine the drive for knowledge in terms of the heterosexual bond.

One of the crucial issues in the debate about women in philosophy is that our culture has established a very firm dichotomy between the feminine and the notion of 'rationality'. In other words, the fact of being a woman has traditionally been assessed as a terrible handicap for a human being who aspires to higher cultural and theoretical achievements. It can be demonstrated today (Irigaray, 1974) that the feminine from Plato to Freud has been perceived in terms of matter, *physis*, the passions, the emotions, the irrational. The actual terms of the discussion as to female 'nature' evolved with time, from the initial question of whether women had a soul—and could consequently be considered as part of the human species—to the problem of their ability to behave ethically.

What was at stake in the question of women and ethics was their status as citizens, that is to say their eligibility to political and civil rights, which would grant them first-class membership in the private club of mankind.

Until the end of the nineteenth century the binary opposition of women and rationality persisted as one of the most venerable mental habits of Western political and moral thought (Moller-Okin, 1979). It seems to me that dualism cannot be dissociated from the question of power, and its corollary—domination and exclusion. I would argue consequently that it is not because they are rational that men are the masters, but rather that, being the masters, they have appropriated rationality as their own prerogative. The denigration and exclusion of the feminine in philosophy, in other words, is just a pretext for the great textual continuity of masculine self-glorification: the mysterious absent entity which grants full grounds for existence to the masculine knowing subject. In a very interesting paper Genevieve Lloyd (1979) demonstrates quite convincingly that the idealisation of rationality is coextensive with masculinity and that it usually turns into a list of grievances against the feminine. The feminine is reduced to that which is 'other-than' and whose difference can only be perceived in terms of pejoration and inferiority.

47

Although it would be possible to read the history of Western philosophy as a variation on the age-long theme of female oppression, against which feminists have taken a stand, I would rather not spell out all the discursive atrocities philosophers have committed against the feminine and against women. It would be a rather depressing task indeed. I prefer to concentrate on the binary logic itself—the dualism implicit in our respective and mutual perceptions of the feminine and the masculine, as they have been structured within our culture. In doing so, I am not releasing the philosophers from their historical responsibility as agents of repression. On the contrary, following Italian feminist Carla Lonzi in her highly provocative essay called 'Let's spit on Hegel!' (1974), I would demand of them an explanation. The question is what sort of explanation, if any, women are prepared to settle for.

After all, the mental habit that consists in turning the feminine into a set of metaphors for 'the other' is not just a small omission which can be remedied by goodwill and some quick repair work. No amount of inclusion of women into theory politics, society could palliate the effects of and compensate for the centuries of exclusion—moreover, compensation is not the feminists' primary goal.

From a feminist standpoint, the inadequacy of the theoretical model of classical rationality is that it is oblivious to sexual difference in that it mistakes the masculine bias for a universal mode of enunciation. The sexual neutrality it professes conceals a fundamental and un-spoken phallocentrism. To condemn this mode of thinking on the ideological level—as being sexist—does not suffice as a conceptual analysis. It is rather that, as a consequence of its phallocentric assumptions, this binary logic produces faulty and incomplete notions, untruths, scientific misjudgments—it is just not good enough as a system of thought.

One of the most instructive things about *Kinflicks* is that, although most of the action in the novel takes place among women, the context within which their exchange occurs is totally masculine. The essential problematic of the novel is thought out in terms of the women's relationship to male, white, middle-class theoreticians who are actually absent. They act as the silent, invisible, all-pervading masters of the game of discourse.

If we take the three main characters of our drama and see how they experience and organise their desire to learn, we can classify them according to the sort of relationship they establish with philosophy as a discursive institution.

Miss Head wishes to be let into the Hall of Fame and be allowed to rest alongside the great thinkers. She crystallises some of the worst dangers awaiting women who dare enter the sacred grounds of high culture. Her energy and creativity are wasted in sterile imitation of patterns of conceptual behaviour that have been invented and institu-tionalised by men, for themselves. Like a sleepwalker acting out someone else's script, she is caught in a perfectly mimetic structure of repetition. The relationship between Miss Head and Ginny is in some ways a replay of the darker side of the female oedipal configuration: the older woman is both the object of sterile love and the subject capable of exercising a normative, prescriptive function—a small-time leader who does not set the rules but knows how to apply them. Like the 'bad' mother of Freudian psychoanalysis, she is the one through whom the Law of the Father is applied and enforced upon the descendants, against their will if necessary. One of the marks of patriarchal culture is precisely the fact that the original bond between the mother and the child must give way to their joint acceptance of a common master: the husband, the father, the man.

Ginny is motivated by the desire to make philosophy the best of all possible disciplines. She believes in it with all the intensity of the neophyte, and were philosophy ever to fail her she would dedicate herself to the mission of reforming it, so as to make it live up to her own expectations. Had she not met Eddie, she would probably have become a moral philosopher and she might have adapted classical philosophical concepts to the analysis of some feminist topic. I can imagine her writing, for instance, a paper about 'the moral and philosophical issues raised by abortion'. Although Ginny is repre-sentative of the pre-feminist state of mind, it would be a mistake to dismiss her attitude as merely naive. The reformist work accomplished by women like Ginny is a reality that cannot be ignored today. In many subtle ways this type of promotion of women within the status quo is changing the structure of our society and of its discursive practices. This phenomenon often makes me think that women as a political movement are not nearly dangerous enough to the socio-political system. At other times it just leads me to believe that, in so far as they are part and parcel of this very system, women are condemned to being signifying agents within it. In other words women are doomed not only to speak, but also to have something to say; if they are to be producers of signs, however, it is their responsibility to choose the ways and means of their discursive production. It is up to women to make their 'difference' work in new and powerful ways wherever it chooses to express itself.

The third position, represented by Eddie, is radical feminism. It is, of course, no coincidence (is it ever?) that Ginny's break from the maternal bond coincides with her meeting this Nietzschian separatist. In a very direct way, she deconstructs all of Miss Head's attempts at systematising reality into a neat, exhaustive conceptual framework. The radical feminist attacks the phallocentric bias inherent in our culture, which manifests itself particularly in the tendency to leap from the particular to the universal and to associate the latter with the masculine. Eddie refuses the notion of universal truths. She posits the deconstruction of metadiscourse (Lyotard, 1978) and asserts the priority of multiplicity and discontinuity over linear and monolithic discourse. For instance, in so far as the preoccupation with 'woman as other' is all-pervading in Western thought it can be used as the paradigm to illustrate the interaction of rationality with norms of regulation, domination and exclusion.

In the radical feminist perspective, therefore, 'woman as other' is the prototype of all that is excluded from ruling modes of thought. Accordingly, it can be argued that the dominant order of discourse in modern thought—that of scientific rationality—is a normative model for all the sciences. 'Rationality' has been thought out in a binary set of oppositions which works by assigning to the negative pole all that is different, or 'other-than'. A connection is to be made, therefore, between the normative power of reason and the rational character of violence; both of these are instrumental to masculine power and to the age-long war it has waged against 'woman as other' and against the 'feminine'.

It seems to me that the radical critique of philosophy unveils the power structures implicit in the theoretical processes and that it does so form a sexualised standpoint. In other words, all philosophical claims to universality are deconstructed by pointing out the complicity between the masculine and the rational. This implies that philosophical discourse, far from being universal, suffers from the most partial onesidedness: a sexual and conceptual bias in favour of the masculine.

The feminist analysis of rationality in terms of normative power assumes that patriarchy has set up the categories of thought it most needed in order to legitimate itself, passing off as 'nature'—that is to say the 'other' of cultural order—a good half of mankind. To sexualise a discourse is therefore a practice of disclosure of vested interests: like the little girl who declares that the emperor is naked, Eddie sees through the power games involved in the theoretical process. The feminine 'dark continent' that puzzled Freud is thus read as the flip side of masculine self-legitimation in discourse.

The question then becomes: can rationality be freed from its hegemonic connotations? Is it possible to take the theoretical and political standpoint of feminism to bring about another regime of truth?

In order to explore the implications of these complex questions I will spell out three different sets of distinct, though related, problems: first of all, what are the specific aspects of the feminist practice of philosophy? Second, what are the repercussions for feminism of the practice of this discipline and how has the presence of feminism affected male philosophers? Third, I shall stress the importance of the ethical question as a point of junction between feminism and philosophy.

On the empirical level the changes brought about by feminism in the field of higher culture and education are obvious: some 50 years after Virginia Woolf's inspiring words (1938), women have gained access to the institutions of learning and are now present in most branches of knowledge. The effective presence of female scholars has caused basic alterations in the practice as well as the discourse of the sciences.

As far as philosophy is concerned, the contribution of someone like Simone de Beauvoir can no longer be ignored by professional philosophers, no matter how hard they try to resist. This new theoretical genealogy of women means not only that academic courses about women in philosophy are possible today but also that the question of women's relationship to learning, and the individual woman's handling of her desire to learn, is being structured differently. The presence of real-life women in positions of authority and knowledge is opening up new possibilities for self-image and identification in women. Thus, if young Ginny went to university today, she would probably have at her disposal some new models of women as fully fledged theoreticians in their own right. The novelty of the pedagogical relationship in which women play the leading roles deserves close scrutiny as the experimental grounds for new ways of thinking about and dealing with philosophy as an intellectual discipline.

It seems to me that feminists need to think more carefully about the transmission of the feminist insight as a critical stance, as well as a thematic or a content that can be formalised. In other words, feminism has the potential to provide thinking women with some critical distance vis-a-vis the structures of power and knowledge in which they are caught. For instance, the interplay of conflicts and desire at work in the pedagogical relationship between women often functions as both the catalyst for and the re-enactment of specifically female patterns of behaviour: oedipal and other dramas that tend to defy expected norms. This double interaction—on the one hand between women and masculine institutions of discourse and, on the other, between each woman involved in the process—stresses the complexity of the issues relating to both feminine and feminist identity.

Here psychoanalytic theory can, once again, provide some useful insight into the political implications of the process of construction of human sexual identity in general and of the feminine one in particular. If we view the discourse about the 'otherness' of femininity as one of the trans-historical and cross-cultural constants of patriarchal culture, then we can take the Freudian scheme as a fairly accurate description of the mechanisms of masculine authority—an analysis of the subjective grounding of patriarchal power.

For instance, in her article about the fantasies of erotic domination Jessica Benjamin (Eisenstein & Jardine, 1980) analyses the mixture of violence and desire that marks the process of identification and of differentiation of the child from his/her parents. Unless the mutual recognition of each other's subjectivity occurs, the need to achieve separation and individuality is doomed to take a violent turn. Benjamin stresses also the lack of symmetry between the two sexes, particularly when it comes to the notion of 'separation': the male child seems more prone to deny his dependence on the mother and, through the denial of this bond he also fails to acknowledge the other as a subject in her own right. In this paradoxical knot of violence and love lies the groundwork for the fantasy of the erotic domination, which can come to fruition in the adult sadomasochistic relationship. In a very interesting and quite daring argument, Benjamin suggests that the matrix of the desire to dominate and humiliate the (m)other, in other words the knot that ties together desire and violence, is related to the original failure to recognise the mother's subjectivity.

This vaguely Hegelian scheme applies perfectly well to our heroine Ginny, who is caught in the double bind of mother-love: loving and hating, life-giving and yet murderous, the maternal space is the threshold of the most fundamental psychic conflicts in one's life. The dialectical struggle for mutual recognition carries on until, in the oedipal triangle, the third party comes to break it up. In *Kinflicks* the tragedy is highlighted by the fact that Miss Head refuses to come to life in her own right. Ginny would be more than willing to recognise her, but the teacher recedes into her strictly functional dimension and, once her transitive task is over, she fades out of existence. Her self-denial not only prevents Ginny's recognition of her as a subject, it also slows down the development of her own individuality. The young woman builds around Miss Head a conflicting web of adoration and aberration, which finally escalates into a full-scale war between the mother figure and her daughter. It is as if one cannot grow without the other. Or else, to use one of Irigaray's more poetic images, one cannot stir without the other (1984). The primacy of the erotic bond with the mother leads to a vicious circle and the child's original attachment results in a structural ambivalence which is particularly violent for the baby girl.

This fundamental ambivalence gives a specific feminine inflexion to the question of interpersonal relationships: how do we explain the 'excessive' nature of women's love? How do we explain that the stuff love is made of is also what hatred is made of? How can we account for the coextensivity of power and desire?

I think that the question of the mother–daughter relationship has been latent in feminist thinking ever since the early days of the movement, when ideas such as 'sisterhood is powerful' seemed self-explanatory. It has, however, become more prominent of late, in a large number of publications, which is in itself quite significant. Like a boomerang, the return of the complex problem of the maternal signifies clearly that something had been missed.

Recent attempts at assessing the evolution of feminist thought on the mother–child relationship have spelled out the different stages of the feminist case for the politics of sexuality (Snitow et al., 1983). The transition from the very early consciousness-raising groups that praised the politics of experience and spoke out against female oppression, to the return of the debate on the double bind of femininity occurred through the lesbian separatist phenomenon.

Notions such as 'woman-identified woman' (Koedt et al., 1973) became the focus of a heated debate about the symbolic homosexuality represented by and built into the women's movement. Thus the insight that 'the personal is the political' acquired a sharper edge of controversy over the choice of erotic objects. The distinction and yet also the connection between personal sexual liberation and the politics of sexuality remains a crucial question for many feminists today. The complexity of the problematic has led, in the highly charged context of the socio-economic recession and the conservative backlash of the 1980s, to question the very notion of feminine identity in relation to the mother's body. It was at a rather critical point in time that the analysis of the mother–child relationship emerged as a powerful site of feminist thought, supported by the psychoanalytic insight into the construction of human subjectivity in terms of symbolic structures. The very formulation of the problem is a symptom of some deep discontent within feminist thought and practice.

When it comes to the question of the mother–child relation I feel quite resistant to two extreme though opposite solutions: one that consists in concealing the molecular complexity of the problem behind a sociological type of analysis (cf. Dinnerstein, Chodorow, etc.), the other being the mystifying idealisation of the woman-identified bond as a 'politically pure' identity, which reduces the mother–daughter problematic to an elaborate analogy for lesbianism.

It seems to me that a way out of this false alternative is a political analysis of sexuality as an interrelated set of power, knowledge and desire structures that are centred on the body—along the lines suggested by Michel Foucault in his *History of Sexuality*. In Foucault's view the interplay of body, discourse and power is positive, that is, it is not to be understood in terms of repression, but rather as active production of forms of knowledge about the bodily subject. Foucault focuses on the historical forces that shape the production of discourse, but at the same time he stresses the idea that 'historical contingency forms a substantial part of the sexual life' (Person, 1980). The attention thus paid to the complexity of the interplay of history and human subjectivity allows Foucault to go further than the traditional analyses of oppression. Within feminist thought, for instance, there exists a militant line (Brownmiller, 1975) that resolves the most problematic aspects of female sexuality—for instance the issues related to sadomasochism, power and domination—by reading them as marks of patriarchal oppression which women have turned inwards. In Foucault's perspective, on the other hand, the question becomes: what does it mean to turn something like this 'inwards'— into what? And out of what?

Foucault's work can be particularly useful to refute the tendency, displayed by some current trends of feminist thought (Daly, 1978) to define women as completely excluded from (dominant) culture and, as such, innocent of and uncontaminated by its values and signifying practices. This view has led, in its most radical separatist form, to the assertion of an authentically female sexuality that could and should be retrieved by women. The liberation of this sort of sexuality is then presented as the principle of legitimation for separatist feminist politics: feminism is the question, lesbianism is the practice.

It seems to me that the conjunction of sexual identity with the question of the politics of desire calls for a more complex discussion. As far as the question of sexual identity is concerned I feel very strongly that, although heterosexuality is the dominant 'lie' about women today (Rich, 1979)—and one which is perpetuated and enforced by an entire social system—it is not the only one. The homosexual separatist alternative is in no way qualitatively or politically 'better'. I do not believe that any purity is possible in a system as coded as ours, where categories such as 'sex', 'race' and 'class' carry normative connotations. There is no 'outside' in the material and discursive system that structures our subjectivity; all a political movement can aspire to is a strong sense of strategy in the Foucauldian sense—as the constant, multiple and dispersed quest for critical standpoints and points of resistance.

The suspension of belief in fixed identities of the sexual, cultural and political kind seems to me an essential step towards a critique of rationality as a normative notion. All identity is just a game of masks that conceals and yet at the same time also conveys the representations of our conscious thoughts and our unconscious thinking. Furthermore, the suggestion that identity is partial and fragmentary may help the feminist movement to avoid the pitfalls of dogmatism and prescription, from which it is not immune—as recent developments in 'feminist theology' and 'woman-centred mysticism' seem to indicate.

The stakes are high: the issue of sexual identity questions the legitimacy of the women's movement as a political force and as a critical stance. How can clear-thinking feminists justify and authenticate their political beliefs today? What evaluation should be made of recent feminist analyses and experiments with identity? Where should we draw the line between personal fantasies, the politics of solidarity and political utopias? These questions are a two-way mirror that reflects both on feminist theory and practice and on contemporary philosophical investigations of human subjectivity. The question I would like to raise here is: what happens to theoretical discourse when women refuse to play nature to *their* culture (Krueger, 1983)? What changes are brought about in an intellectual discipline when some of its main figureheads are women? What happens to the notion of rationality as a guiding principle if women are at last perceived as masterful minds? As Helene Cixous put it (1979), what will happen to their church when the stone on which they built it suddenly collapses?

In turn, how does contemporary philosophy contribute to feminist thought? What are the points of contact and of divergence?

PHILOSOPHY AND WOMEN—THE MISSING LINK

There is as yet no unified problematic about women and philosophy; the fragile conjunction *and*, which links the two terms of reference, does not fulfil a conjunctive role—rather it performs a disjunctive act, marks a categorical, qualitative leap between two discourses and two referents: philosophy/women.

An additional difficulty involved in formulating the problematic is also due to a remarkable coincidence, the emergence and the merging, in the last 30 years, of two phenomena: on the one hand the revival of the women's movement throughout the Western world which led to new analyses of the role, the life conditions and the discursivity of women; on the other, something quite internal to the theoretical field and to philosophy itself—the crisis of rationality. Although it was announced at the turn of the century by the apocalyptic trinity of critical thinkers—Marx, Freud, Nietzsche—this crisis acquired greater relevance and gathered momentum after the Second World War and particularly in Continental philosophy. I do not think this is a simple historical coincidence, but rather an extraordinary concurrence of effects: the new feminism and the philosophical urgency to question the epistemological groundwork of philosophical discourse. The movement to bring philosophy back to its specific historical context was very strong in France. Michel Foucault (1984a:80) summed up this shift of philosophical orientation as follows:

> I would say, then, that what has emerged in the course of the last 10 or 15 years is a sense of the increasing vulnerability to criticism of things, institutions, practices, discourses. A certain fragility has been discovered in the very bedrock of existence, even and perhaps above all in those

aspects of it that are most familiar, most solid and most intimately related to our bodies and to our everyday behaviour. But together with this sense of instability and this amazing efficacy of discontinuous, particular and local criticism, one in fact also discovers something that perhaps was not initially foreseen—something one might describe as precisely the inhibiting effect of global, totalitarian theories.

The structural fragility of discursive practices has led Foucault to reconsider critically the function of philosophy today. His main concern has thus become the questioning of power (1976–84): power as it operates within theoretical discourse, as a political economy that allows certain ideas to emerge as true and others to be excluded as false, in a regime of truth which works through socio-economic and symbolic institutions alike; the specific power exercised by the idea of rationality in its claim to universal validity as the dominant mode in Western philosophy; power as a concept particularly relevant to political philosophy and more particularly to the idea of governmentality—is there a connection between reason and power? how does the ideal of rationality relate to notions such as revolution and liberation?; power as coextensive with the body meant as a field of interacting social and libidinal forces—the body has emerged, in Foucault's thought, as a cognitive field, an object for theoretical and political analysis; it could even be argued that he is committed to working out the philosophical implications of Freudian epistemology, that is,the insight into the bodily, rather than rational, framework of human subjectivity.

Through these questions Foucault expresses the idea that we cannot go on thinking adequately about our historical existence within the categories of thought we have inherited from the past. In the light of the feminist strategies in philosophy that I have pointed out earlier Foucault's work on the body and power represents a clear point of contact between women and philosophy. His microphysics of power casts some new light on the dialectical opposition of the feminine to rationality and stresses the paradigmatic nature of dualistic thinking for Western philosophy.

Although I cannot develop here the details of Foucault's analysis of the 'feminine', I do wish to stress the significance of this point of intersection between philosophical inquiry and the theoretical issues raised by feminists. Let me illustrate this point of contact by a series of other statements made by contemporary thinkers, about the role and function of rationality in philosophical work. The first is taken from Foucault (1976–84:xii):

> These questionings are those which must be addressed to a rationality that makes universal claims while developing in contingency, which asserts its unity and yet proceeds only by means of partial modification,

when not by general recastings, which authenticates itself through its own sovereignty, but which in its history is perhaps not dissociated from inertias, weights which coerce it, subjugate it. In the history of science in France, as in German critical theory, what we are to examine essentially is a reason whose autonomy of structures carries with itself the history of dogmatism and despotism—a reason which, consequently, has the effect of emancipation only on the condition that it succeeds in freeing itself of itself.

The next extract comes from Paul Feyerabend (1975:32):

> We must invent a new conceptual system that suspends or clashes with the most carefully established observational results, confounds the most plausible theoretical principles and introduces perceptions that cannot form part of the existing perceptual world.

The following is taken from Gregory Bateson (1972:437):

> If I am right, the whole way of thinking about what and who we are and what other people are has got to be restructured. This is not funny and I don't know how long we have to do it in. If we continue to operate on the premises that were fashionable in the pre-cybernetic era . . . we may have 20 or 30 years before the logical reductio ad absurdum of our old positions destroys us . . . The most important task today is, perhaps, to learn to think in the new way. Let me say that I don't know how to think that way yet.

The final quotation comes from Adrienne Rich (1976:290):

> I am convinced that there are ways of thinking that we don't yet know about. I take those words to mean that many women are even now thinking in ways which traditional intellection denies, decries or is unable to grasp. Thinking is an active, fluid, expanding process; intellection, 'knowing' are recapitulations of past processes. In arguing that we have by no means yet explored our biological grounding, the miracle paradox of the female body and its spiritual and political meanings, I am asking whether women cannot begin, at last, to think through the body, to connect what has been so cruelly disorganised.

Reading these passages one after the other one is struck by their similarity, as well as some fundamental differences. The philosophers seem to come to a consensus on the urgency to rethink the very foundations of theoretical discourse; their cry of alarm is addressed specifically to the tradition of philosophical thought as an established institution. In other words, their interlocutor is the history of philosophy itself and they all situate themselves within this tradition as speaking subjects. The fact that the tradition which legitimates their position is going through a radical crisis is reflected in their own concern for their place of enunciation. They seem to experience the crisis of modernity as a problem of representation and self-legitimation (Lyotard, 1979). In different ways and to varying degrees they see themselves as carrying the heavy historical burden of 'freeing reason of itself' (Foucault); of suspending and confounding established scientific dogma (Feyerabend); of saving what is left of rationality before it's too late (Bateson)—Cassandra's voices echoing within the city walls.

Maybe there is no alternative left to philosophers in times of crisis than questioning the legitimacy of their discursive practice. Speaking as a feminist I think it must be very uncomfortable to be male, white, middle-class and a philosopher at a time in history when many oppressed groups are beginning to question the very foundations of Western subjectivity. It must be very painful to be cast back in the role of the oppressor and to be asked to account for it.

And yet the philosophers' concern can also be read as a sort of envy-in-disguise: were they oppressed, they could participate in the ferment of ideas of their culture; if they could join in the great work of critical deconstruction of some cultural and theoretical assumptions they might relinquish the guilt and the anguish that come from having been forced to realise the historical role men have played in perpetuating the oppression of women.

If one argues, from the feminist stand, that philosophy has been until yesterday a masculine prerogative that was passed down from the 'fathers' to the 'sons' as one of the intellectual attributes of masculinity, and that as such it excluded women as signifying agents, if then we go on to assume that a specific historical context of crisis has brought feminism and philosophy together, we can only conclude that the discourse of modernist philosophy does not necessarily have the same implications for feminists as for the philosophers. Much as I appreciate the conscious efforts of some male thinkers to develop a more critical outlook on their own cultural tradition and to deconstruct dominant modes of conceptualisation, I also maintain that this is not quite the women's story.

It seems to me that a double symmetry has emerged within critical thought between feminist thought and philosophical investigations of the status of philosophy in general and of its 'feminine' in particular. Feminism has evolved beyond the recognition and condemnation of a factual reality—the patriarchal oppression of women—towards a more active critique of the theoretical models imposed by their culture: the very status of discursivity, rationality and consciousness have been called into question. I would say that, in so far as women are still fighting for basic rights, they have tended to sexualise discourse, to point out its complicity with masculine power.

On the other hand, avant-garde philosophers, confronted by the need to renew their discipline, tend to argue for the dissolution of all models and discursive practices based on phallo-logocentric premises.

They stand before the void of the contemporary crisis of rationality calling for structural transformations in terms of what J.F. Lyotard recognised as one of the things at stake in feminism, namely the deconstruction of metadiscourse.

Some 'post-modern' thinkers display also the tendency to think about feminism and philosophy as a 'lucky coincidence'; a good example of this sort of mystification is a recent article by Craig Owens (1983:59)

> It is precisely at the legislative frontier between what can be represented and what cannot that the postmodernist operation is being staged—not in order to transcend representation, but in order to expose that system of power that authorizes certain representations while blocking, prohibiting or invalidating others. Among those prohibited from Western representation and denied all legitimacy, are women ...
>
> Here, we arrive at an apparent crossing of the feminist critique of patriarchy and the postmodern critique of representation.

In this passage, the intersection of women and philosophy is understood in the light of the problem of representation, of truth and its legitimation. The specificity of the female problematic is implicitly denied by being melted into a sign—a symptom?—of masculine preoccupations.

The feminist stand that I have been pointing out leads me to think that one cannot ascribe easily to the endless 'theories of representation' that our culture has produced and perpetuated about women. I will therefore contest this new metaphorisation of women as the unrepresentable of the process of representation; this position as a sign of unrepresentability is not structurally different from all the other signs to which the feminine was confined in the classical mode (the irrational, the emotional etc.). Women are still perceived as the 'blind spot' of the theoretical and signifying process, the 'dark continent'— and the basic dualistic logic of the signification process itself remains unchanged. The danger implicit in this position is precisely that it does not call into question the hegemonic model which sustains its mental habits; as such it carries on with the age-long metaphorisation of women by the masculine subject of enunciation.

I should rather think that feminism and philosophical modernity can be understood in dialectical terms, that is to say in terms of power and strategy. Thus I believe that the urgency felt by many contemporary philosophers to criticise their own discursive premises betrays their increasing awareness of the discursive presence and power of women and of feminist thought. They seem to have displaced their problematics accordingly.

The question I would very much like to be able to answer is: why is it that as soon as feminists began thinking out loud for themselves, male thinkers took up the 'feminine' as their own cause? What made them want to embark on this sudden 'feminisation' of their own modes of thinking? What is involved in this dramatic change in their place of enunciation? What is being exorcised by it? Why does the subversion or deconstruction of the subject of rationality seem to imply the transition via the 'feminine'?

The most important difference between the feminist stand and contemporary critical philosophy in the Continental tradition lies in their respective awareness of their place of enunciation. It is as if the feminist thinkers were actively involved in the process of bringing about—both in theory and in practice—some radically different notion of subjectivity meant as the conditions of possibility for some other history, some new mode of thought. It seems to me that this difference in inflexion has profound ethical implications. Feminism thus defined stands as the mark of desire for a new way to conduct human affairs, to think about the human being as an entity, as well as being the expression of a political will to achieve justice for women. As such it calls for a redefinition of the status of difference in our system of theoretical, moral and socio-economic values.

If we assert that feminism can bring about an open-ended quest for difference meant as a multiplicity of differences, it follows that what is at stake in feminist theory today is not female sexuality as much as the complex interplay of truth and power and the politics of desire in terms of the discursive and material institutions that shape it.

As our century draws to its end, several intellectual paths seem to converge on the questioning of the 'other' and the need to establish new possibilities for truth. If we are to believe the critique of power in/and discourse as a possible political position, then feminism can be seen as playing a major role in laying the foundations of post-modern ethics.

PART II
The Challenge to Liberalism

5 Selfhood, war and masculinity

Current debate on the implications of equal opportunity programmes for women has thrown up some conceptual complexities about sexual equality and sexual difference. Equal opportunity demands that there be no exclusion from job prospects on the grounds of gender; and the wider demands of equality of citizenship seem to require that there be no civil rights reserved exclusively for men, and no special exemptions for women from civil duties. But sexual equality sometimes cuts across what seem legitimate demands for the recognition of sexual difference. Having granted that there are none so prone to see sexual difference as those who are disinclined to grant sexual equality, there do seem nonetheless to be some unresolved dilemmas here that go beyond the operations of prejudice in individuals or groups, pointing to something deeper in our conceptualisations of gender, our ideals of citizenship and our understanding of the public/private distinction. The question of admitting women to combat positions in the armed forces—combining, as it does, issues of morality, of the demands of citizenship, and of equality in employment opportunity—poses these dilemmas in particularly stark form.

To get some of these issues into focus, I want to begin with a quotation from General Robert H. Barrow, commander of the US marines, on the admission of women to combat positions in the US military. 'War,' he says, 'is a man's work. Biological convergence on the battlefield would not only be dissatisfying in terms of what women could do, but it would be an enormous psychological distraction for the male, who wants to think that he's fighting for that woman somewhere behind, not up there in the same foxhole with him. It tramples the male ego. When you get right down to it, you have to protect the manliness of war' (Quoted in Hartsock, 1982).

The defence of manliness is a familiar response from those opposed to equal employment opportunity. What is unusual about this case is that male chauvinists are not alone in their conviction of the manliness of war. It is, after all, a familiar theme in some of the rhetoric of contemporary feminist peace groups. But protecting, or acquiescing in, the manliness of war is not on the face of it easy to reconcile with sexual equality in citizenship. The response of some feminists has been to bite the bullet and insist that full political equality demands extending to women the right and the duty to bear arms. If that fits incongruously with our traditional ideas and ideals of femininity, so much the worse for those ideals; they rest on misguided views of women as passively dependent on male protection, lacking the character traits of courage and persistence required for military service. Other feminists are only too happy to leave war as a male preserve, adopting a high moral tone from the sidelines: men are programmed towards militarism and death, women are somehow naturally peaceful and life-affirming. Others, somewhat uneasily trying to create a middleground on the battlefield, have explored the possibility of endorsing the admission of women to combat positions in the hope that the presence of womanly traits may have a pacifying effect on the military (see Ruddick, 1983).

Both war and citizenship have, of course, been traditionally male preserves in Western culture. And the source of some of the complexities that are now surfacing is that the masculinity of citizenship and the masculinity of war have been conceptually connected in Western thought—and connected through some of the most central ideals of the philosophical tradition: individuality, selfhood, autonomy, the concern with 'universal' moral principles, the transcending of 'private' interests. To claim that citizenship has been hitherto masculine only because of a perverse desire to exclude women from status and power, while war is somehow masculine on a deeper level, overlooks these conceptual connections, and fails to confront the full dimensions of the maleness of Western political ideals. The maleness of citizenship goes rather deeper in our conceptual structures than we may like to think. For this reason, the exploration of the ways in which philosophers of the past have connected war, citizenship and gender is of more than antiquarian interest. Their conceptualisations have fed into the social construction of gender and are still very much with us. General Barrow's doubts about 'what women could do' on the battlefield may well be an expression of mere prejudice. But his sense of the incongruity of women 'up there' in the same foxhole, rather than 'back there' behind the men, cannot be so lightly dismissed, if we want to understand the complexities of sexual equality and sexual difference.

To bring out some of the connections between ideas of gender and ideals of selfhood I am going to look at three points in modern Western philosophy where concepts of selfhood have intersected with thought about war, gender and citizenship. I will look first, very briefly at Rousseau's story of the Spartan woman in the opening sections of *Emile*; then at a passage from Kant's *Critique of Judgment* on the 'sublimity' of war; and, finally, at Hegel's treatment of the connections between self-consciousness, war and gender in the *Phenomenology of Spirit*.

A Spartan mother—so goes Rousseau's story—had five sons with the army. A helot arrives with news of the progress of battle. Trembling the mother asks his news. 'Your five sons are slain.' 'Vile slave,' she responds, 'was that what I asked thee?' 'We have won the victory,' comes the amended bulletin. 'She hastened to the temple to give thanks to the gods.' 'That,' comments Rousseau, 'was a citizen' (Rousseau, 1911:8). The story is meant as an extreme illustration of the demand that citizens set aside self-interest for the good of the community. War represents the ultimate mark and test of the capacity to transcend self-interest—whether it be through the readiness to risk our own lives or, as with the Spartan mother, through the readiness to sacrifice those we love. War is the ultimate offence to natural feelings of self-love and love of one's own. This is what gives war its moral overtones and also what sets it at odds with what, in the Western tradition, is symbolically associated with women's reproductive capacity. It is fundamentally at odds with the overwhelming love of one's own that is represented by motherhood.

The Spartan mother's way of resolving the tension between citizenship and motherhood is not endorsed by Rousseau. Her chilling suppression of natural feeling is far from his own ideals of citizenship; a society imbued with the fervour of the Spartan mother would be a nightmare. Rousseau's own version of a good civil society demands the preservation and fostering of the closeness to nature epitomised by motherhood. But the role of woman as symbol of natural feeling is not just accidentally related to those other notorious features of Rousseau's political thought—the education of women around male needs, their containment to the domestic sphere. The role of woman as symbol of closeness to nature demands that actual women be excluded from the public arena, not only to protect it from the dangers of uncontrolled passion—the 'disorder of women'—but also to protect from the corruptions of public life the good 'natural' feelings symbolised by woman. The love of one's own, epitomised by nurturant motherhood, can then be tapped for the public good. Men, influenced in the domestic sphere by good women, will transform the corrupt social order, bringing it closer to nature (see Lloyd, 1983b; 1983c; 1984).

We can already see here the glimmerings of a containment of the feminine that is not just practical but conceptual. The conceptual framework demands that woman be 'back there' out of the public arena; and femininity is constituted by that containment. The nature of the exercise in symbolism becomes more explicit and more elaborate in Hegel. But before moving on to its more explicit version there is another dimension of the connections between selfhood and war which I want to get into the picture. So far we have seen the idea that war is the ultimate antithesis to concern with self-interest, demanding the setting aside of a very basic kind of self-love, for the sake of the public good. But at the same time that it opposes that self-love, war is supposed also to offer the gratification of a self-love of a very different kind. It is in fact supposed to offer the prospect of achieving true selfhood. It will help get this second theme of selfhood and war into view if we look at a passage from Kant's *Critique of Judgment*:

> For what is it that, even to the savage, is the object of the greatest admiration? It is a man who is undaunted, who knows no fear, and who, therefore, does not give way to danger, but sets manfully to work with full deliberation. Even where civilization has reached a high pitch there remains this special reverence for the soldier; only that there is then further required of him that he should also exhibit all the virtues of peace—gentleness, sympathy and even becoming thought for his own person; and for the reason that in this we recognize that his mind is above the threats of danger. And so, comparing the statesman and the general, men may argue as they please as to the pre-eminent respect which is due to either above the other; but the verdict of the aesthetic judgment is for the latter. War itself, provided it is conducted with order and a sacred respect for the rights of civilians, has something sublime about it, and gives nations that carry it on in such a manner a stamp of mind only the more sublime the more numerous the dangers to which they are exposed, and which they are able to meet with fortitude. On the other hand, a prolonged peace favours the predominance of a mere commercial spirit, and with it a debasing self-interest, cowardice and effeminacy, and tends to degrade the character of the nation. (Kant, 1952:112–13)

War then has something 'sublime' about it. What exactly does this mean? The concept, as Kant uses it, strictly applies not to nature itself, but to our ideas. It is the disposition of soul evoked by an object, not strictly the object itself, that is sublime. And the sense of the sublime is in fact supposed to make us more aware of what differentiates us from mere nature. Kant defines the sublime as that in comparison with which all else is small. But the point is not that the human mind, in contemplating the grandeur of nature, feels itself to be small. Kant's point is that, in contemplating something sublime, the imagination has always to move on to something greater than it has already encompassed; it never reaches a point where it has got it all together. And what this brings home to us is the superiority of reason over imagination.

In contemplating shapeless mountain masses towering over one another in wild disorder, with their pyramids of ice, or the dark, tempestuous ocean, or such like things, says Kant (1952:105), the mind 'feels itself elevated in its own estimate of itself on finding all the might of imagination still unequal to its ideas'. Our rational understanding reaches ever beyond what can be encapsulated in a representation of imagination. The sublime 'represents all that is great in nature as in turn becoming little; or, to be more exact, it represents our imagination in all its boundlessness, and with it nature, sinking into insignificance before the ideals of reason, once their adequate representation is attempted'. So from the contemplation of the sublime there comes a kind of self-esteem that is grounded in a sense of our status as autonomous rational beings, superior to mere nature. We apprehend nature as something that inspires fear, but at the same time, at another level, as something that has no dominion over us.

> [T]he irresistibility of the might of nature forces upon us the recognition of our physical helplessness as beings of nature, but at the same time reveals a faculty of estimating ourselves as independent of nature, and discovers a pre-eminence above nature that is the foundation of a self-preservation of quite another kind from that which may be assailed and brought into danger by external nature. This saves humanity in our own person from humiliation, even though as mortal men we have to submit to external violence. (Kant, 1952:111)

It is this sense it conveys of nature as having no dominion over us that makes the sense of the sublime akin to moral consciousness. It falls short of the full sense of ourselves as autonomous rational beings, bound by universal principles, which are for Kant the mark of moral consciousness. But it points in that direction. Moral consciousness transcends self-interested concerns; it has as its scope what is common to humanity as such—what pertains to reason alone, in transcendence of natural feelings. The delight we take in the contemplation of the sublime is akin to the delight the autonomous Kantian will takes in the universally binding moral law. It does not depend on anything true of the individual contemplator that is not also true of other minds.

When Kant says that war has something sublime about it, then, he means to associate war with the consciousness of universality. The soul-stirring delight of the apprehension of danger makes it aesthetically akin to the contemplation of raging torrents and precipices. The special reverence associated with the soldier comes from his supposed perception of death as a 'might that has no dominion'. War is associated with a kind of autonomous selfhood that escapes domination by mere nature. The soldier is at real risk of death; that is the whole point. But the self-esteem of this idealised soldier is grounded in the sense of himself as a rational being, and that transcends his fear of death. The idealised soldier has moved from the 'effeminacy' of debasing self-interest to a self-esteem that is bound up with attachment to universal principles. His self-esteem is grounded in the sense of self as rational being, transcending mere nature. Through overcoming the fear of death he has attained a higher form of selfhood—a kind of self-consciousness which transcends what distinguishes self-interested individuals from one another, being focused rather on what they have in common as rational beings.

None of this is really meant by Kant as an ultimate endorsement of war. Elsewhere he makes it clear that he sees war not as itself an exercise of supreme reason, but as a necessary stage of conflict that elicits the more advanced stages of the development of reason in human history—a stage to be ultimately left behind, a mark of the immaturity of the human race. But war nonetheless has 'something of the sublime' in it, evoking the sense of human capacity to transcend nature. War gives us the idea of a transition from mere self-interest and the fear of death—the ultimate threat to self-preservation—to a higher form of a selfhood, to which death is of little consequence. For Hegel the role of war goes beyond this vague intimation of the possibility of a higher kind of selfhood; it becomes the condition of its attainment. And the connections of war with gender also become of much more consequence than either Rousseau's use of woman as symbol of natural feelings or Kant's passing reference to the 'effeminacy' of self-interest.

For Hegel, as for Kant, ethical consciousness is associated with transcending mere self-interest; it eschews particularity in favour of universal principles. And war plays a crucial role in forming and maintaining ethical consciousness in its self-conscious form. For Kant, as we saw, the contemplation of what is sublime in war induces a disposition in the mind which is akin to ethical consciousness. As a case of the sublime, war inclines the mind towards the development of the exalted kind of self-consciousness associated with reason. Hegel goes further, presenting the state's capacity to wage war as the ultimate source of the self-conscious individuality of its citizens. This capacity of the state is the actuality that casts its shadow back through less substantial social structures contained within it—private association, family life—to render human consciousness self-consciously ethical. And that self-conscious form of ethical life is explicitly associated with male consciousness.

To see how this intricate meshing of themes—self-consciousness, ethical life, individuality, gender—comes together we must have in mind both Hegel's famous treatment of the emergence of self-consciousness in the master–slave story and his later account of ethical life in the sections on the family (Hegel, 1977:chs 4, 6). The treatments of self-consciousness in the two sections mirror one another and, for our purposes, the most important connecting thread between them is the role of confrontation with death in the achievement of self-consciousness. In the master–slave story, Hegel is describing the process by which consciousness passes from its lower forms—sense-perception, understanding—to sustained self-consciousness. In this stage of the story of nature's development into spirit, consciousness comes to apprehend itself as confronted not just with enduring static objects, but with living, organic things. This emerging self-consciousness takes the form of desire. Self-consciousness involves awareness of objects which are 'other'—objects which it must endeavour to incorporate, cancelling their otherness. But with each negation or incorporation of the other, selfhood falls back into a lesser stage. The satisfaction of desire cancels the otherness of the object, thus sustaining the sense of selfhood; but with the disappearance of the other, selfhood also subsides. So if the project is construed as achieving stabilised self-consciousness, the negation or incorporation of the other has to be seen as inherently self-defeating. Selfhood resides in the overcoming of otherness; so the very being of self-consciousness demands that there be an other there to overcome. The only way out of this impasse is for the object set over against consciousness to 'engage in its own negation'. It must allow itself to be overcome without thereby ceasing to exist; and the only way for that to be achieved is through the recognition of one consciousness by another. 'Self-consciousness achieves its satisfaction only in another self-consciousness' (Hegel, 1977:110).

In the next stage of the story it quickly emerges that this mutual recognition is inherently conflict-ridden. The mutual need of the other's recognition—demanding, as it does, that each engage in its own negation in order to sustain the other's self-certainty—means that the two must 'prove themselves and each other through a life-and-death struggle'. The rest of the story traces the inevitable twists in the power struggle. The two rival consciousnesses are transformed in different ways by the life-and-death struggle they live through. One survives as master, the other as slave. The consciousness of the master turns into a dead end as far as development into further stages of self-conscious spirit is concerned. For the existence of the subjected slave consciousness cannot serve the purpose that the struggle is supposed to achieve—stabilising self-consciousness. The servile consciousness of the slave cannot provide the master with the reflection he requires of independent self-consciousness. In fact the servile recognition he receives back from the slave is detrimental to the project of sustaining awareness of self as free, independent consciousness. The self-certainty of the victor is once again under threat; the victory turns sour. The slave, on the other hand, has mirrored back to him, for as long as it can be maintained, the free consciousness of the master. But what is more important is that the slave, through his enforced labour on things in the service of the master, is able to transform his immediate relation to the world into self-conscious awareness of things. So the master is deprived of what for the slave will prove the ultimately successful externalisation of self that enables selfhood to be maintained—the capacity to labour on things and thus make them over in one's own form.

Clearly there are several aspects of this story that could be made salient: the twists of the struggle for dominance between rival consciousnesses, the role of intersubjectivity in achieving self-consciousness, the significance of work for selfhood. What I want to focus on here is the role Hegel gives to the confrontation with death in achieving self-consciousness (see Gadamer, 1976:54–74). For him self-consciousness is directly connected with the awareness of life. It has in fact a common structure with the concept of life—both involve the grasp of 'unity in difference'. And according to Hegel the awareness of both life and selfhood arises from the confrontation with death. By living through the fear of death consciousness transcends absorption in the immediacy of life. It becomes conscious of life as something not exhausted by the particular determinate forms it takes on. Thus it is the confrontation with death that gives the slave the crucial capacity to make of his labour the means to successful achievement of stabilised self-consciousness. His work would have no significance for that enterprise unless the fear of death had already 'shaken everything stable in his world to its foundations'. He is now aware of life as something not exhausted by the immediate and particular vanishing moments of experience. His work can now become a way of actually bringing about the 'dissolution of the stable', a reworking of natural existence in his own form. Work becomes 'desire held in check', 'fleetingness staved off'. Through forming and shaping things the slave acquires what eludes the master—'an element of permanence'. He discovers himself in the forms his work imposes on objects. Work becomes a source of a kind of permanence—a leaving of self in the world—that transcends the possibility of his death.

The sense of life as something not exhausted by any particular determinate form it takes on is the other side of the coin to the awareness of death as a real possibility, and this is fundamental to being self-conscious. Selfhood is thus achieved not just through the endeavour to annihilate the rival consciousness, overcoming otherness to make self present in the world, but also and more importantly through the elevation of one's own being above being attached to life. It is this aspect of the story that is crucial for the subsequent treatment of war and the family. The ethical overtones of war come from its associations with transcending a certain kind of attachment to life. By giving up the attachment to life involved in making self-preservation paramount, consciousness breaks through to a higher kind of selfhood. Self-consciousness must risk its life, not only because of its unavoidable conflict with the other, but because it is unable to achieve true selfhood without overcoming its own attachment to life. Only by annihilating itself as mere life, mere nature, can it become certain of itself. By bringing this sense of its own selfhood as transcending mere life to the experience of labour, consciousness is able to move into richer stages of spirit. It is able to 'work off', as Hegel puts it, its attachment to natural existence. It asserts itself, transcending dependence on mere nature. Consciousness is then able to cancel out the forms that things have independently of consciousness—to leave, and find, itself in the world. It makes the world over in its own shape. Through rising above attachment to natural existence, self-consciousness is able to impose itself on nature.

In later sections of the *Phenomenology of Spirit*, Hegel integrates this account of the emergence of self-consciousness through confrontation with death into his treatment of war, the family and the contrasts between male and female consciousness. Ethical life, he says, occurs in two forms, one associated with male consciousness and civil society, the other associated with female consciousness and the family (see Lloyd, 1983a; 1984). Woman represents 'unconscious' ethical life, as opposed to its self-conscious existence embodied in the wider life of society, where the ethical 'shapes and maintains itself' by working for the universal. In the master–slave story, Hegel presented self-consciousness as demanding an externalisation of self, so that it finds itself in the outer world. In the lack of this externalisation, self-consciousness remains tenuous, liable to slip back into immersion in mere life. That contrast is echoed in Hegel's later treatment of female consciousness. For ethical life to be self-conscious it must be externalised into the public realm, beyond the particularities of family life. It is sustained through access to the wider life of society, beyond the confines of the family, where men—but not women—'work for the universal'. In relation to the family, this external activity of the male has a negative role 'expelling the individual from the Family, subduing the natural aspect and separateness of his existence, and training him to be virtuous, to a life in and for the universal' (Hegel, 1977: 269).

The Hegelian individual is 'actual and substantial' only through this richer dimension of universality, associated with life as a citizen. In so far as he is not out there in the public realm of citizenship, the individual is only an 'unreal, impotent shadow'. In the master–slave story the ultimately successful way in which self-consciousness externalised itself was through work in conjunction with the awareness of life that came with living through the fear of death. In the treatment of self-conscious ethical life there are parallels to this crucial role of action, informed by awareness of death. The shadowiness of the individual, in so far as he is contained within the family, is linked with lack of effective action. Where no 'deed' is committed, the particular individual counts only as a 'shadowy unreality'. Selfhood is associated with breaking away from the realm of women, echoing the way, in the master–slave story, self-consciousness is achieved by breaking out of attachment to mere life. The two spheres—outer society and the inner world of the family—are sundered into hostile opposition! '. . . the two laws being linked in essence, the fulfilment of the one evokes the other and—the deed having made it so—calls it forth as a violent and now hostile entity demanding revenge' (Hegel, 1977:283). Each sees the demands of the other as outrageous. But the one that must prevail is the consciousness that 'looks to human law', to the 'commands of government', which have a 'universal public meaning open to the light of day'. It must prevail over the other law 'locked up in the darkness of the nether regions', which manifests itself as 'the will of an isolated individual', a 'wanton outrage' against the demands of society. So 'womankind' is constituted as a principle of hostility to society, constituted through male transcendence of the private domain.

The superior form of ethical consciousness associated with the male 'in its universal existence is the community, in its activity in general is the manhood of the community, in its real and effective activity is the government'. And it maintains itself by 'consuming and absorbing into itself the separation into individual families presided over by woman-kind' (Hegel, 1977:287–88).

> [S]ince the community only gets an existence through its interference with the happiness of the Family, and by dissolving [individual] self-consciousness into the universal, it creates for itself in what it suppresses and what is at the same time essential to it an internal enemy—womankind in general. Womankind—the everlasting irony [in the life of] the community—changes by intrigue the universal end of the government into a private end, transforms its universal activity into a work of some particular individual, and perverts the universal property of the State into a possession and ornament for the Family. (Hegel, 1977:288)

The 'other' has to be incorporated if self-consciousness is to be maintained. But that means it has to be there to be constantly overcome. Self-conscious ethical life, likewise, must have womankind there to transcend in order to be what it is. And there is an analogue, too, of womankind 'performing its own negation'. But first let us see how death comes into this ethical version of the emergence of self-consciousness.

Ethical self-consciousness and death are linked. But what exactly is their relationship? Death frees the ethical individual from his sensuous reality. After a long succession of separate disconnected experiences, the individual concentrates himself into 'a single completed shape, and has raised himself out of the unrest of the accidents of life into the calm of simple universality' (Hegel, 1977:270). In dying the individual achieves a complete shape, a calm, simple universality, removed from the unrest of life. But it is not dying as such—not dying, construed as a natural process—that achieves this shaping of the individual. Construed as a natural process, death is an outrage to self-conscious beings, the ultimate deprivation of autonomy which throws the individual back out of the self-conscious freedom of spirit into the brute necessity of mere nature. It is not dying itself, then, that bestows this much-to-be-desired calm, simple universality, but rather the significance that can be given to death in a social context. 'The wrong which can be inflicted on the individual in the ethical realm is simply this, that something merely *happens* to him. The power which inflicts this wrong on the conscious individual of making him into a mere thing is Nature ...' (Hegel, 1977:278). To rescue the conscious individual from this outrage, death must be given social significance. What gives death its power to bestow a 'complete shape' on the individual is its appropriation by the family, so that it becomes an action 'consciously done'.

> The duty of the member of a family is on that account to add this aspect, in order that the individual's ultimate being, too, shall not belong solely to Nature and remain something *irrational*, but shall be something *done*, and the right of consciousness be asserted in it. Or rather the meaning of the action is that because in truth the calm and universality of a self-conscious being do not belong to Nature, the illusory appearance that the death of the individual results from a *conscious* action on the part of Nature may be dispelled, and the truth established. (Hegel, 1977:270)

The family takes on itself the responsibility for death—takes on itself the 'act of destruction' of the individual, thus rescuing him out of the grip of mere nature for spirit. '[T]he *dead*, the universal *being*, becomes a being that has returned into itself, a being-for-self, or, the powerless, simply isolated individual has been raised to universal individuality ...' (Hegel, 1977:271).

That the family has this power to salvage its dead from the outrage of death depends, however, on its containment by the wider structures of the state, and on its subjection to the needs of the state. That death can be a source of individuality—that it can have ethical significance at all—is ultimately due to what the state can make of death through war. War shatters the isolation of individuals and calls them out of their shadowy existence within the family. War plays for ethical consciousness the same role that the possibility of death in general plays for self-consciousness: it shakes consciousness out of attachment to mere nature into spirit:

> The Spirit of universal assembly and association is the simple and negative essence of those systems which tend to isolate themselves. In order not to let them become rooted and set in their isolation, thereby breaking up the whole and lefting the (communal) spirit evaporate, government has from time to time to shake them to their core by war. By this means the government upsets their established order, and violates their right to independene, while the individuals who, absorbed in their own way of life, break loose from the whole and strive after the inviolable independence and security of the person, are made to feel in the task laid on them their lord and master, death. Spirit, by thus throwing into the melting pot the stable existence of these systems, checks their tendency to fall away from the ethical order, and to be submerged in a (merely) natural existence, and it preserves and raises conscious self into freedom and its own power. (Hegel, 1977:272–73)

The focal point for this exertion of State power through the demands of war is woman, representing, as she does, the private concerns of the individual—the shadowy, unconscious form of ethical life which must be shaken into the open day of self-consciousness. She must be got to perform her own negation. She must be got, that is, to agree to the surrender of her men—a violation of all that she stands for. The subversive character of womankind is associated with woman's attachment to private individuals. And this is epitomised in her fascination with the 'power of youth' as the antithesis of the 'earnest wisdom of mature age'. What attracts woman about (male) youth is its commitment to private pleasure and enjoyment, as opposed to care for the universal. 'She makes this wisdom an object of derision for raw and irresponsible youth and unworthy of their enthusiasm. In general, she maintains that it is the power of youth that really counts ...' (Hegel, 1977:288) Her interests embody the attachment to private concerns which the community must repress, but on which it at the same time depends. The community must appropriate the fascination of youth to its own ends. It must recognise the power of youth as the 'power of the whole'. This controlled recognition is achieved through enlisting those brave youths into the nation's wars.

> The negative side of the community, suppressing the isolation of individuals *within* it, but spontaneously active in an *outward direction*, finds its weapons in individuality. War is the Spirit and the form in which the essential moment of the ethical substance, the absolute freedom of the ethical *self* from every existential form, is present in its actual and authentic existence. (Hegel, 1977:288–89)

Thus war appropriates to the interests of the state the hostile private interests associated with womankind, and in the process transforms those interests—summed up in the fascination with male youth—into universal concerns. War takes the brave youth away from woman-kind—whether he be the son whose worth lies in his being the 'lord and master' of the mother who bore him, the brother, who is 'the one in whom the sister finds man on a level of equality', or the youth through whom the daughter, freed from her dependence, obtains the 'dignity and enjoyment of wifehood'. But having taken him away it returns him glorified. 'The brave youth in whom woman finds her pleasure, the suppressed principle of corruption, now has his day and his worth is openly acknowledged' (Hegel, 1977:289).

For Hegel, then, war—the ultimate outrage to self-interest and the desire for self-preservation—is at the same time the means of raising ethical life to self-consciousness, transforming private attachments into the universal concerns of citizenship. What bearing does all this have on our contemporary understanding of sexual equality and sexual difference? Hegel, of course, endorsed the containment of the feminine to an inferior private domain and the associated masculinity of both war and citizenship. But his diagnosis of the cultural constitu-tion of 'womankind' remains a profound insight into the complexities of sexual difference, which can help us to understand better some of the obstacles to genuine sexual equality. Femininity, as we now have it, has been constituted within the Western intellectual tradition to be what is left behind by ideals of masculinity, citizenship and patriotism. But if that is so the idea of a special antipathy between women and war has to be seen as in some ways a product of the very tradition to which it may now seem to be a reaction. It may be salutary to realise that the idea of the feminine that figures in some of the rhetoric of feminist peace groups springs from the same sources as General Barrow's conviction that there is no place for women on the battle-field.

In his elaborate intertwining of the themes of self-consciousness, death and gender, Hegel has articulated a structure of thought which makes some sense of General Barrow's intuitive conviction that woman has to be 'back there', behind the soldier, rather than up in the same foxhole. What underlies General Barrow's unease is the fact that in Western thought the manliness of war goes deeper than the idea that it is manly to defend the weak. The masculinity of war is what it is precisely by leaving the feminine behind. It consists in the capacity to rise above what femaleness symbolically represents: attachment to private concerns, to 'mere life'. In leaving all that behind, the soldier becomes a real man, but he also emerges into the glories of selfhood, citizenship and truly ethical, universal concerns. Womankind is constructed so as to be what has to be transcended to be a citizen. Ethical life has been construed in this tradition precisely as the transcending of the 'feminine'.

I want also to suggest here in passing that we can through Hegel's presentation of the prevailing assumptions of his culture make some sense of phenomenon of patriotic motherhood. He has laid bare one rationale of women's sacrifice of male youth to provide the nation's cannon fodder. His story makes some sense—though horrifying sense—of the at first sight extraordinary fact that the ideology of nurturant motherhood has been so readily enlisted in the cause of patriotism, which seems on the surface to be so much at odds with it. In giving up their sons, women are supposed to allow them to become real men and immortal selves. Surrendering sons to significant deaths becomes a higher mode of giving birth. Socially constructed motherhood, no less than socially constructed masculinity, is at the service of an ideal of citizenship that finds its fullest expression in war.

I have tried to bring out something of the connections between the masculinity of war and the masculinity of ideals of citizenship in the Western philosophical tradition. Woman qua woman—as symbol of attachment to individual bodies, private interests and natural feeling—represents all that war and citizenship are supposed to contain and transcend. Our inherited ideals of ethical life and citizenship—no less than General Barrow's sense of the manliness of war—demand that we leave the feminine behind. Woman as symbol cannot really be inserted into the public arena, or into the battlefield, without creating a major upheaval. But this of course is not just a matter of our symbols being in disarray. The symbolic content of maleness and femaleness has been incorporated into the gender construction of real men and women and remains part of our 'male' or 'female' consciousness. The upheaval results from peculiarities in the operations of symbols in our culture. But it is of course not merely a symbolic upheaval.

6 Sex equality is not enough for feminism

Margaret Mead set up in a clear and general form the problem of the high valuation people put on men's doings:

> In every known human society, the male's need for achievement can be recognised. Men may cook or weave or dress dolls or hunt humming-birds, but if such activities are appropriate occupations of men, then the whole society, men and women alike, votes them as important. When the same occupations are performed by women, they are regarded as less important. (Mead, 1962:157)

To decide whether women's or men's doings are genuinely more valuable, one would need to be able to look at the intrinsic character of the doings, aside from which sex does them. It might seem at first blush that just this attitude—what counts should be the character of the activity, not which sex does it—is fostered by equalitarianism, but I believe this is not so. The reasons stem from the intrinsic limitations of the concept of equality as a guiding ideal for feminism.

Equality is a concept that can only be applied to two (or more) things *in some specified respect*. There has to be a characteristic which both have in respect of which they are said to be equal. Two sticks might be equal *in length*, two persons equal *in height* (*equally long, equally tall*). But if I call my first stick *a* and my second stick *b*, I cannot meaningfully say simply that *a* is equal to *b*; nor can I meaningfully say to Les and Viv simply that Les is equal to Viv—not unless I specify, or at least presume, the particular respect in which they are equal.

In general, equality does not relate objects considered extensionally, but only objects considered under some specified common criterion of measurement. Equality implies commensurability. Where there is a criterion of commensurability, comparisons of *greater than, equal to,* or *less than* may be made. *Equal to* stands essentially in a continuum of comparison—stands at the point between *greater than* and *less than*

These generalisations are about equality of any kind; they must apply with just as much force to equality of the sexes as to equality of length—in so far as equality of the sexes can be made a coherent idea. But insisting on commensurability does not capture the programmatic thrust of the notion of equality of the sexes.

The standard argument for sex equality has three elements: women's nature; the social treatment of women; women's perform-ance. In its dogmatic form, the argument invalidating the subjection of women runs as follows:

Dogmatic Argument for Sex Equality
(1) Women and men have equal natures   *Axiom*
(2) So if women are given equal treatment with men   *Programme*
(3) The outcome will be equal performance   *Goal*

Each of the three steps is internally complex. For instance, (1) does not mean that any woman has an equal nature to any man. What is meant by 'nature' in this dimension is capacity or potential to perform. And in this mode of thought it is not usual to believe that all persons are equal in potential. What is asserted in the equal nature of the sexes is that the *range* of potential among females is equal to that among males. As raw material for social performance females born as a group are equal in nature to males born as a group. The distribution of potentials in the one group will be equal to that in the other group. It is, if you like, a claim about the equality of the statistics of potential to be found in the respective sex groups. In parallel, (2) is not about equal treatment of every human individual, but about an equal pattern of treatment for the sex groups and (3) about an equal pattern of performance for the sex groups.

Human potentiality is not something that can be observed or measured directly—not even in a rough and ready sort of way: just not at all. Performance can be observed, and at least in principle both the specific educational training and the general social treatment of the performer can be observed. Potential has to be read back from performance in the circumstances of treatment. Performance in one task can, of course, be taken as an indicator of potential in others, but here the validity of the inference must depend on establishing a correlation of performance in the two tasks. A supposed instance would be IQ testing.

So the axiom of equal nature (or (1) above) amounts to an absolute confidence that equal treatment (or (2) above) would lead to equal performance (or (3) above). And the same presumed connection can also be used to reason in the opposite direction, to conclude that where performance is not equal, there must have been inequality of treatment, even where it is not at once apparent what the relevant inequality of treatment can have been.

In the context of a programme to bring about sex equality, the axiom of equal nature (or (1)) amounts to an absolute confidence that there is no natural limit to the extent to which raising the social treatment of women up towards the level for men will correspondingly raise up the performance of women till equality of treatment and performance are reached.

PLATO'S SEX EQUALITARIANISM

The essentials of sex equalitarian thinking were laid down in a compact discussion in Part Six (old Book Five) of Plato's *Republic*, which might be said to have set the framework and upward standard of thinking about women's advancement for a couple of thousand years. Such thought as was given to the position of women over that period often represented a retreat from the standard set by this argument of Plato's, but did little or nothing to carry the standard forward. A sex equalitarianism very close to Plato's, though in some ways more equalitarian, is now so entrenched that it might be said to have entered common sense. (Recent feminist thought has come up with some new ideas which go beyond the equalitarian framework, but these do not yet have wide acceptance.)

Plato stresses that the question what male occupations women are also capable of following is decided neither by appealing to what women now do following custom nor by some vague appeal to a difference (unspecified) in nature as between women and men. It is not a matter of whether women's nature is different from men's in any way whatever. It is a matter of what, custom aside, is the nature of women *in such respects as are relevant* to an occupation—whatever particular occupation is in question. Following this approach he claims for women potentialities which are not directly demonstrated in their current social performance. Further, he claims for them a potential for performance relative to men's which is higher than that of the current relativities.

It may be asked of Plato what can be meant by a 'nature' which lies behind women's current performance and which possesses a potential far in excess of that demonstrated in current performance. There are no presocial persons and there could not in principle be any. Real persons cannot take on and put aside social functions or roles as they might change clothes. A real person necessarily grows up as part of a social context; some capacities are developed but others are irreversibly foreclosed in the process. There is no room to leave an unmodified presocial—or extrasocial—individual inside the social individual.

Plato makes it clear that to approach the realisation of their higher potential both absolutely and relative to men, women would need to have something closer of the ideal education, institutions, customs, expectations of the ideal republic. Plato's claims about women's nature can therefore be interpreted—or drawn out—to mean something of the form of a counterfactual hypothetical. Had women had treatment which enabled them to develop their capacities more, they would have performed higher and they would have performed closer to the performance of men who had the same treatment.

Plato's discussion of women has to be taken in the context of the social dispositions argued for by the *Republic* as a whole. Taken in this way, the general position is that in the case of women as in the case of men, the ideal society would provide education, social institutions and expectations such as would bring each citizen to the highest performance of which that person was capable as an individual. Plato was at the same time an elitist committed to hierarchy and discipline; individual rights, liberal individualist diversity, were no part of his vision. But the equalitarian, meritocratic elements of his consideration of the sexes do not logically depend on his hierarchical authoritarianism, and can be detached from it.

Plato, then, rejects the idea that women should be spared onerous, responsible or dangerous social duties on account of their child-bearing and child-rearing role. The proper social and political place of women is clearly seen as interdependent with the question of women's capacities. The question of what occupations women might appropriately follow is clearly distinguished from what occupations they do follow. And the question of what occupations they might follow is clearly framed in the form of what occupations appropriate to men women ought also to be admitted to.

Much of the *Republic* is taken up with considering how men's capacities could be developed and used to better advantage in ideal circumstances, and especially how preparation for the occupation of governing could be radically improved. Thus Plato asks not whether women ought to be educated and occupied like men in contemporary Athens, but whether women ought ideally to be prepared for and admitted to men's occupations as ideally conceived.

Nonetheless the question of the educational and occupational ideal for women is broached very differently from the question for men. The approach is to decide what is the best pattern for men and then turn to women: '...whether it's asked in joke or in earnest, we must admit the question, Is the female of the human species capable of taking part in all the occupations of the male, or in none, or in some only?' (Plato,

1974:206). Women are still associated with the domestic; still today this association sets the context of discussion of appropriate occupation for women. In Plato's world the exclusion of women from the non-domestic was so taken for granted that the suggestion of change was amusing if it was not pressed, shocking if it was. Plato knows he invites ridicule by questioning what seems so unquestionably fitting. But there is another aspect of what is taken for granted that Plato himself accepts without question: in contemporary Athens it is men's occupations that set the standard of serious work and achievement: '. . . is there anything men do at which they aren't far better in all these respects [amounting to quickness at picking up whatever it is] than women? We need not waste time over exceptions like weaving and cooking, at which women are thought to be experts, and get badly laughed at if men do them better' (Plato, 1974:209). This presumption that the occupations that have been associated with women are trivial is projected into the ideal society: the standard of the occupations which ideally develop the capacities of those who do them is to be set by consideration of men. Having established this standard, we can ask whether women should also prepare for and attempt these occupations.

Plato, then, points out that in a matter where there is so much room for people to misunderstand each other's meaning even where they use the same words, it is essential to be very clear what is intended in posing the question of different natures for the sexes. It is uncontroversial that in some sense women and men have different natures, but not all differences between persons are relevant to the question of suitability for a certain occupation. For instance, bald men differ from long-haired men on account of their shortage of hair, but it would be absurd to exclude either group from the occupation of cobbling on that account. Aptitude for cobbling is all that should count. Similarly, women bear and men beget says Plato (1974:207—8), but if a woman and a man both have aptitude for medicine, they have the same nature in the way that should count for admission to the profession of medicine.

This model for understanding how the sexes differ has been influential and remains with us. Biological sex differences—woman bears, man begets; the sex organs differ; the sex acts differ—are seen as belonging to the category of physical, non-psychic, thus trivial differences like the bald/hairy difference (which after all would also have *some* concomitant implications for action such as having to do your hair or not). Assimilation to this model sits well with Plato's low valuation of sex and the sexual passions as components of the good life, their importance for him residing mainly in their negative potential to woo the individual away from the wholehearted pursuit of reason. The assimilation frees Plato to treat biological sex as having in principle very low positive social import—no significant implications for capacity in the practical affairs of life, still less in the capacity that was for him the supreme capacity, what made humans human, the capacity to reason. The radical conclusion is that the subjection of women and the limitations customarily put by society on women's development cannot be justified by good reasons.

Even so, there now arises for Plato the question that must be faced by every person who directs thought to this area. Are important intellectual and practical capacities as a matter of fact more to be found in one sex than in the other? Or (a somewhat different question, but with some of the same bearings in the framework of Plato's argument) are the capacities of one sex of a different *kind* from those of the other? Socrates, Glaucon and their friends in the *Republic* do not pause to consider the possibility of constructing detailed criteria or of going out to investigate as an aid to reaching an answer; there is no hint of the approach involved in modern social science and there is no perceived lack. The answers come at once with a confidence that makes it clear there is no doubt in the minds of the discussants that they can answer at once from their general experience.

The answer arrived at by this method is that the capacities and aptitudes of the sexes are like in that 'natural abilities are similarly distributed in each sex', but that in all 'women will be the weaker partners'. This may seem an incongruous combination of ideas unless it is interpreted to mean that on the one hand women's capacities are of like *kind* with men's and with a similar scatter—similar proportions of women and men respectively will have a capacity for mathematics rather than woodwork, say—but that women on the whole have the capacities in a lesser *degree*. No conclusion will follow as to the relative capacities of any particular woman and any particular man, since 'a good many women are better than a good many men at a good many things' (Plato, 1974:209). But Plato does not canvass the possibility that the limitations put upon women's education and experience might account for *all* the observable differential in the performance of the sexes. Some of Plato's discussion is not dated—with different cladding it is still with us—but the failure to confront that possibility, even to deny it, is something that could hardly occur today.

In modern sex equalitarianism (in what I have called the Dogmatic Argument for Sex Equality) the presumptions have been raised to the point of confidence that equal treatment would bring overall equal performance as between the sexes. Plato stopped short of this supposition. His good society required equal treatment of the sexes up to the point where the differentiated capacities of individuals could be gauged. Some women, he expected, would perform well, but women's performance would on the whole be weaker than men's.

It is worth giving a little attention to this point since it has been the focus of hostility for some recent feminists. To my mind, from the feminist point of view the important positive thing about Plato's discussion is the power it has had to promote consideration of how changed treatment might advance women and reveal their greater potential. The important negative thing is not that Plato did not go all the way in his judgment of women's potential relative to men's but rather that he took male performance as the paradigm in framing the question of the relative capacities of the sexes.

So I am not sympathetic with the way Julia Annas (1976) tackles Plato. As it seems to me she is herself entrapped in the important negative thing from Plato's reasoning—the male paradigm which enters the essential strategy of his argument and has major, though by him unrecognised, implications for policy—she wastes her fire on Plato's judgment that women on the whole have less potential than men on the whole. Even in the direction where she does choose to fire, Annas does not correctly identify the target. The inadequacies of her presentation of Plato's position illustrate the ideological imperatives of the Dogmatic Argument for Sex Equality. The logic of Annas' equalitarian position is to require what I call the Axiom of Equal Natures (1) (see p. 78). The ground of her intolerance of Plato's judgment about women's relative potential is that she thinks Plato has got it wrong in proposing equal treatment on the strength of postulating less than equal natures. Less than equal natures will not justify equal treatment.

Annas fudges the any/all distinction which Plato has been careful to make. She lists the criteria Plato gives for aptitude in learning and picking up skills. On the whole, it is agreed in the *Republic* discussion, men greatly excel women in all these qualities. Annas is not mollified by Plato's affirming that '"many women are better than many men at many things"'. As Annas sees it, 'if men always excel women in these very important respects ... surely there are some pursuits (e.g. generalship) where these qualities are needed in a high degree and which it is therefore not reasonable to open to women'. Soon afterwards she makes the invalid jump: 'If only men excel in a quality,' she says, 'then if efficiency is our aim surely that makes it reasonable to regard a pursuit that requires a high degree of that quality as suited specially to men. The fact that women will not invariably come bottom is neither here nor there' (Annas, 1976:310).

Now there is a sense of the ambiguous 'men always excel' that would do for Plato's meaning, but Plato does *not* say *only* men excel. Further, he is speaking here in the present tense—presumably of women as they are rather than women as they might be. His inclusion of women in the Guardian class of the ideal republic can be interpreted to mean no other than that, at least under changed conditions, some women *will* excel. He does not confront the question whether a woman might, in Annas' terms, come top, but the possibility is not excluded by the logic of his argument. Just the same, when women share in all occupations, he does expect that they will (on the whole) in all occupations be 'the weaker partners'.

As far as validity of reasoning goes, the question between Annas and Plato would seem to be settled in Plato's favour. But the difference between them runs deeper. Annas makes it very clear what is the source of her concern: 'Scientific research into sex differences is an area of great controversy precisely because its results do have important social consequences; if men and women did have different types of intelligence, for example, then different types of education would surely be appropriate.' And a little later, 'it is possible that [Plato] genuinely does not see the disastrous relevance of his claims about men's superior intellectual gifts to his point about distinct fields of activity' (Annas, 1976:310). Here Annas makes another unjustified elision, and this time one that belongs to the more interesting difference with Plato. She assimilates different *types* of intelligence—which one might reasonably take to refer to cast of mind, different kinds of intellectual skills—to different *levels or degrees* of intelligence—a reference to supposed superior male intellectual gifts, supposed inferior female intellectual gifts. She doesn't analyse it in this way but her line of thought can be straightforwardly understood: if women are taken to have anything other than equal natures (especially equal intellectual natures) with men, they will be taken to have different and inferior natures and will be given different and inferior education and training, different and inferior occupations. The occupations to which high rewards, status and interest attach will remain men's occupations. She rightly points out that it is access to men's jobs that have the rewards, status and interest that is the matter in dispute—not women's jobs with the inverse ratings. Given what has happened in history, one can sympathise with her fears, if not her argument.

Annas' implicit appeal is to the corollary of the Dogmatic Argument, as schematised earlier: if women are not performing equally with men, then they must have been treated less than equally (so the feminist programme as she sees it must be completed; the differences of treatment must be located and rooted out). It is strategically a very useful approach, but it requires the Axiom of Equal Natures and it thus provides an ideological imperative to defend the Axiom.

When Plato compares women with men in their social and political potentialities he uses what may be thought of as a *dual grid*. On the one hand there is the *grid of kinds* of capacity—that is to say the maths kind, the music kind, the woodwork kind and so on. Then upon any particular kind that has been isolated, there is superimposed the *grid of degree.* Women and men are said to have the same sorting under the grid of kinds, which is to say the spread of the kinds of capacity is the same for each sex group. But when the grid of degree is applied to the respective kinds, women overall have the respective capacities in less degree. As Plato puts it, '[t]here is . . . no function in society which is peculiar to woman as woman or man as man; natural abilities are similarly distributed in each sex, and it is natural for women to share all occupations with men, though in all women will be the weaker partners' (Plato, 1974:209).

Plato's dual grid retains importance in the polemics of sex equality. The use he makes of the grid of degree detracts from his sex equalitarianism, but his argument nonetheless has a form which can be set out parallel to what I have called the Dogmatic Argument for Sex Equality:

Modest Argument for Sex Equality:

(1a)	Women and men have equal natures on the grid of kinds, but women rate on the whole lower on the grid of degree	*Axiom*
(2a)	So if women are given equal treatment with men to the limit of individual capacity to have their development advanced	*Programme*
(3a)	The outcome will be improved and optimal relativity of performance	*Goal* (Ideal Republic)

It might be thought that unlike the grid of degree, the grid of kinds fails to yield a criterion of measure, since the qualitative distinction between kinds of capacity constitutes incommensurable difference. For Plato this is not so, since he believes some capacities are intrinsically more valuable than others, the capacity for reasoning, or philosophy, being the most valuable—so that to have the capacity for philosophy would rate higher than to have the capacity for wood-work, and so on.

Now Plato aside, some capacities are indeed more important or valuable than others in being of more general application (reason has very wide application, for instance). But it is not pure abstract human capacities that Plato relates to women. Rather it is capacities for certain occupations determined on the basis of considering what would be an ideal occupational breakdown for men. While these occupations are idealised, they are recognisable versions of men's familiar occupations and they come with their status ranking built in by definition. Men's doings as the model of human capacity and excellence are structurally enshrined in Plato's argument.

This does not emerge as nakedly as it might since Plato lays it down that women have equal distribution with men over what I call the grid of kinds. Discrimination would be justified against a sex with poorer representation in high-value capacities, but this possibility is not invoked. Here is the dimension in which Plato can be called equalitarian (but only because he affirms that women come up to the male standard). Because the sex groups are same-level or equal in the kinds of capacities they possess, the good society will offer them similar treatment in education and will make all occupations equally available to those individuals of either sex who are able to perform well in them.

In the grid of degree, Plato falls short of equalitarianism; in this dimension women are held by him to be on the whole less than equal, or weaker, not just in performance but in potential. But only on the whole. Some women are expected to excel, given changed treatment to enable them to do so.

In his equalitarian dimension Plato is thoroughgoing in two respects which remain salient in our day for sex equalitarians. He isolates what are probably the purest of the traditional sex functions—domestic duties for women, soldiering for men. And in these critical cases he is toughmindedly prepared to set tradition aside. Women can and should be detached from domestic duties, at least where they are to have leadership responsibilities, which is to say in the case of Guardian women. Women can and should be attached to soldiering where their capacities suit them for it, as in some cases they will. The traditional dispositions are socially mutable and are not well founded in the natures of women and men.

This is because the highest part of people's natures, the definitive part, the reasoning part, the psyche, is a sexless entity which is lodged within the sexed body. The body, in Plato's more metaphysical way of presenting the matter, inhibits or clouds the operation of reason—we have to strive to remember the truths we knew in a more direct way before the psyche became attached to the body. (The denser cloud made by what he saw as the weaker, inferior female body might indeed be seen as providing a rationale for finding women on the whole inferior in the grid of degree.) Thus the excellence for which these sexless individual psyches can strive is unitary, not sex-relative. Incidentals of the body—baldness, hairiness, female sex organs, male sex organs—do not significantly modify the nature of the psyche or the character of the individual.

In Plato's version of the death of the family—his prescriptions for detaching the Guardians from the domestic—he is faithful to the concept of the sexless psyche, the equal natures of men and women. From his point of view he is even-handed as between women and men in his prescriptions for the end of domesticity. For both sexes the family as we know it is to be abolished. Guardian women will be freed of domestic duties, Guardian men will be freed of their family responsibilities, including responsibility to provide for a family household—his spouse, his children. The community becomes the Guardians' family; it is to the community that the Guardians will feel that deep personal sense of responsibility familiar within the family.

While there is a sense in which this rationale is even-handed as between the sexes, common sense at once perceives that the projected shift for women is much greater than that for men. Relief from petty responsibilities to a few close relations may be essential for Guardians of both sexes, but for male Guardians it will mean relief from what is anyway a minor theme in the lives of male Athenian citizens such as Plato had in mind. For the women it will mean being relieved of their whole way of life, and being empowered to move into the public arena in a way utterly remote from the prospects of female Athenian citizens.

The detailed domestic arrangements proposed by Plato are of interest not so much for themselves as for the way they reveal Plato's evaluation of domestic responsibilities as inhibitors of development of the abilities required for high political and social performance. His denial that the domestic function is biologically determined, and the connection he makes between the restructuring of domestic provision and the entry of women into public life and high responsibility, is a central and enduring part of the equalitarian argument which begins its entrenchment in our thoughts with Plato.

WOLLSTONECRAFT'S VERSION OF SEX EQUALITY

The foundation works of modern feminist theory, Wollstonecraft's *Vindication of the Rights of Woman* and Taylor and Mill's *Subjection of Women*, both make use of the dual grid. Thus Wollstonecraft: 'If women are by nature inferior to men, their virtues must be the same in quality, if not in degree, or virtue is a relative idea; consequently, their conduct should be founded on the same principles, and have the same aim' (Wollstonecraft, 1967:57; see also 58; 72; 75; 94). Here the kind/degree dimensions re-emerge: women are strongly asserted to have the same grid of kinds, even if overall a lower rating on the grid of degree. The key consideration in arguing for equal treatment of the sexes is, as in Plato, that women have the same kinds of capacities as men, that virtue is unitary—the same for women as for men: there is no 'sex in souls' (Plato, 1974:104)—and that reason and virtue belong together: 'In fact, it is a farce to call any being virtuous whose virtues do not result from the exercise of its own reason' (Wollstonecraft, 1967:52).

The general philosophical context is now, of course, very different. Wollstonecraft belongs to an intellectual world where society is viewed, as it were, from the individual looking out, while Plato belonged to a world where the individual was viewed from the point of view of the community looking in. This shift runs parallel to the shift in general philosophy from ontology to epistemology. When Wollstonecraft compares her need to believe that virtue is unitary with her need to believe there is a God (1967:58), she locates herself in the post-Reformation world of individual conscience; her insistence that a being's virtue can only result from the exercise of its own reason is modern and individualist in a way quite foreign to Plato. For Wollstonecraft the final responsibility of reasoned judgment must remain with each individual agent. It is part of this modern perspective that for her the justification for equal treatment of the sexes can be expressed by an appeal to individual rights—equal rights to treatment which would enable the development of those individual reasoning powers and hence the pursuit of that unitary virtue.

In general Wollstonecraft does not see women's role in childcare as a threat to the higher personal development and independence she projects as the right of the female individuals of the future. The new stature of women will enhance the new superior mother–child relationship, she believes (1967:258–59). But women will retain their high degree of responsibility for childcare, envisaged as undertaken in the context of companionate marriage. Is Wollstonecraft simply less tough minded when she imagines the new growth and independence of women is consistent with their continuing unequal commitment of energies to the private sphere? Wollstonecraft spends most of her time considering the general run of people. But she too thought that for both sexes the very highest performance is incompatible with commitment to family responsibilities.

There is a different way of looking at what Wollstonecraft has to say about childcare, procreation and marriage. She can be seen as trying to *envalue* women's doings, to claim that they are unjustifiably degraded in their present form, that they can in principle be elevated and that they ought to be so in the interests of both equal rights and the good society. In seeking to envalue women's doings she can be seen as pointing the way towards radical feminism, at least at an abstract level. But in the concrete she is much closer to those recent conservative feminists (such as Rossi, Friedan, Elshtain and Wolgast) who celebrate certain conventional feminine virtues and affirm the value of the family, thus moving away from the same grid of kinds for the sexes, but in the direction of traditionalism.

Reason (developed as understanding) is essential for the development of virtue in the individual. Women's first duty is to themselves as rational individuals and after that come their civic duties: 'The being who discharges the duties of its station is independent; and, speaking of women at large, their first duty is to themselves as rational creatures, and the next in point of importance, as citizens, is that which includes so many, of a mother' (Wollstonecraft, 1967:218). The duty of self-development as rational individual applies to every individual woman, but the civic duty of a mother is not generalisable in the same total way. It is just the single most important civic duty applying to women as a group. The duty of motherhood and the care of children, Wollstonecraft says, falls on the female owing to her sexual nature. Virtue can only be realised by the carrying out of our duties as citizens, but women's development of their individual intellectual and moral powers is a prerequisite of their realising their virtue in the discharge of the civic duty of motherhood (or any other civic duty) (1967:109, 113–15, 226–27). The prerequisite in turn requires that women be given like men an education and training which renders them intellectually independent; in women's case this will mean independent of men rather than reliant on men's authority. Only with such independence of mind is a companionate marriage possible, one which will be based on friendship once the flames of sexual passion have died. Sexual passion is an unruly and disruptive force and, (1967:64, 67, 105) when it has run its brief course, love of children should take its place on a more enduring basis (1967:121, 228). Friendship, founded as it is on reason and judgment, is the proper basis for marriage (1967:62–63, 65, 70, 121–22). And only with independence of mind will women have the reasoning powers needed for the proper care and upbringing of their children (1967:109, 115, 215).

For Wollstonecraft it is very abstract kinds of capacity—for reason, knowledge and virtue—which are common to the sexes. When given the chance to develop these capacities, most women would apply them mainly in the occupation of mothering, so that at least for these mothering women the reference point for the reasonableness, knowledgeability and virtue of women would be sex-specific skills and activities, a different reference point from men's. What makes reason the same in kind for each individual is something very abstract, the same as what makes an individual an individual: 'Reason is ... the power of improvement; or, more properly speaking, of discerning the truth. Every individual is in this respect a world in itself' (Wollstonecraft, 1967:94). The appeal is in effect to what it means to act, to be an individual agent, to do something on the basis of having decided to do it. Only intentional conduct can be virtuous, so all virtue has reason (in a spare but unitary sense) as a prerequisite. The development of reason (in understanding) is needed for developed virtue.

The problem for this attenuated form of equalitarianism is that it is the element of measure, of coherent comparison of the sexes on some scale of lesser than, equal to, greater than, that is gone. 'She is as reasonable a mother as he is a philosopher' may make rough sense but it cannot make smooth sense. And it is not obvious, for instance, what would count as educational equality or equal training for the respective different performances. The programmatic force of the argument for sex equality is surrrendered when the validity of arguing from same capacities to same appropriate occupations is broken.

TAYLOR AND MILL ON SEX EQUALITY

With Taylor, Mill and *The Subjection*, the dual grid continues to have application. In their major mode, Taylor and Mill are like Plato and Wollstonecraft in wanting to ascribe the same grid of kinds to the sexes. As part of their agnosticism on women's nature, they entertain the possibility that women rate lower than men on the grid of degree. Even so, they argue, women are entitled to an equal chance to compete, since individual women will excel many men. If the lesser claim (same grid of kinds, lower on grid of degree) is sufficient to validate equal treatment, they do not need the stronger claim (same dual grid), which could not anyway be established in the contemporary state of ignorance. For them the ignorance would be dispelled only by empirical evidence. Taylor and Mill have a thoroughgoing empiricist orientation new in feminist theory and it puts a new construction on the grid of kinds.

Mill's liberal individualist philosophy specifies a certain higher order characterisation of the nature of an individual person: this characteristation could be given as *the character the individual arrives at by autonomous self-development*—when the conditions for such autonomous self-development exist. Autonomous self-development is sometimes further specified by Mill as the development of the individual's distinctive *intellectual, moral, emotional, aesthetic potentialities*. What the particular (or first-order) description of the individual's character is must depend on the particular case. So in terms of this Millean position, the question whether female individuals and male individuals have the same grid of kinds would come down to whether those first-order descriptions would have to draw on the same range of characteristics for female individuals as for male individuals. But to know the answer we would need evidence from cases where the conditions for autonomous self-development *do* exist. And because of the subjection of women we lack such evidence, at least in the case of female individuals.

We *are* able to see, as Taylor and Mill point out, that the way women's autonomous self-development is inhibited results in certain gross distortions of their development: 'What is now called the nature of women is an eminently artificial thing—the result of forced repression in some directions, unnatural stimulation in others' (Mill, 1970:148). Taylor and Mill underline the difficulties of founding an understanding of the comparative nature of the sexes on the contemporary state of ignorance (Mill, 1970:150). The principles concerning the determination of women's nature that they enunciate could be recast in the following way: all a characterisation of women's nature can amount to, if it is to have any basis in the knowable, is a hypothesis about the limits of social change of gender character. Where it is the underlying nature of existing or historical women that is in question, all *that* can amount to is a hypothesis about how they might have been if, contrary to what is the case, their circumstances had been different. But it is not mere change or difference that is the issue, rather it is improvement, or the higher development of women. What is to be the standard of improvement or higher development? Again we run up against the need to specify criteria of comparison and again it is as a matter of fact in Taylor and Mill the male standard which fills the need and takes its place as the standard against which to measure. Or at all events, in the dominant mode of *The Subjection* the standard of their 'equal freedom of women' is set by: equal contract in marriage up to the standard for men; property rights like men's; access to occupations now reserved for men; granting of political rights such as men have; equal access to the education men have. The upper standard, the standard to which women's present condition is to be compared, is the standard set by what men do.

Yet Taylor and Mill, like Wollstonecraft, cling to the family as an ingredient of the good society. It is an idealised family with cultivated women in it, but still a family with its economic and political dependency structure left intact. The companionate wife–husband relationship and the rearing of children by cultivated and rational parents are still thought to be compatible with a situation where the mother, by choice, takes the main responsibility for servicing the household and caring for the children, while relying on the father to be the economic provider and to link the household with the public world.

Now in this projected future, however much non-domestic occupations and political responsibilities are formally open to women, it is impossible that women as a group should take up the openings equally with men. And where the justified expectation is that women's non-domestic participation will be low, society will be unwilling to provide an education to fit women for a future standardly foregone. But if women generally do not receive the requisite educational preparation for competing in the public arena, even those exceptional women who would choose the new opportunities will be handicapped by their lack of educational preparation.

Mill and Taylor do put a low valuation on domestic chores as a vehicle for self-development (contrast Wollstonecraft). They describe with some sensitivity the circumscribing effects of domestic life with its humdrum round and the debilitating effects of the woman's being always 'on call', having no time to be her own person. Confined in the pettiness of the private sphere, women do not develop a sense of community spirit, they believe. But Mill and Taylor do not grasp the nettle and call for the dissolution of the family structure they knew. This serious deficiency stems from the power of abstract individualism in their thinking. Too committed to the idea of members of society as individual contractors and choosers, they are unable to think through the implications of the sexual division of labour for women as a social category.

In the minor mode of the essay, which tries to do justice to their agnosticism on the question of whether women's nature differs from men's, Taylor and Mill give equivocal intimations of a possible *different*, but equally valuable, nature for women (a different grid of kinds). The laudatory section on the *practical* bent of women is in this vein (especially 57–58). This practical bent is held to be the real basis of so-called *women's intuition* and further to be the support of a special and admirable cast to the intellect of intellectual women. This is the capability they have for tying the general to particular examples, of seeing that theory keeps its feet on the ground, doesn't get lost in ungroundable abstractions: 'Men who have been much taught, are apt to be deficient in the sense of present fact; they do not see, in the facts which they are called upon to deal with, what is really there, but what they have been taught to expect. This is seldom the case with women of any ability' (Mill, 1970:191). There is alleged to be a complementarity about these intellectual gender bents; each is a corrective to the other. They have the potential to be equally valuable.

There is also, in the discussion of companionate marriage, some suggestion that the dispositions in intimate personal relationships parallel those for the intellect. Where both sexes have been able to develop their capacities, where there is full cultivation, the intimate personal relationships of the sexes parallel those of the intellect in their productive complementarity. The contrast is with things as they are—unhappy exaggeration of undesirable differences, the inevitable outcome of traditional treatment of women (chapter 2).

There is an ambivalence in Taylor and Mill about how to value the supposed special virtue of women's style of thinking, as comes to light in the comparison of the woman's peculiar intellectual character with that of the self-taught man. The intellectual woman, with her practical orientation, is deficient in the speculative ability which can discover general principles. This is what might be expected from her lesser general knowledge, 'exactly the thing which education can best supply'. But we may ask why bother with the extra education if the lesser education had those alternative and complementary good results? To be sure, Taylor and Mill emphasise that they are making a speculative suggestion. Is there anything in it? Because if so, there are different grids of kinds for the sexes and the sex equality argument is fundamentally affected.

The idea they run with is that education may not eliminate all difference of intellectual cast as between the sexes. They find 'the general bent of women's talents is towards the practical', a valuable bent for applying theory to practice, but also for theorising. Women's style of thinking is more generalist, men's more specialist, while at the same time women have 'a rapid and correct insight into present fact' (1970:190), the empirical equivalent of *women's intuition*. Women are better at generalising from their actual experience (1970:190) and at observing what is there to see (1970:191). Women are better at coming up with a battery of instantiations or counterexamples to generalisations, at seeing whether the generalisations fit the world; men are better at thinking up speculative generalisations which get away from their own experience (1970:192). Putting all this together, we might say that a synthetic mental strategy is postulated for women, an analytic mental strategy for men.

Women's mental strategy, as well as having its special advantages for intellectual work, fits women particularly well for practical affairs—a general aptitude that could be applied in public occupation as it is in private domestic work. When it comes to putting theory into practice in the affairs of life, too, women's livelier sense of people's feelings stands them in better stead. A woman is better able to appreciate how a general policy will affect individuals (1970:192).

Taylor and Mill point out that a woman's special intellectual qualities make her a great aid to a man speculator, a thinker up of the generalisations. Julia Annas (1977:184) seizes on this and accuses Mill in effect of thinking of women as superior research assistants rather than as possessors of coequal complementary intellectual powers. But this is too quick. The remark that offends Annas can more properly be seen as a piece of polemic directed to men intellectuals and designed to point out that contrary to general belief they have, even as things are, much to learn from women intellectuals. It is hardly appropriate to project this as the Taylor–Mill vision of women's best future role.

Suppose the complementarity thesis of Taylor and Mill or something like it were true. This is the same as to suppose the capacities of women and men point in at least somewhat different directions and that the development of these capacities would result in different excellences. This takes us back to my starting problem that where there is divergence between the doings of the sexes, society puts a higher valuation on men's doings. From women's having a distinctively different style of thought it does not follow of necessity that this type of mental activity is any less valuable than men's. The presumption of Taylor and Mill is that it is *not* less valuable; as they put it, 'this difference is one which can only affect the kind of excellence, not the excellence itself, or its practical worth' (1970:197–98).

The inferiority of women's distinctive style of thought would follow only from the assumption that men's style constitutes *the* norm of excellence. This is the assumption that is swallowed by Annas when she condemns the Taylor–Mill complementarity thesis: 'As long as one admits that women are intuitive and men suited to reasoning, one's best efforts at valuing women's contribution will be patronising and damaging, encouraging women to think that *the most highly regarded mental achievements* are not for them' (Annas, 1977:185, emphasis added). To this one may respond by asking: *is it true* that those intellectual achievements which are the product of men's style of thinking are *properly* regarded as superior to those in which women excel? However much people believe it to be true, and however great the obstacles this puts in the path of feminists, the question of truth remains. Surely this is not a closed question, as Annas supposes. Annas is pointing to the obstacles, rather than settling the question, when she says the special qualities for which Taylor and Mill praise women 'are created within a male-dominated society, and it is very unlikely that the roles that give them content can within that society achieve a genuinely high value' (Annas, 1977:186). She simply assumes that only traditional women's roles can give content to the distinctive style of thought attributed to women, but this is the point at issue.

At a more general level the point at issue is whether feminism will simply capitulate to the androcentrism of standard liberal equali-tarianism. A start has already been made in unearthing the deep androcentrism of the tradition of thought in which we stand and in exploring the practices which work against the male norm. To fall back on an unquestioning or merely expedient acceptance of that norm is to lose ground.

If the sexes have indeed different excellences, then the educations and the occupational structures apt to call forth the distinctive excellences might be expected to diverge—at least somewhat. This is the determination that the idea of the same grid of kinds was designed to avoid, so Taylor and Mill (in their minor mode) must be counted as implicating themselves in the need to postulate a different grid of kinds for the sexes. What they say about affecting only the kind of excellence, not the excellence itself, only serves to underline this implication. Strict commensurability is gone. Taylor and Mill do not explore, they do not confront, the effect on the equalitarian argument of a different grid of kinds. But explored it must be, if a thoroughgoing agnosticism about the sex natures is to be entertained. And given the continuing state of our ignorance, agnosticism seems to me to be the only defensible position.

GENDER EQUALITY AND SEX EQUALITY

A thoroughgoing agnosticism involves entertaining three distinct possibilities. There is the possibility of completely equal natures, expressed in the Axiom of Equal Natures (1). This sustains the Dogmatic Argument for Sex Equality, but only if it is held dogmatically, only if it is elevated to the status of an axiom. The strategic advantage of this position for a feminist programme is that less than equal performance from women (as compared to the male paradigm) shows women have not yet got fair treatment, that their treatment needs to be improved in some way. Next there is the Modified Axiom of Equal Natures (1a) (see p. 85)—same grid of kinds, women lower on the grid of degree. Used in a worst possible case argument, this sustains the Modest Argument for Sex Equality. For a feminist programme, this has the lesser but still considerable strategic advantage that you can argue against women's *disqualification* in Taylor and Mill's sense—you can condemn any discrimination against women that can be detected. This position is strong enough to justify those forms of affirmative action which can be interpreted as correcting a disqualification. But then, third, there is the possibility of distinctive excellences, potentialities, or natures for the sexes. Ideally developed individuals would be gendered individuals. Where does this third route for the agnostic feminist leave sex equality?

The goal of *sex* equality is the goal of *individual* equality irrespective of sex (though sex itself—woman bears, man begets—is retained). This is not a goal that can be embraced along with the assumption of distinctive natures for the sexes. Such an assumption implies that individuals are necessarily gendered and that their gender will make a difference to what would best promote their development. Even though the genders are thought of as working towards divergent goals, it is still possible to construct an analogue of the sex equality argument, which might be called the *gender* equality argument. The programme of such an argument looks towards an equally enabling or equally empowering treatment for the genders. Concepts that can be used to convey this idea are *equal freedom* and *equal consideration of interests*. Such an argument would look something like this:

Argument for Gender Equality:
(1b) Women and men are gendered by nature (have   *Assumption*
      incommensurable but complementary grids of
      kinds; grid of degree cannot compare women
      with men directly)
(2b) So if they are equally enabled to develop their   *Programme*
      divergent capacities
(3b) They will perform differently but their   *Goal*
      performance will be mutually complementary
      and have comparable value.

The trouble with this programme is that while at an abstract level equal freedom, equal consideration of interests, equal enablement, can apply to sexes with divergent natures, in the real political world this kind of equality has nowhere to come to earth. It does not provide a *workable* principle of comparison. How could one tell whether women had equal freedom or enablement with men or less or more when the exercise of women's freedom is a different manifestation from the exercise of men's freedom (or enablement or whatever)? One can argue that this or that is a liberating or empowering or enabling or good way for women to go, but if it is a gender-specific way, then what is added by trying to assess it in terms of equal to or less than the other gender in some very abstract dimension of enablement?

Thus we can ascertain whether women are being admitted to the public service, we can see what proportions of admissions are of women, we can see if the proportion of women among senior public servants is rising towards equality and so on, which is to say we can test the progress of the sex equality programme. But if we suppose women's gender bent is different from men's, how shall we test the progress of the gender equality programme? What performance among women shall we compare to senior public service performance, say, among men, in order to make a judgment whether women are rising towards equal freedom with men in their self-development? Alternatively, we might see that certain changes in the structure of the public service would favour women's development through the public service. But how would we relate this to gender equality? How much change, which changes, would count as having made the structures equally hospitable to the genders' divergent development through the public service? As a programmatic goal, equality is here stretched beyond its usefulness.

EQUALITY AND LIBERATION

What has happened in recent feminist thought is that *liberation* has entered alongside *equality* as the coordinating concept of the programme for women's advancement. The women's liberation movement has sought to envalue and develop what have been perceived as women's gender-specific potentials and capacities. To this end the movement has not hesitated to be exclusively a women's movement and to foster a whole range of women-only projects, and a culture which explores in a range of art forms a distinctive women's perspective. At the same time there has been an insistence on the equalitarian goal of an end to discrimination against women. Are these goals, are the justifications they rely on, incompatible?

The answer is that they are not incompatible. There is a fundamental asymmetry of social power as between the sexes which has been the starting point for any feminist programme for the advancement of women. In this context the reference point for sex equality has always been how women measure up when taking on men's doings—

since all the established structures have been for men's doings, men's doings have set the standard of performance which shows developed capacity. And the more the evidence comes in, the more uncontroversial becomes what was obvious even to Plato—that women will perform pretty well at men's doings given the chance. So the Modest Argument for Sex Equality does apply and following its programme does yield significant advancement for women. There is at least sufficient overlap between the natural capacities of the sexes for women to be fitted to men's grid of kinds and measured when the grid of degree is superimposed. An end to women's disqualification from men's doings is a minimal requirement for women's advancement and cannot be dispensed with. The question is rather whether this rationale of advancement does full justice to women's potential or whether, on the contrary, gender-specific women's programes *as well* would go further towards optimising women's advancement.

There is sometimes felt to be inconsistency here. A separate women's movement and separate structures exclude men and that's not equality is it? This way of looking at the matter neglects the asymmetry of power as between the sexes, in favour of an abstract individualism that does not engage with the real world. Exclusion on grounds of sex does not have the same import for a man as for a woman, because of the different starting points. Men do not need and should not be given immunity from disqualification when it comes to projects designed specifically for women's advancement.

It is much more difficult to determine what simply advances women than to determine what brings women closer to the male model of excellence. New forms of life which make more of women's potentialities have to be created; they are not necessarily given in the observed performance of men. Some experiments may fail, others prove fruitful. Even the fruitful ones may not all prove compatible with each other. There are many possible ways of advancing—there is not necessarily one absolutely best way. Human life and society are more open-ended than that. What is to count as advancement or liberation will need to be established on the merits of each particular case.

When 'catching up to men' is not the only path of women's advancement, the importance of nature/nurture questions does not disappear completely, but is put in a new light. There do exist gender characteristics—mental, emotional, moral, aesthetic. Whether or not some elements are due to nature, these characteristics are successfully reproduced over generations. We know that many of the detailed elaborations of gender difference are due to social training; we do not know how much underlying structure of difference may be entrenched in biology. Discussing which differences may be due to nature and which to nurture is often taken as tantamount to discussing which are mutable and which (if any) we are stuck with. But this is misleading. If

97

we were to discover some biological mechanisms which underwrite certain gender differences, this would not mean that such differences are in principle inaccessible to change. On the contrary, some types of biological engineering could prove more feasible than some types of proposed social engineering. In contraceptive technology we already have an area cross between biological management and biological engineering, which has had a vast effect on gender relations. It has made possible social changes in areas which had proved very highly resistant to change by social engineering alone. Examples abound, but one would be the social valuation put on virginity and the behaviours associated with this valuation. So with biological engineering, too, it becomes a question of what changes that prove to be feasible are actually contributory to the advancement of women.

Liberationism abandons the ideological set which requires a faith in projecting *the same* performance from the sexes. It abandons the belief that nature is by definition immutable. This equalitarian position (which liberationism supplements) when taken on its own is vulnerable to any future empirical work which might establish that there is indeed some biological difference between the sexes which influences their performance in matters other than bearing and begetting. Liberationism is not vulnerable in this way. Liberationism fully accepts the genders as they are as the starting point of feminism; its agnosticism about nature/nurture befits the state of contemporary knowledge.

Sex equality, or the removal of women's disqualification, does nothing in itself to explore new societal forms which build on the distinctive gender characteristics of women. Liberationist projects can do the exploratory work which may retain separate momentum and/or show what modifications are needed to the established social structures to make them more hospitable to women's achievement.

Women *should* be allowed to do the things that men do. But when they are, their subjection may still not be at an end. We must look beyond equality to liberation.

JANNA THOMPSON

7 Women and political rationality

I

Down through the ages political philosophers have argued that women are not equipped by nature to make sound judgments about public affairs. Generations of liberal feminists have countered with arguments which have also been employed to oppose other forms of discrimination: There is no good reason to believe that women (or Jews or black people) do not have an equal capacity to make rational judgments. But even if women (or Jews, or Blacks) were found to be intellectually inferior, this would not justify excluding them from politics. Nor could it justify preventing individuals of these groups from competing for public office and other positions of power and prestige.

The principle which governs how all these cases are treated is stated by John Stuart Mill in *The Subjection of Women*. In modern society, he says, 'human beings are no longer born to their place in life, but are free to employ their faculties, and such favourable chances as offer to achieve the lot which may appear to them most desirable' (Mill, 1980:16). If we approve of this, 'we ought to act as if we believed it, and not to ordain that to be born a girl instead of a boy, any more than to be born black instead of white, or a commoner instead of a nobleman shall decide the person's position through all life' (Mill, 1980:18).

But this principle, which many people find so convincing when applied to people of other races and religions, has never had the same power to persuade in the case of women. Most people do not think that the sex of a person is irrelevant to how she ought to be treated and how her talents ought to be employed. In fact, Mill didn't think so

99

himself: 'Like a man when he chooses a profession, so, when a woman marries, it may in general be understood that she makes the choice of the management of a household, and the bringing up of a family, as the first call upon her exertions . . . and that she renounces all other objects and occupations which are not consistent with the requirements of this' (Mill, 1980:48). What nature doesn't rule out directly, it rules out indirectly.

Is Mill here exhibiting a failure of nerve, a reluctance to live up to the full implications of his liberal convictions? Or is his 'lapse' better understood as a recognition of the difficulties which real natural differences between the sexes pose for a more uncompromising application of his principle?

Biology cannot determine social destiny in the way that having certain genes determines eye colour, but virtually all social groups regard differences in sexual function and characteristics as a reason for treating women and men differently. An individual's goals, desires and character are formed according to his/her identity as a male or a female. To insist that being born a girl or a boy should in no respect determine a person's social destiny is to require radical changes in the way people understand themselves and live their lives. It seems to require that women and men become more alike in their attitudes, interests and personalities—otherwise they will not in any real sense have the same freedom and opportunities. For those who want women to play a larger role in social decision-making, it seems to require that women become more like men, since in our society the ways of life and consciousness which are derived from a woman's sexual function have restricted her entry into public life. Social conservatives are not alone in thinking that such a change would be a real loss. But if feminists give ground, if they admit that this kind of equality with men is not what they want, then they seem to be giving comfort to those who assume that sexual differences disqualify women from full participation in those activities which are supposed to be the glory of the human race and in those affairs which determine our political destiny.

My purpose in this chapter is not so much to resolve this dilemma— to tell feminists what they should be fighting for—as to account for its existence, to criticise ideas about politics and rationality which help to establish the framework in which we think about the implications of sexual differences.

What kind of loss would a persistent attempt to apply the liberal principle entail? The anti-feminist answer to this question is well known. For Carol McMillan in *Women, Reason and Nature* (1982) the important sexual difference is that women can have babies and men can't. It is true that from this bare biological fact nothing prescriptive emerges; nor does McMillan think that women have by nature a mothering instinct. But nevertheless, she thinks that things will go better for individuals, their children and society as a whole if biology is taken as a basis for social conventions which divide the labour of women and men. Since her biology already gives a woman a unique and individual relation to a newborn infant, it seems reasonable that she be the one who devotes herself to its needs. Being able to do this well requires that a mother be a certain kind of person; that she be nurturing, sensitive and loving, rather than objective, detached and self-seeking. And therefore it is important that girls have a different kind of upbringing and education from boys; that a woman find fulfilment in serving the needs of others; that mothers be discouraged from engaging in work outside the home.

The mistake feminists make, she says, is to regard traditional conventions and values as an imposition on women and a hindrance to their freedom. But this is to treat one's own body as something external to oneself, to forget that these conventions and values are deeply embedded in the way in which men and women understand themselves, find meaning in their lives and satisfying relations with each other. The natural facts of human existence, she concludes, ought to continue to play a central role in our ethical life (1982:92).

McMillan's defence of tradition depends on the conflation of two views. The first is the familiar, but not very convincing, argument for conservatism: that we have certain relationships and conventions which are so deeply embedded in our social life and in our ways of understanding ourselves that it would be enormously damaging, disrupting, and hence wrong, to change them. It is incidental to this argument whether the conventions in question are based on biology. The other view is more attractive, but its ethical implications are more difficult to appreciate. This is that individuals will be better off if they acknowledge the fact that 'man is a natural being whose life is therefore always subject to certain limits and conditions ... he must remain steadfastly bound, through all time, to facts that know no movement and do not change: birth, suffering, death, the conflict between freedom and necessity and so on ' (1982:155). But whatever this means, it is not an argument for traditional sex roles. For if detachment from natural, sensuous existence is a problem, then men are in a far more perilous state than women, since they, it seems, have gone further down this road; and thus feminists who say that men should take more of a share in housework and childcare are doing them a moral favour.

How we should set about appreciating the facts of our flesh-and-blood existence as women or men is not very clear, but it is not only anti-feminists who criticise liberals for ignoring them. Moira Gatens (1983:152) complains that liberalism 'neutralises' sexual differences, and has thus led feminists to regard the equality of the sexes as their primary political goal. But this pursuit of equality misfires because it ignores 'the social and personal significance of male and female biologies as lived in culture . . .'

What exactly is the complaint against liberalism which Gatens and McMillan are making? Liberals will, of course, deny that a demand for the equality of the sexes has to mean ignoring differences. They allow that women, like the handicapped, may need special treatment in order to make use of their freedom and enjoy their opportunities. In fact, by placing an emphasis on the individual, on her own needs, wants, goals and abilities, the liberal can, with some justification, claim to be combating a pernicious use of abstraction, a neutralisation of differences which has done a lot of social harm. To treat all women, or all men, as members of a category is to ignore differences that exist among individual women and among individual men. A lot of tyranny has been practised in the name of 'Woman'; and therefore liberal weapons for combating it are a necessary part of any feminist armoury.

It is true (liberals will admit) that there is a sense in which their treatment of individuals does neutralise sexual, and other, differences. An individual appears in their calculations as someone rational and self-interested who happens to have certain physical and psychological characteristics, certain interests, desires and needs. But his/her worth, entitlement to rights, liberty and justice rests simply on being an individual, and not on being a man, a woman, a Christian, an Anglo-Saxon, or whatever. This way of regarding people is undoubtedly different from the way people usually think about themselves. A woman does not regard herself as an *individual* who just happens to be a *woman*—especially if her life revolves around her conception of what it is to be a woman. But liberalism, its supporters will insist, does not require people to have a certain kind of consciousness. It can respect and allow expression of the interests and desires of both the women who want to be 'women', and the women who want to be more like men.

This is one face of liberalism. There is also liberalism militant—the liberalism which does have ideas about what individuals should be like. And women, it is clear, have never measured up very well. Liberal feminists have often vied with misogynists in their recitations of female failings. 'No other class of dependents,' says Mill, 'have had their character so distorted by their relation to their masters' (1980:21). The fact that some women do not mind their servitude is the worst aspect of this distortion. And so, Mill in *The Subjection of Women* is not only concerned with doing away with legal restrictions on women's activities, but with bringing about a state of affairs in which women can develop as 'progressive beings'.

To have views about how individuals should develop is as unavoidable in politics as it is in everyday life. As long as children have to be raised and societies have to be governed, those responsible will make, more or less thoughtfully, decisions which determine what kinds of lives and opportunities others will have, and thus what kind of people they can become. Even the most laissez faire of liberals, the most earnest devotees of negative freedom, will advocate policies which are bound to have an influence on the way people develop their interests, wants and goals, now and in the future. Like most liberals, Mill's ideas about what a progressive being is are linked to his view about how political rationality can be achieved.

One of the complaints that Mill makes against women, as he finds them, is that when they do have an influence on political affairs it is usually a bad one: 'She neither knows nor cares which is the right side in politics, but she knows what will bring in money or invitations, give her husband a title, her son a place, or her daughter a good marriage' (1980:38). To be a responsible citizen, especially one who deserves to be entrusted with political decision-making, Mill says in writings on political representation, you need to be 'free from narrow or particular views and from any particular bias' (Mill, 1977:45). What keeps women from achieving this is not any deficiency in intellectual capacity, but a bad education and a situation in life which hinders them from exercising this capacity.

Women are not the only group of people whom Mill thinks are disadvantaged by their social situation. An employer of labour, Mill judges, is likely to be more politically capable than a labourer, since he must work with his head and not just with his hands; a skilled worker is likely to be better than an unskilled labourer, but most capable of all are likely to be members of the leisured class—those who have the time, education and the detachment to make political judgments which are good for society as a whole (Mill, 1977:475).

What makes members of the leisured class the best prospects for political leadership is, first of all, their higher level of education. They are more likely to have, or to be able to acquire, knowledge about economics and other subjects which a practical politician must master. But more important, members of the leisured class are in a better position to understand what is good for society and the individuals in it. One reason for this is that they are more likely to be impartial. Unlike the worker, the housewife, or even the employer of labour, they do not have the preoccupations which tempt people to put their own interests above the interests of society as a whole. Secondly, the leisured class is more likely to contain the progressive beings which Mill hoped would become more and more numerous. Leisured individuals, free from the bondage of pressing material needs, free from the daily grind of toil, are more likely to develop their creative powers, their intellectual and aesthetic capabilities; they are more likely to be able to experiment with new forms of life. To the extent that they are progressive individuals and know what happiness in its higher form is like, they are in the best position to seek the good for other individuals, that is, to bring about those conditions which will encourage other people to become progressive individuals too.

Mill has no doubt that women can become progressive individuals and political leaders, but the fact of the matter is that women, even in the leisured class, are far less likely to be in a situation in which they can develop in this way. In the home they will be preoccupied, as they should be, with 'narrow' concerns and interests. McMillan is inclined to believe that there is a psychological incompatibility between being a mother and exercising 'rational' detachment. When Mill suggests that women can best contribute directly to the political process after they have finished raising their children, he is perhaps acknowledging that such an incompatibility exists (Mill, 1980:100).

Modern liberals usually turn their backs on Mill's theory of political representation and argue that political rationality arises not from a particular social location, but from a state of mind. Impartiality is achieved through an exercise of the imagination: by thinking oneself into the position of others, taking into account each person's interests and desires, and then weighing all these preferences in order to decide on a course of action that will bring about maximum satisfaction (Singer, 1981); or by imagining that you and other rational, self-interested individuals have to make decisions about basic social principles in ignorance of your particular social position, special interests, sex, race, etc. (Rawls, 1972). These techniques for achieving rationality, to the extent that they work, enable us to arrive at general principles or political judgments which are impartial in regard to the interests and goals that people happen to have. But they ignore what I have argued is inescapable in politics: views about what interests and goals people *ought* to have. Mill, on the other hand, takes this problem as central, and his theory of political representation is meant to establish a way in which sound judgments can be made for the ultimate good of all individuals. The theory therefore does not deserve to be dismissed simply as elitist, but it is clearly open to a number of criticisms.

The most obvious of these is that the leisured class is a doubtful source of political rationality. The detachment, the independence of this class is open to question, along with its 'objective' knowledge and its views about what it is to be a progressive being. Intellectuals and their systems of thought only came into existence in the first place, say Marx and Engels, because of a historically achieved division between mental and manual labour: 'From this moment onwards consciousness can really flatter itself that it is something other than consciousness of existing practice . . .' (Marx and Engels, 1978a:159). But this independence is an illusion. Even the economic thought of these intellectuals is influenced by their class position; and so is their idea of what it is to be a progressive being. It is understandable why members of a leisured class should think that being free of manual labour, of the work necessary to satisfy one's needs, makes it easier to be a progressive being. But this idea of progress depends upon a division of labour. By bringing this division into question Marx and Engels also raise questions about a view of the good life which takes the division for granted. Freed from the restrictions of class society, so they claim, individuals will be able to develop both their physical and mental capacities in cooperative labour; they will become all-round individuals with a wide range of capacities and needs.

By bringing into question the impartiality of the upper classes and their ideas about progress, Marx and Engels are also, in effect, challenging ideas about political rationality which tend to discount the outlook of those who occupy other positions in society. Why not apply this challenge to the case of women? It is true that for historical reasons women, especially those in traditional roles, have not participated much in political affairs and have not often related their concerns to political ones. But if we abandon Mill's views about where good political judgments come from, then there is less reason to think that a woman's interest in her children and her involvement in family and community life should, as such, be a hindrance to her development as a politically rational being. Why shouldn't we even suppose that her interests and involvements can be a source of a point of view that deserves to be called rational? This was, in fact, what Marx and Engels were prepared to argue on behalf of the working class. How much aid can marxism provide to those who are looking for a view of politics which includes the outlook of women?

II

What makes the materialism which Marx and Engels introduce in the *German Ideology* seem such a promising foundation for an alternative approach to politics is its insistence that consciousness, including consciousness of political objectives, arises out of the needs, constitution and capabilities of human beings as biological creatures, and out of the means by which a society develops these needs and uses these capabilities. What keeps this promise from being fulfilled—so feminists have often complained—is the emphasis that Marx and Engels, from the beginning, put on one aspect of material existence. For it is labour, especially productive labour, which quickly takes the centre of the stage, and those other aspects of our material existence: our development as sexed and sexual beings, giving birth, raising children, etc., are mentioned hardly at all and given virtually no role to play in the account of the development of the forms of consciousness which Marx and Engels are interested in.

What it means to give primacy to labour depends on what materialism is supposed to do. Is it a theory of history? a theory about social structures? an explanation of ideology? or a more general theory about the development of social consciousness? Marx and Engels' cryptic general remarks about the forces and relations of production and their relation to 'superstructure' have been interpreted in various ways by marxists, and it is easy to come to the conclusion that there is no such thing as a general materialist theory; that there is merely marxism—the special theory about capitalism, its development, nature and eventual demise.

As far as this theory is concerned, it is not difficult to understand why productive labour is regarded as the prime mover of social life. 'The bourgeoisie cannot exist without constantly revolutionising the instruments of production, and thereby the relations of production, and with them the whole relations of society' (Marx and Engels, 1978b:476). And so the bourgeoisie bring into the world techniques and new social forms which shatter traditional relationships, including the 'natural' relation of women to men and of both to nature. It is simply not true that flesh-and-blood matters know no movement and do not change; but the forces that move them come from outside.

Our society can be called by a number of names—racist, sexist, etc.—but it seemed obvious to Marx and Engels, as it does to most marxists, that understanding its capitalist nature was the key to understanding its 'laws of motion'; and that the working class, because of its position in the relations of production, would play the leading role in capitalism's overthrow. The primacy of labour doctrine, so understood, is an empirical theory about society, a hypothesis which has been criticised from a number of points of view, including feminist ones. But along with this empirical theory go political objectives which arise out of Marx and Engels' materialist foundations, out of their views on labour and consciousness which they formulated in their earlier writings. The primacy of labour doctrine appears there in a different guise.

Marxism is a view about how society can be changed for the better, and as such it cannot avoid being concerned with the question which also exercised the bourgeois political philosophers: how can individuals and groups with their particular interests and aims arrive at a rational understanding of, and willingness to achieve, a common social good? In the *German Ideology* Marx and Engels show that they are well enough aware of the problem: 'This subsuming of individuals under definite classes cannot be abolished until a class has taken shape which no longer has any particular class interest to assert against the ruling class' (Marx and Engels, 1978a:198). But in a class-divided society all classes have particular interests and are in opposition to each other because of these interests. So how can the working class be assigned the role of humanity's vanguard?

According to the *German Ideology* what makes the working class capable of representing humanity in the struggle against capital depends more on what it lacks rather than what it has. This lack is most obviously a material lack. The working class has no control over production and no hope under capitalism of achieving this. And thus any attempt to be self-active requires the appropriation of the totality of instruments of production. The very limitations of the working class bring about the opposite—an overstepping of all limitations.

Along with these material conditions goes a consciousness which in a negative form prefigures the emancipation of a communist society. What imprisons individuals of other classes within the narrow confines of their group interests is that they get some satisfaction out of having the identity that their group provides. 'With the community of proletarians, on the other hand, who take their conditions of existence and those of all members of society under their control, it is just the reverse; it is as *individuals* that individuals participate in it' (1978a:197–98). They can do this because as members of the working class they have been 'robbed of all real life content, have become abstract individuals but who are, however, only by this fact put into a position to enter into relations with one another *as individuals*' (1978a:191). Even the fact that their work is unpleasant and of indifference to them encourages this development, for it prevents them from falling into 'a slavish relation' to their labour as craftworkers of earlier times have done (1978a:178).

Thus capitalism has in reality put the working class into a position which modern liberal philosophers have merely pictured in their imagination. By being shorn of particular identities, loyalties and interests, they have become abstract human individuals—fit to be the measure of the general good. The German ideology still lingering in the *German Ideology* is the only thing which could make it seem possible to found a movement of revolutionary change on a negation. In fact, Marx and Engels have a problem in common with modern liberals: there is not enough content left in their notion of an individual in order for it to be used as a basis for an idea about social progress. There is an enormous gap between this presentation of the working class and the political objectives which it is supposed to realise.

Their more positive attempt to establish the working class as the progressive class depends on a philosophical view about the relation of labour to human progress: 'Men can be distinguished from animals by consciousness, by religion or anything else you like. They themselves begin to distinguish themselves from animals as soon as they begin to produce their means of subsistence' (1978a:150). It is through labour that homo sapiens becomes human. By means of labour individuals are continually making and remaking their own identities, their needs, skills, relationships. Man makes himself, and also makes nature into his image. He doesn't lie back and take it. By labouring he is thus more active, creative, more energetic in separating himself from the merely natural than in any of his less dynamic encounters with material existence. What is important about the working class is not simply that it is an 'under class' but that it is in an intimate relation with those forces of production which are unfolding and increasing human capabilities and expanding human consciousness.

From time to time in their later works, Marx and Engels try to explain why individuals who have this relation to the mainstream of material progress will also be capable of developing something more than a narrow class interest. In the *Communist Manifesto* they stress the way in which bourgeois society has forced workers into cooperative relationships, made them receptive to all sorts of influences and ideas—unlike the rural idiots who labour in their social backwaters. In *Capital* Marx argues that Modern Industry—industry based on the use of power machinery—has encouraged workers to become more versatile and all-rounded, more knowledgeable about scientific and technical matters, to the extent that 'there has developed a contradiction between the technical necessity of modern industry and its capitalist form' (Marx, 1954:487).

What makes this kind of labour such a fertile basis for the production of consciousness is not simply its capacity to create social wealth and material progress, but its potential to encourage the development of working-class individuals who are rational, active, many-sided, scientifically minded, and in general capable of understanding and promoting a progressive view. Marx has two reasons for regarding the working class as humanity's vanguard: the intimate relation this class has to the forces which are responsible for human development and its ability to free itself from those traditional loyalties, bonds and ways of thinking which make individuals one-sided and narrow.

Marx, like Mill, has a view of how to be politically rational which involves appointing a particular group of people to be the promoters of social progress. Like Mill's theory of representation, this account puts women on the sidelines. For it takes as central work which is more likely to be done by men than by women, as well as a position in the relations of production which men are more likely to fill: work which is cooperative and public (as opposed to work done in families or small communities); work which is based on science and high technology (as opposed to work based on traditional skills); work which is constantly producing new products and using new techniques (as opposed to work which binds a worker to particular unchanging products). Traditional women's work fails to be liberating labour because it is backward; it doesn't develop new skills, capacities and new needs. Moreover it restricts a woman's development as a universal individual by giving her a 'slavish' relation to those particulars which her labour is devoted to serving.

For the same reason Marx and Engels rush past the more humble aspects of our relation to nature in order to get to labour. Such things as giving birth, raising children, developing as sexual beings, becoming old, ill, facing death—those aspects of life which women have traditionally presided over—are limitations which bind us to nature and fate, something man is struggling to overcome through labour. In so far as we are caught up in them, they hinder us from realising our *human* potential.

Marxists do not deny that women can play an equal role in politics. But they can do so only by joining the workforce and becoming a true member of the working class. Even then they are not likely to be engaged in labour which is truly liberating, but are more likely to be working in those subordinate, low-technology, service areas which are behind the frontline of man's encounter with nature and his struggle with capitalism. The vanguard always seems to be where women are not.

Mill's account of how political rationality is possible gives those who work with their hands a subordinate role in politics as a special interest group. Marx, with his materialist passion for setting things on their feet, turns this account half-way round and transforms humble handworkers into the vanguard of human progress. What is positive about this rotation is that it broadens our idea of what a progressive being is; it shows one way in which living a good life can be related to our physical existence. What is questionable about it is that it retains the idea that some social group by virtue of its position is best fitted to represent the good of all; it assumes that some of our capacities and activities are more *human* than others. Marx is in no better position to defend this idea than Mill. The more he distances himself from idealism, the more he sees the working class as consisting of real individuals rather than abstractions, the more obvious it becomes that their understanding and political aims come out of a particular perspective which is as limited and as subject to historical vicissitudes as the perspectives of others.

From our vantage point it is easier to question the connection marxism makes between material and human progress and to doubt whether the working class will ever develop the will and consciousness to struggle for a society which will abolish all human oppressions. We are also aware of how aspects of life which have traditionally been women's concerns—education, welfare of families, care of the old and sick, childbirth—have become political matters. Thus it has become more difficult to justify excluding from politics the views about social good arising from the perspectives of women. There are also many other voices clamouring to be heard.

Practically speaking our faith in humanity's vanguard has vanished. Philosophically it was never justified. But if we rid ourselves of the idea that some group of people by virtue of their social position or state of mind are best able to comprehend the general good, we put ourselves in a position which political philosophy has tried to avoid. We are faced with the prospect of having before us a number of well-founded but contrary views about the general good and no way of deciding which is correct. Traditionally, political philosophers have solved this problem by finding ways of limiting what can be taken to be a legitimate view of the general good. This chapter shows how their way of doing this marginalises women and their traditional concerns. No real solution to the problem of political rationality will ever be found without including the perspectives of women.

No one has ever explained how women can be political animals without becoming part of the brotherhood of man. And no one has satisfactorily described what a general human good would be like which incorporates the perspectives of women. It is always possible, of course, that there is no such thing as a human good, that all talk about such a thing is ideological—an attempt by one group of people to pass off their interests as general interests. If all interests are merely sectional interests, then rational decision-making would be, as utilitarians have always imagined, a matter of management.

In my view, the only current political philosophy which provides an account of how genuine participatory democracy might reach a rational and agreed result is Jürgen Habermas' theory of discourse and rationality. Habermas argues that truth, as far as political and moral goals are concerned, is reached through a discourse in which everyone can participate fully, free of external and internal constraints. The virtue of Habermas' position is that it recognises that a political point of view can arise from a person's own experiences; it also recognises that there are restrictions, some obvious, some more subtle, which prevent people from being able to convert their own perspective into a contribution to a political dialogue. On the other hand, the 'ideal speech situation'—the situation in which all external and internal constraints are lifted—is a notion too abstract to be of much use to feminists or anyone else. What is at issue in the debates I have been concerned with is precisely what counts as an external or internal constraint. The problem is that the vantage point from which questions of validity are supposed to be decided, according to Habermas' theory, is remote from the situations in which social issues are ordinarily discussed.

But Habermas sometimes has another way of presenting ideal discourse which doesn't suffer from a loss of contact with the issues which divide real historical individuals. He imagines the participants to be real people facing the problems of their times—individuals who differ from us only in that they are being as rational as they can be, which means not only that they are willing to freely communicate and criticise, but that they are committed to removing restrictions revealed by attempts to deal with their problems. To the extent that the ways of life of women (or of men) are found to be a hindrance to their participation, social changes have to be made.

Once discourse is conceived as a historical event rather than a linguistic ideal, it becomes much more difficult to see how it could issue in consensus. Sceptics will point out that the problems of one group of people are not the same as those of another; the social relationships which feminists regard as problematic are seen by others as natural and satisfactory. But this pessimism, when it is used as a reason for denying all possibilities of discourse, assumes from the start that political interests are bound to be sectional interests and that each group has exclusive rights to identify and discuss the problems which belong to them. The autonomous women's movement sometimes misconceives its task as a defence of political territory.

The fact is that women's problems are not just women's problems. Feminism in its modern form—the form that began in the seventeenth century—was a response to the dislocations caused by the rise of bourgeois society and the Industrial Revolution. Women have experienced these dislocations in a particularly severe way, and are therefore more likely to be aware of some of the serious social contradictions caused by them. But the problems are general ones: the rift between human beings and nature—the issues raised by the environmental crisis, reproductive technology, as well as the debates about the significance of male and female biology; and the problems caused by the conflict between demands for individual liberty and the need for social cohesion. If there are going to be rational solutions to these problems, that is, solutions which are not simply an imposition of one group's interests on everyone else, they will only be discovered through the kind of discourse which Habermas envisions. This discourse cannot be rational without the participation of women, and women have every reason for wanting to be participants.

8 Desire, consent and liberal theory

That the personal is political has become much more than a slogan for feminist activists in liberal democracies: this is the rubric of new feminist theory, in which the perspective of inquiry is extended by women's knowledge. In treating the personal as political, esteem is accorded women's reality and legitimacy sought for appropriate methods of explanation of this reality. That 'the personal is political' challenges the claim to universality in philosophy, poetry, language and all scholarly inquiry. It is a challenge which is seriously made, and must be seriously met, in public and in private. The separation of the public and private spheres, and the identification of the former as male and the latter as female, is fundamental to liberal democratic life. So are the lower status and actual confinements of the private sphere and so too are the emancipationist demands for a progress of women into the public sphere. If the actual source of women's lower status is not the public/private division but the sex-specific nature of the categories, a 'gender-neutral, gender-equal public/private' division is a haven from a heartless world without the 'pedestalisation' of women. Another is the ambisexual world of Le Guin's *Left Hand of Darkness*: in these constructs the private realm might still be considered subordinate to the public, but not women to men as a consequence of the division (Nicholson, 1981; Simms, 1981; Lasch, 1977).

Like the social relationship we call private property, in liberalism specific gender characteristics are treated as necessary and fixed, whether seen as divinely ordained or scientifically validated. In feminist theory, personal relationships are political not only because they can be assessed 'according to ideals of the public world' (Nicholson, 1981:91), but because they are structured by those ideals:

'It is precisely because sexuality is so often the vehicle for the expression of power relations that sexuality is, by its very nature, a subject for political inquiry' (Person, 1980:606). Even the most confined definition of 'political', as to do with power and the allocation of resources, can be usefully applied to the study of personal relationships (Huston and Cate, 1979; Hatfield et al., 1979). This kind of work is conservative in the sense that structural dynamics are reinforced by findings which frequently are further demonstrations of personal inadequacy. Feminist theory must go further: new political concepts are needed to explore rather than simply affirm what has been sensed so painfully by women. Feminist theory can examine why personal problems are interpreted as the symptoms, or effects, of individual weakness, and search for the source of problems so perceived in the gendered structure of liberal society.

There is no better evidence of the ahistorical and conservative nature of a political analysis focused exclusively on the public sphere than the demonstration of the private effects of the approved behaviour of public life. The concept of human nature asserted by Thomas Hobbes in the seventeenth century, endorsed by John Locke, remains the model for the liberal citizen: the man–city/woman–home structure is the historical product of Hobbes' technology of social organisation. Hobbes believed that the mechanism of society he advocated was deduced from the 'facts' of human nature. His definition of that 'nature' has been realised in the shaping of gender-specific personal traits by the gendered institutions of liberal society. To Hobbes the primary human motivation was acquisitive desire, and the reason for restraint, fear. The state of nature was a chaos of unrestrained desire to acquire and unalloyed fear for one's acquisitions and one's life. In the state of nature the original dominion was that of the mother over her child. Hobbes slips from the suggestion that this right derived from bearing the child to the assertion that the mother's dominion depended on her nurturing the child rather than exposing it. He is thus able to connect maternal dominion in 'meer Nature' with paternal dominion in civil society. Public 'terrour' paradoxically protects private nurturing:

> For the Lawes of nature (as Justice, Equity, Modesty Mercy, and (in summe) doing to others, as wee would be done to,) of themselves, without the terrour of some Power, to cause them to be observed, are contrary to our naturall Passions ... [I]f there be no Power erected ... every man will and may lawfully rely on his own strength and art, for caution against all other men. (Hobbes, 1968:223–24)

It is at this point that Hobbes introduces the gendered mechanism within his model of human behaviour. Acquisitive desire is both basic motivation and legitimation of the restraining power of the Leviathan:

this 'human' trait is thus appropriated in civil society as male. The parallels between Hobbes and Freud are no curiosity (Flax, 1980:30): Freud's assumptions are Hobbes' assertions, by which women are assigned as other, other objects of acquisitive desire. This is a civil structure, contrasted with the 'disorder' of the unlimited desire of women as well as men in the state of nature. In Hobbes' litany of 'voluntary motions', (1968:ch. 6) we are left in no doubt that desire includes sexual desire; and the suppressive effect of the imposition of civil law on female desire is a function of his reasoning that superior strength conveys authority.

There is another effect of the construct of a civil world in which social virtues are nurtured in private and a calculus of prudence rather than a love of goodness is the ideal guiding public behaviour. As Elshtain (1981:108–114) argues, Hobbes recasts the language of politics: his vocabulary is drained of *public* moral evaluation and moral terms are relegated to the private arena. The nurturing virtues are there dependent on protection by public power. This split discourse is implicitly linked to the split desire within civil society in that the privileged segment is male.

Locke's contract theory of government is built on Hobbes' 'facts': a logic of acquisition requires that assurance of security of property and person which government provides by restraints on this individual liberty. The Lockeian contract is a contract for the propertied. By treating labour as property, Locke was able to extend the contract to most men, but not equally to women, who remained at one remove from the public agreement to be governed. From Locke we read consent as the entry, by choice, into the civil contract. Choice is an important problematic as the concepts of consent and of contract have been employed in liberal theory (Beitz, 1980; Martin, 1980; Pateman, 1980a). The difficulty of identifying consent in the absence of choice has been avoided by assuming consent, by ignoring non-consent or reinterpreting non-consent as consent. The special problems for women in liberal theory, and law, have been discussed by Pateman; the treatment of submission as consent depends on a scenario in which '[t]he "naturally" superior, active and sexually aggressive male makes an initiative, or offers a contract, to which a "naturally" subordinate, passive woman "consents"' (1980:164). Although Locke rejects Sir Robert Filmer's justification of patriarchy as a 'natural' principle for public rule he retrieves the idea of the 'natural' subjection of women, 'a Punishment laid upon Eve'. His recourse to a 'natural' legitimation of authority is only applicable specifically to conjugal relations if the private domain is split off from the political world (Elshtain, 1981:124).

The feminist critique of liberal theory is both a response to women's experience of a society constructed on this basis and an acknowledgment of the difficulty of explaining this experience. Most readily, the critique is geared to repairing the split, rather than explaining women's experience of it. This emancipationist approach has been useful in clarifying the nature of the split liberalist world, revealing that women's path from the private to the public domain is choked with obstacles. What has been less clearly revealed is that the other path is wide open and well used: there is an everyday movement of men, and a potent transmission of values from the public into the private domain. The conversion to a two-way path was prominent as a demand of women's movements in the 1960s and a generation later, is prominent as a response from reformist legislatures.

The preoccupation of feminist theory is now with the problem of explaining the experience of women: it is not only the split world, but the split discourse, of liberalism which is the vital field of investigation. The relegation of women as 'other' by the simplistic but devastating process of sex identification earlier focused attention on the social attribution of characteristics justifying that relegation. The use of the category 'sex' to refer to the biological state of being male or female and the category 'gender' as the accretion of socially attributed characteristics of masculinity and feminity was predicated within the reformist mode, and linked the transcendence of class and race with that of gender. This environmentalist/essentialist dichotomy, rooted in liberalist discourse, continually caught back the feminist critique into that split discourse. The theorisation of difference involves a radical fracture of this process (Gatens, 1983; Salleh, 1984). A focus on the specificity of female experience requires an adjustment of Hobbesian distrust of a desire which requires restraint by phallic law, a restraint to which Locke argues all consent (although women are faced with the denial of desire). It is the focus on the significance of somatic experience which reveals the processes of confirmation and denial of sexual desire as Hobbesian, and the waxing and waning of the appearance of validity of Lockeian consent. 'Desire' and 'consent' are key concepts in the study of private as well as public liberalist life, and both studies are of political behaviour. When we examine institutions predicated on desire as given, and consent its necessary ameliorative, we are studying the developed dynamic of possessive individualism, the fuel of liberal democracy. The forms of this public behaviour are the dies of our analytic tools—and politics is studied as the use of power over others, the allocation of resources, the permutations of the playing out in society of desire to acquire as male, and dominant. How well are personal relationships 'explained' using the same tools? This mode of explanation of liberal sexual relationships depends on the power of public behaviour to permeate the private domain, so that we can explore the political nature of sexual desire and sexual consent as reflections and reinforcers of desire and consent in the public sphere.

Locke reasons after Hobbes that the protection of person and property by law is needed where unlimited acquisitive desire is the basic human motivation. The social contract rather than the strength of the Leviathan justifies the law as long as the governed consent to the contract. How well does this construct serve as an analytical framework for sexual relationships in liberal society? Male sexual desire is understood as an acquisitive and powerful drive; the sexual contract called marriage is seen as a restraint on male desire and a security and protection for women, an exchange to which each is required to consent. This sexual contract is predicated on the assumption that male sexual desire is much greater than female desire, so that a man purchases sexual satisfaction. A woman need bring only her person to the market; in exchange for protection of her person and access to property she yields up some rights to her person.

This construct of liberal marriage has historically been starkly revealed in the broad disjunction of imagined and bodily experience. In her 'deromanticization' of Victorian marriage, Karen Horney linked the enforced demand for monogamy to the social sanctions against infidelity and the economic sanctions against female independence (Garrison, 1981:681). The idea of the virtuous wife, as 'Mary', was at a peak point of contrast with the sexual 'Eve', the locus of passion, of 'forgetfulness of duty, place and public obligation' (Janeway, 1980). Hobbes' desiring woman belonged in the state of nature, not in civil society; in Machiavelli woman was at best capricious, at worst disgusting. Both Rousseau and Hegel recoil from the wanton and disordered figure of 'Eve' (Pateman, 1980b; Moller-Okin, 1980:Part III). The elevation in Victorian society of the 'Mary' stereotype to priestess status, and the denial of prostitution, were an insistent declaimer of the moral superiority of women, of the notion that women were by nature modest and virtuous (Houghton, 1978:348–53). The cost to women was considerable, for '[p]assionlessness was on the other side of the coin which paid, so to speak, for women's admission to moral equality' (Janeway, 1980:579).

The literary, economic, legal and social dimensions of the ascension of the 'Angel in the House' are well known. For men, public life was acquisitive, competitive, tough, active and individualistic. Man maintained the Hobbesian haven where women served in her sanctuary of sharing, responsiveness, nurturance and passivity, (Houghton, 1978:341–48). The power of proscribed sexuality for women was a current across the polarity of class, with the home as haven a social ideal to both sexes. The burden of his wife's material aspirations on the man of substance was a reinforcement of the structure of gender relations (Houghton, 1978:184–89) and their transmission across the world and down the generations. Victorian women were less 'God's police' than state police, in that the sexual contract was in many ways enfunctional to an industrialising economy.

Sexual relationships thus susceptible to the influence of public behaviours are one place where women's opportunity to acknowledge the disjuncture between experience and explanation emerges. Liberal society even at its Victorian peak has never succeeded in proving Hobbes' point to women, nor in securing women's universal or permanent consent to the sexual contract. The Victorian family was not a 'school of sympathy', and neither is the modern marriage: it is the institution by which a man confers social identity on a woman (Bridenthal, 1982:225–35; Tavris and Offir, 1977:218–32). She is changed from a waiting maid, from 'the former Miss X', consummated by the transforming power of sexual relations with a man. Liberal marriage is an institution for the penilisation of women, it is not a symmetrical partnership, and it is an effective agency of control (Simms, 1981:319; Firestone, 1970:17; Pateman, 1980a; Ehrenreich and English, 1979:94–95)—especially in a society where housework is seen as public punishment (Lekachman, 1975:94). Victorian women responded strongly to their opportunity with feminist protests against marriage and a precursor to modern consciousness-raising groups in the 'No Secrets' movement (Zaretsky, 1981:230–33). Dora Russell, Stella Browne, Charlotte Perkins Gilman and Emma Goldman were among those feminists who made powerful statements of their knowledge of the oppressive 'contract' of marriage: but this was never seriously accepted as political while the intellectual agenda was drafted by men. The experience of men was public, and thus political women had the obstacle of dismantling man's construction of women's experience of sexuality, of motherhood, of marriage. The sites of significance located in these experiences remained faults in the liberal framework, potential sites of rupture.

Analysis of the influence of capitalist production is useful in studying the process of family change from the seventeenth century in domestic and city architecture, the development of towns, in law, health, education and other public phenomena. The examination of the effects of privatisation, commoditisation and individualism on personal life is an important development from such analysis, but is still not sufficient basis for explanation of the agency of women in either the social or the sexual contract. Why did women accept exclusion from the public sphere? Why did women pay with their sexuality for a commission in the state police? What were the personal effects of the attitudes of men to women, and of the cross-current of attitudes from public life brought home, and taken to bed? The fragments of experience of women who resisted and our own experience at the same sites of opportunity are illuminated by the feminist

117

critique of liberalism which extends beyond both marxist and psychoanalytic explanations and suggests that the struggle with Hobbesian desire and Lockeian consent is of central importance. The function of these concepts not only explains the public face of possessive individualism but reveals its private parts in their historical shape as well. But this is only what we know, only bringing our consciousness up to date with our suppressed acknowledgments, only reclaiming a conquered territory (Ward, 1984:118).

The liberal sexual relationship is a genre within which are types of encounter differentiated by the use of male power, whether that be physical, economic or institutionalised. All such uses of power are political, though unexamined in the narrow liberal definition. Incest, sexual harassment and rape are predicated on superior male force, whether manifest or not. Where force is the only factor, there is no Lockeian contract and thus the concept of consent is (logically) irrelevant in the forcible sexual use of females. Hobbes' notion of the duty of obedience to superior strength would be more appropriate in clarifying the historical relevance of consent in identifying rape. As Pateman shows, in practice threats, including those which are accepted as instilling terror, do not legally establish non-consent (1980b:157). Hobbes' legitimation of government by 'terrour' is an unexamined but powerful influence in such legal reasoning. That influence is transmitted from criminal law to sexual lore, for in feminist analysis 'rape is revealed as the extreme expression, or an extension of, the accepted and "natural" relation between men and women' (Pateman, 1980a:161). Force might sometimes be used by men, or rape or harassment alleged by women, when breach of contract is the unarticulated complaint, but where women are without the power to define consent, and the contractual nature of social relations are beyond the scope of political inquiry, law remains blind. Whether force is or is not part of sexual harassment, the superior public position of the initiator is an essential element. The detriment in those situations stems not from actual bodily harassment but from the initial proposition which victimises its object. Ultimately the superiority of the liberal male position is justified by Hobbes and effected by the 'auxiliary' position of women reconstructed in liberal society and liberal sexual relations. The analogy of authority in society and the authority of man in marriage was often drawn by Locke's contemporaries. The liberal model of a marriage contract is one in which a husband provides protection and access to property and the wife provides sexual and other personal services. Where the wife is not economically dependent the model is amended in practice, but more important is the effect if female sexual desire is equal to male sexual desire. An analysis beyond that of political economy is necessary to examine this problem in libidinal economy (Barker-Benfield, 1972).

While sexual desire is acknowledged as male and acquisitive, sexual relations are formulated like Hobbesian civil relations and reinforced by liberal institutions, like liberal marriage. It is not only our self-image but our most intimate relations which are subject to shaping by, and serve as supports for, liberal society. Private life is thus violated by public life: the home may be haven for men, but it is a universe of experience for women. The liberal moment of patriarchy is not passed when women enter the sphere of men.

Marriage 'helps men and hurts women' (Tavris and Offir, 1977:143) but lack of self-esteem and dependency might be the product of liberal sexual relations rather than institutionalised family life despite the importance of reformist feminism on issues concerning the restrictions of mothering—abortion, contraception, childcare. It is not only the social construction or economic enforcement of gender roles that confines us, but the processes of affirmation, or denial of processes of negation, in which we are actively engaged as thinking and feeling subjects. Sexual relations in a liberal society are the crucial sites of the affirmation/denial process. It is not the separation of public and private worlds, nor the gendered nature of that separation, but the concealed violation of sexual relationships by rationalised public behaviour which is the vital effect of liberal doctrine. This effect is redefined in feminist theory where the 'facts' of women's lives are revealed as 'manufacts', if the context and tendencies of women's experience are not treated as conquered or passive. The 'tyranny of facts' (Lukacs, 1971:172–73) has a special power where gender roles are concerned. Most seriously, moments of potential change are diffused when women image themselves as necessarily powerless, managing to accede to putatively universal understanding in which their knowledge and being is marginal. Women described and explained within masculine parameters are 'other': the negative connotations of words for women have served this subjugation of woman, and female sexuality (Spender, 1980:18–19).

The view from Freud, of female desire lived as an attempt to acquire a penis equivalent, is alien to, and alienating of, female sexuality. But unfortunately not necessarily. The 'objective' social construction of female sexuality is, logically enough, alien and alienating, and in denying the possibility, let alone necessity, of the female as subject in explanation of female sexuality, offers Hobbesian desire as the authentic form (Irigaray, 1981c:99). No wonder passion was the price of Victorian respectability, still no wonder women's bodies are the battlefields where men's explanations confront women's experiences, for 'the body can and does intervene to confirm or deny various social significances in a way that lends an air of inevitability to patriarchal social relations. A thorough analysis of the construction of the specificity of female experience, which takes account of the female *body*, is essential to dispelling this "air"' (Gatens, 1983:149). An important element of feminist writing is the expression of female sexuality: this affirmation of woman as subject has long been vital to the protest of women. The dominance of the Freudian phallacy in the twentieth-century social construct of female sexuality (Miller and Fowlkes, 1980:785; Ward, 1984:101–117) has not destroyed the vital message in that writing of women for women, although the absolute disallowance of the idea of a feminine libido in Freud has served to disconnect women from their own words and their own knowledge. Karen Horney's challenge to Freud strengthened the analysis of the function of culture in psycho-sexual development, and affirmed the principle of female sexuality:

> Historically the relation of the sexes may be crudely described as that of master and slave ... a girl is exposed from birth onward to the suggestion ... of her inferiority, an experience which must constantly stimulate her masculinity complex ... Owing to the hitherto purely masculine character of our civilization ... it seems to me impossible to judge to how great a degree the unconscious motives for the flight from womanhood are reinforced by the actual social subordination of women. (Horney, 1927:325)

Freud, rather than Horney, informed subsequent work, and the concept of derivative female sexuality continued to reign in 'scientific' literature (Person, 1980:787–89). That female sexual pleasure is studied at all is traced in Janeway's analysis to the decline in the economic importance of chastity, and cultivation of the imagery of woman as sexual object—'Mary', as social object rather than social subject, has outlived her moment and that the opportunity for development in feminist theory of an authentic paradigm of female sexuality might permit women to reject merely that recovery of Eve (Janeway, 1980:579–86).

The relation of sexuality to identity, and in particular the importance of genital sexuality to the gender identification of men, is recognised in feminist theory (Person, 1980:618–19). The possible influence of women's monopoly of childcare is a central controversy of vital importance to the thesis of infantile dependence as the major limitation on sexual liberation (Dinnerstein, 1976; Ruddick, 1982:91). Nevertheless, occupying centre stage of new feminist theory is the idea of a different female sexuality: this theorisation gives coherence to all previous writing and searching and talking about female desire. The explanation and restoration of the integrity of pleasure/knowledge/meaning so painfully disassembled for the purpose of constructing liberal society, of controlling the construct, and of analysing/reinforcing the control, is of immense importance. Not the least significant is the destruction of the semblance of equity in the sexual contract by the affirmation, by women, of their sexuality, supervening arguments centred on the access of women to capital.

Woman's social power, and access to property, entailed her complicity in denying her sexuality. It is the sexual contract based on Hobbesian desire and Lockeian consent which produces the female eunuch, the bourgeois variant of an ancient theme. For not acquisition, but adjunction (a denial of appropriation) characterises female sexuality (Irigaray, 1981c:104). In this view, the sexual pleasure of women cannot be calculated: its diffuse nature makes it too elusive for the sexual contract. It is as much because of the nature of subjective female experience, rather than that women were not supposed to experience desire, or were supposed always to experience less desire than a man, that female sexuality was liable to be discounted by women in liberal relationships. For '[p]roperty and propriety are undoubtedly rather foreign to all that is female. At least sexually' (Irigaray, 1981c:104).

All the words which have protected the idea of female sexuality and spoken to women's experience, like Kollontai's 'Great Love', Anais Nin's 'Eroticism in Women', Adrienne Rich's journey from 'The phantom of the man-who-would-understand the lost brother, the twin-' breaking through patriarchal reality to the *Dream of a Common Language*, are gathered from 'the little structured margins of the dominant ideology' (Kollontai, 1972; Nin, 1976; Rich, 1978; Irigaray, 1981c:104). The decrepit sexual concepts of bourgeois desire and consent might be swept from sight when our language and our lives realise the meaning of the word *jouissance*, the motif of the French feminists' writing (Marks and de Courtivron, 1981:36–37 n.8; Kristeva, 1981:16 n.6). Perhaps this is the long-sought key to clearing the conceptual obstacles between the personal and the political.

Jouissance nominates a desire which is the counterpoint of desire to acquire: the sense of curious and delightful play in a baby's learning and an adult's loving. Recovering the path Descartes devalued as 'low rationality', learning with our lives as well as our abstract processes of thought is to burst the bonds of liberal desire, with implications for our political behaviour at both personal and public levels. Similarly, undoing Lockeian consent reveals the miserable thing acquiescence is, and dissolves the justification of many a so-called contract, both the personal and the public variety. The availability of an acknowledged alternative procedure is essential to Lockeian contract theory. To be free and equal is to be able to choose to accept or reject a form of civil contract, or a form of sexual contract. The expression of desire is the expression of that freedom, and the guarantee of choice once we transcend the limitations of liberal theorisation (Lloyd, 1983a; 1983b; Thompson, 1983; Salleh, 1984).

The reconceptualisation of 'desire' and 'consent' is a promising direction in post-liberal thinking as a means of addressing political problems beyond the range of liberal tools of inquiry. Working in this direction disarms a tradition of knowing which, through a gendered public/private split has served, by the severance of 'public' reason and 'private' passion, to confine the possibilities of knowledge and experience.

PART III
The Challenge to Academia

ELIZABETH GROSS

9 Philosophy, subjectivity and the body: *Kristeva and Irigaray*

Julia Kristeva and Luce Irigaray are two of the most widely recognised French feminists outside France. Both women share a number of sources, points of reference and broad similarities—which is hardly surprising given the shared context of post-1968 French political and social theory. Among some of their common concerns are their interests in developing accounts of the processes of production and constitution which create male and female subjects as distinct in personality, subjectivity and social position. Both are thus strongly influenced by the work of the notorious French psychoanalyst and enfant terrible, Jacques Lacan (1978a; 1978b; 1982). His seminars on Freudian theory were attended by virtually an entire generation of French intellectuals, including both feminists; with the publication of his most significant, and outrageous, papers and seminars in 1966 as the *Ecrits*, he has exerted an enormous influence over the interests of feminist theory in both France, and, through the overwhelming success of Juliet Mitchell's text, *Psychoanalysis and Feminism* (1974), in Anglo-American and Australian contexts as well. Since 1968, or after, feminists have attempted to understand the psychic *internalisation* and reproduction of patriarchal power relations, and positions of male superiority and female inferiority by means of the Freudian conception of the unconscious and sexuality. Both Kristeva and Irigaray use many of the methods, techniques and insights of psychoanalytic theory to develop their own projects: in Kristeva's case, the development of a theory of the *speaking subject*, a being capable of understanding and articulating language, a being constituted as a social subject by being subjected to the laws of langauge; and in Irigaray's case, the development of a theory of sexual specificity and identity for the two sexes. The speaking subject is, for Kristeva, paradoxically both the agent of coherent, cohesive discursive or representational 'texts' and systems; and, at the same time, can be seen as the site for the transgressive rupturing and transformation of systems of meaning and representation. In Irigaray's case, she will attempt to use psychoanalytic methods to interrogate the 'repressed' or unacknowledged elements of psychoanalysis and a whole history of philosophy that has been based on the effacement of women's autonomy and specificity.

Besides this common use of psychoanalytic theory and some of its practical or therapeutic components (NB both feminists are practising psychoanalysts as well as theorists), Kristeva and Irigaray also share a background in a series of challenges to the question of texts, reading, interpretation and meaning, initiated in the first instance by Ferdinand de Saussure early in this century, and developed by a number of writers from the 1950s—among them, Claude Lévi-Strauss, Emile Benveniste, A.J. Gréimas, Roland Barthes, and, most recently, Jacques Derrida. Derrida's elaboration of the techniques by which philosophical and literary texts may be 'deconstructed' has particularly exerted a powerful common influence on both Kristevan and Irigarayian projects. Derrida argues that these privileged texts of the West reveal an unacknowledged excessive textual play which, if sought out, may be capable of undermining the logic of each text's explicit commitments and claims. His challenge to the domination of metaphysical thought, structured in terms of binary oppositional categories, has provided a number of methods and goals recognisable in the work of both feminists. Above all, his critique of logocentric identities and values, his assertion of a radically heterogeneity of *difference* (or *différance*. See Derrida, 1979) and his attempts to undermine the foundational assumptions of vast systems of knowledges, directly link with the Kristevan assertion of a subversive, libidinal force underlying all discourse but unspoken by it. For Kristeva, deconstruction has helped to establish a decentring of all social identities—personal, sexual and symbolic—as her theoretical object and goal; for Irigaray, deconstruction has provided a series of methods for interrogating philosophical categories and oppositions which contribute to women's theoretical containment within patriarchal or phallocentric models.

While remaining key reference points of sociological, methodological and epistemological influence on Kristeva's and Irigaray's work, their respective projects and interests cannot be merely reduced to or explained by the openly virile frameworks of psychoanalysis or deconstruction. Both feminists develop beyond their male predecessors in a number of significant respects, using their methods more as points of departure than as systems which must be reverentially accepted. Among these developments can be included: the use of psychoanalytic and deconstructive theory in an openly *political* context, using these otherwise therapeutic or critical techniques to explain, and change, oppressive social relations and systems of representation; an attempt to integrate an account of sexuality with an understanding of language and signification; an attempt to focus on and acknowledge what has been obscured, repressed or silenced, both in relation to Western patriarchal texts in general, as well as in relation to the texts of Lacan, Derrida or others, more particularly. Psychoanalysis and deconstruction are only part of the intellectual repertoire of the work of these feminists; they, and other sources of influence can be seen as intellectual raw materials for their own, very different aims in theoretical production.

Yet, although Kristeva and Irigaray share a concern with masculine and feminine forms of subjectivity and sexuality, as well as a fascination with the social debt owed to an unarticulated maternity, and with procedures of textual analysis, reading and interpretation, there are a number of points of tension or contradiction between them that forbids too close an identification of their divergent positions on the question of women, femininity and the female body. For two feminists whose interests are in principle so similar, Kristeva and Irigaray are nevertheless committed to incompatible projects, being opposed both politically and in terms of their relations to their various intellectual predecessors. I intend to examine these differences, by focusing on the position each accords to women and femininity in their theoretical systems. I hope these differences may prove instructive for Anglo-Saxon feminists in their theoretical enterprises, for this disagreement may clarify broad disagreements and lines of intervention and interaction between two distinct forms of feminist theory.

KRISTEVA AND THE FEMININE

As a semiologist, a theorist of literary production, as well as a psychoanalyst, Kristeva brings together a psychoanalytic account of the psychic and social production of subjectivity with a structural and post-structural analysis of textual or discursive production. These two interests coalesce in her object of analysis, the *speaking subject*. She relies upon psychoanalytic accounts of infantile sexual development, the distinction between pre-oedipal 'feminine', polymorphous sexuality and oedipal, phallic, masculine, orgasmically directed sexuality, for the key features of the two orders or processes she claims govern all individual, social and signifying unities. The earliest pre-oedipal sexual phases in the child's life—those specified as oral, anal, phallic, scopophilic, sadistic, or epistemophilic by Freud (1905)—are roughly correlated with the unspoken, repressed foundation of signification, which Kristeva calls 'the semiotic'. The later oedipal overlaying of this pre-oedipal, anti-social, narcissistic sexuality is called 'the symbolic' by Kristeva, in accordance with Lacan's understanding of this term: the symbolic order is equivalent to the social, the order of law, language and regulated exchange. The child enters the circuits of social law, language and exchange clearly long before the oedipal phase (which psychoanalytic orthodoxy places at around the age of five); yet this entry is not, at this initial point, a regulated, ordered, articulated or rule-governed immersion. The child is not yet positioned as a subject within the symbolic order; it has not yet subjectively assumed the social spaces pre-designated for it as a subject of a particular type (class, race, sex) within a particular culture. To acquire, or to accept this as one's position is to resolve the oedipal demand to renounce the immediacy of pleasures and gratifications demanded by the pre-oedipal child in exchange for the deferred gratification afforded by a stable place in language and culture.

The *semiotic* and the *symbolic* orders are both necessary for there to be a stable speaking subject, a stable discursive product or an agent of social unities, institutions and practices. However, while the West can accept the necessary reliance it has on law- and rule-governed, meaningful, productive, masculine functioning, on the symbolic, Kristeva claims it is incapable of accepting its necessary dependence on a fragmented, chaotic, bodily, libidinal, feminine energy. The feminine or semiotic foundations of all social functioning must remain dis-avowed, unspoken and unrepresented for these social unities to function as such. The semiotic and symbolic are thus ambiguously and strategically located both on the levels of individual, psycho-sexual operations—that is, on the level of fantasy, dream, symptom, desire, and so on—and on the level of social, cultural and signifying operations—in the production of all social objects, whether these are texts, images or commodities. The semiotic is equated with the energetic, rhythmic, bodily contributions of the pre- or anti-social individual—libido and unharnessed bodily energies—as well as with the contributions of the usually neglected phonic, graphic, corporeal supports texts, social practices and institutions rely upon but do not admit to. The symbolic, by contrast, is the replacement of the anarchic, perverse, polymorphous libidinal impulses by their hierarch-ised, regulated, subordination to the primacy of genitality—that is, by the subsumption of a feminine plural *jouissance* by a singular, regulated order of phallic sexuality. The symbolic is the domain of definite positions and propositions, the social site for the creation of unified texts, discourses, knowledges and practices constituting social life by subsuming individual, and sub-individual energies into collec-tive, compromised, social forms. Crudely put, the semiotic is the input of an undirected body, while the symbolic is the regulated use and organised operation of that body in socially recognised tasks.

Both Kristeva and Freud consider the pre-oedipal or semiotic phase as feminine and maternal. The mother is the primary object of love and libidinal attachment for the child's spasmodic, incipient sexual drives and ego boundaries. She is the love-object and 'other' for the child, satisfying its needs and constituting its desires. Freud designates the pre-oedipal phase as a 'feminine', 'dark', 'shadowy' region over-layed and 'whitewashed by time'. It is a 'Minoan-Mycenean' founda-tion of ruins, supporting an oedipal, masculine, paternal or Greek civilisation, a 'dark continent', a tribalised Africa to the white, civilised Europe! Given the repressed and fragmentary nature of this period in our individual prehistories, the semiotic or pre-oedipal can only be reconstructed or inferred from the existence of ruptures, symptoms, 'flaws' (parapraxes)—the limits of oedipal, symbolic dis-course. It is only through the symbolic that we can have any post-oedipal access to the semiotic. It is only through the symbolic that the semiotic is capable of gaining any expression, a voice, a mode of articulation, just as the pre-oedipal infantile phases must be recon-structed through the analysis of the post-oedipal adult. Kristeva considers the semiotic feminine and maternal in several senses. It is an order or phase predating the imposition of sexual (that is, oedipal) identity; it is dominated by the mother's body, or at least its 'parts', as well as its symbiotic relations with the child's body; it is pre-phallic, pre-paternal, existing before the father is regarded as symbolic source of authority; it is, moreover, ambiguously and undecidably active and passive, subject and object, self and other, distinctions which are not yet oppositions, nor yet equated with the preferred characteristics of each sex (Freud suggests that the child is socialised so that subject, active and phallic are aligned and, consequently, object, passive and castrated are integrated with male and female development respectively.)

The semiotic, like the pre-oedipal, can be located in two distinct processes or sites: on the one hand, the semiotic as lived and experienced in the earliest phases of infantile life constitutes the unspoken raw materials repressed by symbolic functioning; on the other hand, the semiotic is capable of reappearing in the breaches, ruptures or disturbances of the symbolic order, in the form of an excessive, multiple overflow or trangression of symbolic norms (a form of the 'return of the repressed'). The semiotic is thus both the precondition and the excessive overflow of the symbolic. It is neces-sary for symbolic functioning, but because it cannot be spoken as such, it also continues to exert a possible resistance to and subversion of symbolic norms. The semiotic, maternal, feminine is thus both the unspecified prop or support of social production, as well as the site of its disruptive or revolutionary supersession.

The rhythmic, energetic, dispersing bodily force, multiplying and proliferating pleasures, sounds, movements, gestures—the semiotic is thus, on Kristeva's understanding, the raw phonic and gestural material of language. Yet it must be renounced, sacrificed, repressed or censored in order that the pre-oedipal child acquire a stable social position and identity through its submission to paternal, oedipal edicts. Yet, like the repressed itself, the semiotic can return through, across or by means of symbolic ruptures. Like the dream or symptom, a repressed irruption in the discourse of consciousness, the semiotic threatens, at certain privileged moments, to transgress its subordinated, unacknowledged position, breaching the limits of textual intelligibility and destabilising symbolic efficacy. These privileged moments are witnessed by the dispersive, decentring practices of the avant-garde, in whose texts and creative practices Kristeva locates the emergence of the play of rhythms, forces and matter over the primacy normally accorded to the text or work of art as a system of expressing meaning. The symbolic is a superimposed order, regulating, ordering and stabilising the fragmentary energies of semiotic flows in order to produce meaning, coherence, identity in language.

In short, the sphere of the symbolic, oedipal or patriarchal modes of organisation owes a debt of existence to an unspeakable, pre-linguistic, repressed bodily domain of semiotic, libidinal, 'feminine', 'maternal' flows. This is a debt which cannot even be acknowledged, let alone repaid. It is significant that Kristeva posits the semiotic as both feminine and maternal. It is feminine in so far as it is pre- or proto-patriarchal; it is maternal in so far as the mother, the maternal space and material support of the child's desire, is the *semiotic chora*, the space and receptacle defining its limits, the boundaries of its psycho-physical existence. For Kristeva, however, there can be no specific or determinate relation between this powerful semiotic, maternal structuring and structured space, and *women*.

On the one hand, Kristeva acknowledges this patriarchal symbolic debt to maternity and femininity; in this sense, she is among the first to signal the unspoken yet crucial role of both in the development of speech in the child in particular, and in all social/symbolic functioning, more generally. Yet, on the other hand, she relies uncritically on the Freudian/Lacanian effacement of women as an autonomous sex: the pre-oedipal mother dominating the semiotic is the *phallic mother*, the mother as a 'neuter' or sexless subject. The feminine is also paradoxically a term seen by her as *sexually* indifferent—distributed independent of sexual identity, predating the sexually distinguished positions of phallic, active, male, subject and passive, castrated, female, object. She *disembodies* these designations, seeing them as independent of the female body, sexuality or subjectivity. As she sees it, femininity is a series of processes, positions and desires that are equally attributable to male and female children. Pre-oedipal sexuality, predating the child's psychical recognition of sex differences, is equally visible in children of both sexes. Even more ironically, Kristeva's model of maternity is not based on the specificities of the female subject, or indeed, any subject at all. For her, maternity is a subjectless, fragmented and fragmenting series of bodily processes, splitting and fusing cells, genes, micro-parts. Becoming a mother is in fact the abnegation of being a woman: 'Within the body, growing as a graft, indomitable, there is an other. And no one is present, within that simultaneously dual and alien space, to signify what is going on. "It happens, but I'm not there." "I can't realize it, but it goes on." Motherhood's impossible syllogism' (Kristeva, 1980:327).

Kristeva claims that the maternal body, and feminine energies, cannot be identified with women's specificity. Where women have an access to the subversive forces of the semiotic, in their experiences of ecstasy, *jouissance*, women are not able to articulate or to provide it with a symbolic context. In so far as woman is seen as representative of the feminine semiotic, or the maternal *chora*, Kristeva confirms the psychoanalytic, especially Lacanian proposition that woman, in experiencing a pleasure 'beyond the phallus' (Lacan, 1982), yet can know or say nothing about it (Lacan, 1982:146). She seems to accept without question that men alone can represent, speak, symbolise the subversive underside of social unities: 'At the intersection of sign and rhythm, of representation and light, of the symbolic and the semiotic, the artist speaks from a place where she is not, where she knows not. He delineates what, in her, is a body rejoicing' (Kristeva, 1980:242).

The implication is that the poet, artist, theorist, avant-gardist, the trangressor of social, artistic and representational norms, is necessarily male. Men alone occupy the position of both speaking subjects with stable positions of enunciation, and transgressive subjects, whose discourses broach the limits of cultural tolerance. This is because, given Kristeva's adherence to the psychoanalytic model, it is only men who accede to the symbolic, in order to be able to subvert it. It is only from a position within the symbolic that its limits can be transgressed, if only to be later re-established elsewhere. The male writer takes on the representation of the unspoken energies and forces of the feminine and the maternal, thus always risking a loss of the stable position of identity assured for men within patriarchal culture. (He risks, on the one side, fetishism, the libidinal attachment to phallic maternity; or on the other, psychosis, the identification with the phallic mother [Kristeva, 1976:70].) Her argument is puzzling in feminist terms, to say the least: her ideal model of a transgressive subjectivity articulating itself is a male who has identified with and taken upon himself the representation of a femininity women can't speak: man mimicking the woman who reproduces man!—man unable to accept his difference from, and his debt to the maternal space which bore him.

The avant-garde or revolutionary male, it can be claimed, is unable to accept his difference and separation from the maternal space, remaining in some libidinal, identificatory and projective relation to the (phallic) mother. He cannot recognise this debt, for he is unable to accept his otherness from her. The woman's body, speech and creative energies, channelled into and alienated from her in a (constricted, patriarchal) maternity, are 'transferred' to or articulated by the son who refuses to accept her femininity, remaining thus attached to a phallic, maternal counterpart or *doppleganger*. The male 'representative' of femininity turns out to be the male unable to accept women's differences, whether bodily, psychic or social.

The role and status of women's bodies and subjectivities seem to be the crucial points of disagreement between Kristeva's understanding of the feminine and Irigaray's. There is an implicit desexualisation of identity, subjectivity and social practices in Kristeva's description of the semiotic and symbolic registers, a reduction of sexual, bodily characteristics to the features of 'gender' (cf. Gatens, 1983). Yet her simultaneous elevation of a de-sexual 'feminine' and her acceptance of the patriarchal definition of women as lack, negative or castrated may themselves be symptoms of a broader problem in Kristeva's understanding of the feminine: her relation to male systems of representation, knowledge, reason and even revolution. In relation to the work of Lacan and Derrida, Kristeva seems to adopt the position of protégé—accepting the fundamental framework and ideals of Lacanian and Derridean projects while 'applying', reorganising, contesting, adapting some of their details. Her account of the semiotic and symbolic, for example, involves taking over the Freudian/Lacanian categories of pre-oedipal and oedipal phases, or imaginary and symbolic orders, disputing some of the boundaries of these categories (for example her notion of the semiotic can be located earlier than Freudian primary narcissism (Freud, 1914b) or the Lacanian mirror-stage or imaginary order (Lacan, 1978a:chs 1–2); her concept of the symbolic places the oedipal dynamic at an earlier age than psychoanalysis (Kristeva [1984] challenge the duration of these psycho-sexual stages) but leaves the broader, more problematic issues and methods unquestioned (for example, the problem of the female oedipus complex, female castration and the derivation of feminine characteristics by the logical manipulation of masculine characteristics—if male is active, female is passive, if male is phallic, female is castrated, etc.). While relying less explicitly on Derrida's work, Kristeva is nevertheless strongly influenced by/with Derrida's invocation of the subversive, revolutionary potential of textual practices in the face of a metaphysics of identity or presence. Kristeva takes on the Derridean project of undoing the metaphysics of identity, with none of the strategic irony of Derrida himself. In full recognition of the impossibility of displacing identity with difference, its subordinated counterpart, yet locating his challenges to those dominant assumptions and methods of philosophy, Derrida recognises deconstruction as, at best, a provisional or tentative untangling of the oppositional strands in metaphysics. Kristeva uses the Derridean challenge to identity by posing it with respect to feminist or women's struggles for identity:

> [W]omen cannot *be*: the category woman is even that which does not fit in to *being*. From there, women's practice can only be negative, in opposition to that which exists, to say that 'this is not' and 'it is not yet'. What I mean by 'woman' is that which is left out of namings and ideologies. Some 'men' know something of it too ... [C]ertain feminist arguments seem to resuscitate a naive romanticism, believing in an identity (the opposite of phallocratism), when compared to that of experimentation with each of the dual boundaries of sexual difference which we find in the dual discursive economy in Joyce, Artaud ...
> (Kristeva, 1980:166)

Feminist struggles for identity, for a discursive, theoretical space for *women's* self-recognition are 'naive' compared to the subversion of sexual identities achieved by Joyce or Artaud! The feminine is, for Kristeva, a term released only in the destruction of identity, male or female. The feminine is 'liberated' by men's experimentation with their (male) identity; yet the dissolution of female identity does not have the same strategic or subversive effect as the subversion of male identity—the destruction of the identity that women have not yet achieved must be compared to the destruction of the identity of the slave, which makes *political* sense only when the slave is no longer a slave. It is, in all other respects the call for the extermination of all possibility of group resistance to oppression—a significant counter-move at precisely the first moment in Western history when women as an (international) group are agitating for the right to construct an identity for and self-representations of women (cf. Gross, 1982).

IRIGARAY AND THE FEMININE

Although Irigaray is also interested in the contributions of the feminine to social and individual existence, she remains committed, as Kristeva does not, to affirming the intimate, necessary relation between the repression of the feminine and the oppression of women. Irigaray's work, like Kristeva's, is informed by Lacan and Derrida; yet, unlike Kristeva, Irigaray seems to *use* Lacan and Derrida, where their works are tactically relevant, without actively reproducing their positions or values. Where, for example, Kristeva will rely upon the Derridean concept of *différance* in her attempts to dissolve the category of identity (both male *and* female), Irigaray will use the term as a mark of *women's specificity*, autonomy and independence from men. Irigaray's concern throughout all her works is the articulation of a femininity, an identity or subjectivity which is women's. Kristeva sees feminism as one among many social ruptures and upheavals expressing a more general and diffuse crisis in Western culture; feminism, moreover, may not be seen as the most effective or far-reaching of the movements of social subversion, given its restriction to a politics of identity. Instead, the avant-garde experimentations in representational forms and signifying practices bring into doubt far more efficiently the principle of unity, or social cohesion. Irigaray, by contrast, is concerned above all with the positions, experiences, the exclusions and silencing of women effected by patrocentric cultural and theoretical norms.

Irigaray's work can be situated at the interstices of the concepts of language or representation, power relations, and bodies. It questions the adequacy and relevance of our received histories of thought, systems of knowledge and modes of representation for expressing or characterising the specificity of women. Her object of critical analysis is the system of phallocentrism: the network of images, representations, methods and procedures for representing women and the feminine in some necessary relation to men and masculinity, a series of presumptions about the representation of one sex from a perspective deemed universal by the other sex. Her work is thus an attempt to reveal, challenge and undermine the domination of phallocentric conceptions of femininity. These conceptions submerge feminine perspectives, interests, experiences under masculine criteria of value and validity. At the same time as thus attempting a deconstruction of phallocentrism, Irigaray explores a new theoretical space and forms of language which enable women to see and represent themselves in positive, self-defined and self-judging terms. In disentangling the reliance patriarchal power relations maintain over women's bodies, sexualities and experiences through the development and use of systems of representation, systems of meaning to inscribe the female body as a negative, dependent, lacking object, Irigaray attempts to explore some of the possibilities of different, positive representations contesting the inscription of women's bodies with meaning in challenging patriarchal power.

While Irigaray uses a number of elements of Derridean reading and deconstruction, she remains autonomous in her critical objects of analysis and in her development of these elements into a 'style' of interrogation and analysis all her own. Deconstruction becomes one among a number of critical tools she uses to reread the key texts of psychoanalytic and philosophical theory. But in her hands, it becomes an openly political weapon, directed to the politics of female self-representation—the politics of sexual difference.

With respect to psychoanalytic theory, far from attempting to slot women into its predesignated masculine categories for example, uncastrated women=masculinity complex; normal femininity= castration), nor simply ignoring psychoanalysis, Irigaray uses it. She takes psychoanalytic theory as an critical object of interrogation, as a symptom of a broader phallocentric malaise that infiltrates all its traditions of knowledge and forms of representation; moreover, she uses psychoanalytic techniques—free association, the analysis of the lapsus, parapraxes, 'symptoms', etc.—as among her methods of interrogation, a critical tool used against itself. In short, she demonstrates psychoanalytic theory's internal ruptures, points of elision, its own repressions. She deconstructs psychoanalysis.

Like Derrida, her aim is to undermine, provisionally overthrow the reign of dichotomous oppositions, those that define women, femininity and the various qualities and properties associated with them in some form of dichotomy with masculinity. Yet her aim is not merely the endless transgression of boundaries, motivated by an interest in the play of the text, an aim Derrida and Kristeva seem to share. Rather, Irigaray's project is much more clearly political in so far as it is directed to providing an intellectual or discursive space in which women can explore, experiment with and go beyond the experiences that distinguish them as oppressed in patriarchal culture. She wishes to participate in the creation of a speaking position (or many), a conceptual perspective and discursive space where women can articulate their specific needs, desires and contributions. Clearly such a space does not yet exist, or, if it does, then this space exists now only as marginalised, a 'private space' outside the scope of publicly validated interactions. The possibility of carving out such a space depends on clearing away much of the domain of representation that men, who claim to be speaking universally, have constructed: 'the articulation of the reality of my sex is impossible in discourse, and for structural, eidetic reasons. My sex is removed, at least as the property of a subject, from the predicative mechanism that assures discursive coherence' (Irigaray, 1985b:146).

Her project is ultimately impossible, but necessary. Through her deconstruction of phallocentric or sexualised discourses, theories, images, representations, she demonstrates their production from and reproduction of a specifically sexual position, which remains unacknowledged as such. In analysing how the domination of the right to speak 'universally' has been appropriated by men, Irigaray suggests the procedures by which the male body is evacuated from or disavowed by phallocentric discourses and signifying practices. In so far as phallocentrism represents itself as disembodied, universal or true, the specific attributes and interests of men are capable of being presented as if they were universal. To compensate for this absence of the male body, women are considered the corporeal, bodily, material substratum supporting male intellect, reason, theoretical structures— male immateriality. It is only by reinserting the male body back into the discourses from which it has been expunged that femininity and women may be able to establish a discursive space or position from which to speak (of) their sex.

Irigaray's project thus involves the specification of a kind of sexual difference that has no place in Kristeva's work. Kristeva abstracts the concept of sexual difference from a sexualised and sexed body. Irigaray's understanding of difference, by contrast, is always related to, and inscribed upon the experiences of the sexed body. Irigaray specifies an account of the body's *morphology*; the body is not considered an anatomical, biological or neuro-physiological body—a body that is the object of the sciences of biology. Rather, her object of analysis is the body as it is lived, the body which is marked, inscribed, made meaningful both in social and familial and idiosyncratic terms, the body psychically, socially and discursively established: the body as socially and individually significant. This body is considered to be built on biological raw materials out of which are produced meanings, sensations, desires, pleasures, by its interaction with systems of social meaning and practices. To separate the feminine from a female morphology, while useful in some contexts for strategic purposes, is misguided, both thoretically and politically. It is politically misguided in so far as it enables the reproduction of the phallocentric privileging of male representations of femininity, the male prerogative of speaking on behalf of women; it is theoretically misguided in so far as it presumes a self, or drives, or forms of identification to function *independent* of the particularity of the bodies in which they arise. Such an account cannot explain why femininity inscribed on a *female body* is necessarily different from 'femininity' inscribed on a *male body* (see Gatens, 1983).

Both Kristeva and Irigaray affirm a polyvocity, plurality and multiplicity which normally lies dormant or repressed within prevailing systems of representation—an uncontrolled, excessive, irruptive textual force or materiality. In opposition to Kristeva, Irigaray regards this plurality as a productive site hitherto unoccupied by women. Her aim is to allow women some place *as women* within it, and elsewhere, introducing a genuine plurality into a monosexual universe.

Irigaray's claim is that the masculine can speak of and for the feminine only because it has emptied itself of any relation to the male body, and its specific modes of material existence, its morphology and social meaning. This process of 'evacuation' creates a virtual or fantastical space, a distancing space of reflection and specula(risa)tion in which the male can look at itself and the world, as it were, from the outside. This space established between masculine consciousness and reason and the male body is precisely the kind of space required for the production of *metalanguage* and *metadiscourse*, the conceptual space of philosophy and other knowledges. It is a hierarchically structured space, involving distinct logical levels, whereby one is able to govern and regulate the other. This space is the one required for the creation of knowledges as they have been developed in our culture.

Metalanguage functions to establish clear-cut boundaries, borders and limits beyond which hierarchically subordinated object-language is not 'permitted' to trespass. Metalanguage can remain on a purified, uncontaminated level, judging but itself being incapable of being judged. Irigaray's strategy is to refuse the existence of such lines of demarcation dividing object and metalanguage. Where such boundaries occur, they are a result of forms of fixation which attempt to regulate the inherently ambiguous, polyvocal, nature of language. The products—knowledges—of this form of male self-distance are thus *isomorphic* with male sexuality and alien to a femininity defined in its own terms.

> [A] feminine langauge would undo the unique meaning of words, of nouns: which still regulates all discourse. In order for there to be a proper meaning, there must indeed be a unity somewhere. But if feminine language cannot be brought back to any unity, it cannot be simply described or defined: there is no feminine metalanguage. (Irigaray, 1977b:65)

The reign of the 'proper'—proper names (the Name of the Father), proper nouns, with their fixed meanings, property, and propriety— regulates the domain of male self-representations and images, with the effect of relegating women to the position of the improper, the impure, the unclean, with no proper names of their own, no property properly theirs, produced by and exchanged within an economy not regulated by the phallic. The proper-ness of the masculine can only be constructed and ensured if men's access is secured by women's exclusion. Women's impropriety is the guarantee of men's proper reign over them. Irigaray seeks an adequate language and modes of representation by which this 'impropriety' may be expressed, a language beyond the hierarchical regulation of metadiscourse.

Instead of a language which refuses its own materiality to see itself as pure neutral medium, Irigaray asserts the materiality of the text. The text has been regarded as transparent, formalisable, capable of transliteration into other forms without loss of meaning. It is a language seen on the model of, or as *isomorphic* with oedipal, phallic sexuality. In opposition to this prevailing conception of knowledge as a neutrally expressed body of information produced by a sexually indifferent subject from an unspecifiable perspective, Irigaray attempts to clear a space within language for another voice, body, pleasure, other forms of sexuality and desire, other forms of discourse, different forms of reason can be articulated. She demonstrates the violence to which masculinity resorts in appropriating discourse, meaning, sexuality and desire to itself. This violence is an unspoken feature of the persistent historical dominance of particular styles, modes, and procedures of knowledge rather than the many others possible. She wishes, not to reappropriate this domain as 'properly' feminine, but instead, to create discourses and representations of women and femininity that may positively inscribe the female body as an autonomous concrete materiality. To demonstrate not only the existence of alternative models of women and femininity, but the seizure of the power of definition by some models bound to masculine forms, that is, to make explicit what phallocentric domination is based upon, is to reveal the limits of phallocentric thought, the impossibility of its self-representation. A language isomorphic with female sexual morphology must both undo phallocentric domination and assert positive alternatives which can show women in women's terms.

Irigaray refuses to speculate on or represent what a feminine (use of) language may be. This would involve speaking *for* other women, which amounts to speaking *as* a man. It is a tactic to evade or refuse difference (cf. 1985b:156). Nevertheless, some negative indications about a feminine subversion of discursive regimes may be extracted from her work. Such language would challenge rather than conform to patriarchal or phallocentric values. It would not be organised according to many of the dominant norms or ideals of knowledge today: it may avoid a singular, hierarchical structuring either syntactically or semantically, the subject–predicate correlation, adherence to a normative grammar, ideals of textual transparency or intertranslatability. These phallocentric commitments are made possible only because of men's capacity for self-distance, their disavowal of corporeality:

> Nothing is ever to be *posited* that is not also reversed and caught up again in the *supplementarity of this reversal* ... we need to proceed in such a way that a linear reading is no longer possible: that is, the retroactive impact at the end of each word, utterance or sentence upon its beginning must be taken into consideration in order to undo the power of its teleological effect, including its deferred action. (Irigaray, 1985b:79–80)

To speak *as*, not *for* women is in itself to begin to undo the reign of the proper, the self-identical, singular phallic organisation. To speak to evoke rather than designate, to signify rather than refer, to overburden oppositional dichotomous categories by refusing their boundaries or borders is to occupy the impossible 'middle ground' excluded by logic and reason in their present forms. This is not to create a discourse *without* meaning, but rather to proliferate many meanings, none of which could hierarchically unify the others. Irigaray's aim is not to specify or provide a model for such a discourse, but rather, to create a space in which the exploration of many discourses and many women's voices can articulate themselves—and force others to listen.

DIFFERENT FEMINISMS

To return now to the question of the relations between Irigaray and Kristeva, and the relevance of their differences for English-speaking feminists. Their similarities and points of association indicate major domains of philosophical and political interest that may need further emphasis in many Anglo-American feminist texts. Both their projects are located in the relations between the networks of language, bodies and power relations. These concepts may be most constructively considered, not as independent, external 'entities' but as ones fundamentally and inextricably bound together in social and political existence. These domains indicate key points of focus and contention around which most contemporary feminism revolves. Both Kristeva and Irigaray have indicated that language, discourses, texts, utterances are not simply empirical acts, like all other human actions, but serve to fundamentally ground, represent and make social/natural life meaningful. Neither neutral nor transparent modes of *reflection*, they are active agents of the processes of inscription, *'worlding'*, categorising and valuing the world. Kristeva and Irigaray both highlight the complex mutual interactions between these discursive or representational systems and bodies, the crucial but neglected role of the body in the lived and structural reality of oppression. For Kristeva, the body provides the unacknowledged and resistant input for the functioning of all symbolic systems; its drives, libidinal flows, partial, fragmented and spasmic processes, not considered involved in the processes of social production but in fact the vital but repressed 'feminine' components are the foundations of all social production and the sites for its radical upheaval and undermining. The body, before it is structured and hierarchically unified under the category of a single sex, is the source of both social limits and their transgression. For Irigaray, by contrast, there is no 'universal' or sexually undifferentiated body. All bodies must be male or female, and the particularities, specificities and differences of each need to be recognised and represented in specific terms. The social and patriarchal disavowal of the specificity of women's bodies is a function, not only of discriminatory social practices, but, more insidiously, of the phallocentrism invested in the regimes of knowledge—science, philosophy, the arts—which function only because and with the effect of the submersion of women under male categories, values and norms. For Irigaray, the reinscription, through discourses, of a positive, autonomous body for women is to render disfunctional all forms of knowledge that have hitherto presented themselves as neutral, objective or perspective-less. Significantly, neither Kristeva nor Irigaray consider the body as a biological, anatomical or natural object. Their differing views both entail that the biological provides at best a foundation or bedrock, 'raw materials' overlaid, worked upon, produced, constructed as a body of a specific type, with specific capacities, skills, social values and positions as a result of discursive, familial and socialisation practices, both conscious and unconscious.

English-speaking feminists have long been wary of affirming the corporeality or materiality of women, or women's bodies. The overly close association of women with their (frail and limited) bodies has been a tactic of patriarchal oppression for many centuries. The charges of biologism, naturalism or essentialism are justifiably directed to accounts of the body which render it impervious to social, political and individual transformation. However, both these feminists have shown that *some* concept of the body is essential to understanding social production, oppression and resistance; and that the body need not, indeed must not be considered merely a biological entity, but can be seen as a socially inscribed, historically marked, psychically and interpersonally significant product. Without a thoroughgoing analysis of the interaction of discursive systems and the psycho-physical sexed body, feminists may challenge prevailing practices with only limited success. Until systems of meaning and signification are understood and challenged, women will remain the objects of male definition and scrutiny. Without some challenge to those systems of meaning which guarantee that 'identical' behaviour of the two sexes will continue to be valued differently, unequally, any struggles by women for autonomy are ultimately futile. Both Kristeva and Irigaray signal the serious problems involved in women's struggles for equality to men. Both assert the *irreducible differences* between masculine and feminine (for Kristeva) or male and female (Irigaray) that render naive and suspect any attempt to force a formal equality on their differences. Such an equality can only be postulated by the reduction of one (or both) terms, subordinating one to the other. Both feminists, in contrast to a feminism of 'sameness' or equality, nominate a feminism or politics of difference, of specificity—a politics involving the recognition of the differences *between* men and women, (or women themselves, for Irigaray) or the differences *within* each man and woman (Kristeva).

While these similarities between the two French feminists are instructive in these general respects, the details of their major differences—the differences within their accounts of difference—may highlight problem areas within Anglo-American feminisms. Above all, the differences within their strategic accounts of sexual difference locate the major role that not only the body, but the specificity of the *female body* must play in the understanding of women's oppression within patriarchal civilisations.

In the work of Kristeva, because sexual difference is located in the *interior of the subject*, fracturing the subject into two sites of discourse, two modes of organisation, two kinds of sexual attachment, one feminine, plural, multiple, material, the other, phallic, hierarchised, singular, unified, law-abiding, it is a sexual difference within a sexually *in*different subject and body. This *androgynous* model of human subjectivity in fact serves, as do all versions of androgyny, to cover over and deny any *specificity* that might be accorded to *women*. It is a way of accepting women's demands for recognition while neutralising the desire to be recognised *as women*. Women's universal commonness, humanity, universal species-existence shared with men can be accepted by her, but not those specificities, particularities of experience, social position, morphological inscription that mark women as different from men. For Kristeva, to advocate sexual difference is to elevate the polymorphous, pre-oedipal rhythms, libidinal flows and spasms—located in all subjects, independent of sex—over the more rigidly ordered norms of symbolic functioning. She proposes a project for the dissolution of *all* identities, sexual, social and discursive. Her conception of difference is simply that which underlies and threatens to overwhelm all identity. Thus any affirmation of difference involves asserting the heterogeneity latent in male and female 'identity', the diverse modes of semiotic/feminine and symbolic/masculine and their fundamental irreducibility. This disembodiment of the feminine from the female, the affirmation of an androgynous intra-subjective interplay, puts into question the struggles of women for the right to an identity, or position in culture as autonomous beings that women have struggled so bitterly so achieve. Written at the same time as the emergence of second-wave feminisms, Kristeva's work functions to strategically question and undermine its political raison d'être. In signalling the crucial role that men, and only men, are able to play in subverting symbolic by semiotic processes, Kristeva unwittingly guarantees the maintenance of social and sexual relations in their present, phallocentric forms. Ironically, she constructs a 'feminism' that functions to actively silence women and devalue their forms of socio-symbolic and discursive intervention. As a consequence, men, at least those who risk some of the stability of their masculine social positions, are thus able to act as the best representatives of a 'feminine' mode of speech, a feminine form of subversion of the symbolic (cf. Gross, 1982).

By contrast, Irigaray locates *sexual* difference *sexually*—that is, she uses this concept in her attempts to articulate feminine specificity. It is only, by implication, as a result of the oppression of women that the feminine can be accorded a subversive, radical or disruptive social or conceptual effect. The processes of social and familial inscription on the sexed body of the child *construct* the male body as virile, full, unified and the female body as passive, castrated or lacking as the necessary precondition of patriarchal social relations, 'naturalising' and rationalising this historical domination. The categories 'masculine' and 'feminine' are directly related to these inscribed, sexed morphologies; their dependence on the social positions of the two sexes can only be neglected through a most serious political oversight—one which effaces the reality of women's individual and social oppression. Yet, on the other hand, in Irigaray's conception of male and female bodies and subjectivities, there is no presumption of a biologically or naturally *given* body or identity for women (or men). The identities, bodies and experiences of the two sexes are inscribed, in the first instance on the neonate's biological raw materials—but materials which possess no form, order, organisation or meaning before the processes of social inscription.

Psychical, social and interpersonal meanings thus mark the body, and through it, the identities or interiority of sexed subjects. The female body is inscribed socially, and most often, individually experienced as a lacking, incomplete or inadequate body; this body internalised in the form of an image (an imaginary) forms the limits or boundaries of the subject's ego or sense of self. It is *lived*, experienced and understood as a body, as one's own, only by means of these traces of meaning marked upon it. Women's oppression is generated in part by these systems of patriarchal morphological inscription—that is, by a patriarchal symbolic order—in part by internalised, psychic representations of this inscribed body, and in part as a result of the different behaviours, values and norms that result from these different morphologies and psychologies. Irigaray's aim in interrogating systems of philosophical theory is to destabilise the presumed norm of masculinity, is to speak about a positive model or series of representations of femininity by which the female body may be positively marked, which in its turn may help establish the conditions necessary for the production of new kinds of discourse, new forms of knowledge and new modes of practice.

Irigaray embarks on the task of clearing a space in which these images, practices and positivity can come about. This space can only be developed if feminists *engage with* the phallocentric system of thought which has so actively subordinated women; in mastering and going beyond phallocentric norms and methods, Irigaray suggests that women must not be trapped within the systems they must subvert. Unlike Kristeva, she seems to have a firm grasp of the commitments that 'Master Discourses'—whether these are Freudian, Marxist or Saussurian—imply for those who undertake to work within their frameworks. These commitments involve an immersion within their phallocentric norms, unless there is a way in which they can be harnessed that does not commit one to accept their underlying assumptions and values. Kristeva's work, in spite of its many insights, is itself a phallocentric representation of women and femininity; her dissolution of sexual identity posits a universal or quasi-egalitarian concept of subjectivity; her admiration of a (male) avant-garde over the articulation of women's specific experiences is an oppositonal model that is also phallocentric. Irigaray makes clear that unless these basic models of representing the two sexes are questioned, all discourse, whether feminist in intent or not, will reproduce the prevailing models of phallocentric knowledge.

Irigaray suggests, not a pious, respectful or subordinate role for women in relation to male knowledges, but a more 'excessive' outlandish one—parody, mimicry—to both engage with and outstrip phallocentric models (cf. 1977b;1985b). Mimesis entails a duplicitous process: on the one hand, to be able to mime something, one must be able to 'go through the motions' which signify it. To mime philosophy entails the production of philosophy according to the accepted norms and standards of the discipline; to mime a system is to understand its principles, be able to reproduce its form, as would a disciple; yet it also implies going beyond that system, exceeding its limits and norms, overburdening it with the ambiguity that consists in both reproducing and not reproducing it. To mime is to both remain within a system and also to remain outside it. To mime is not merely a passive reproduction, but an active process of reinscribing and recontextualising the mimicked 'object'. It is to position oneself both within and outside the system duplicated to produce something quite other than and autonomous from it, using recognisable actions for new purposes.

Her work is thus both a deconstruction of phallocentric systems of philosophical and psychoanalytic thought and a strategy to develop points of view, intellectual methods and insights relevant to women's definitions of self and the world—a reclamation of the domain of theory in which women have participated either as objects of male speculation, or as themselves surrogate men. Unlike Kristeva's project of un-localising and disconnecting the feminine from women, Irigaray does more than simply reproduce variations of the dominant intellectual paradigms. Women's demands for a *femininity* that is defined by women not only contests patriarchal models of knowledge, but also the received values of intellectual and discursive models of understanding. Both feminists show that language, representations and systems of meaning are not incidentally connected to social order and its subversion; yet Irigaray's challenge to prevailing norms is directed to a political goal absent in Kristeva, the creation of autonomous images models and representations of women and femininity.

CATRIONA MACKENZIE

10 Simone de Beauvoir: *philosophy and/or the female body*

Woman does not entertain the positive belief that the truth is something *other* than men claim; she recognizes, rather, that there is *not* any fixed truth. (de Beauvoir)

Feminist philosophers, including Michele Le Doeuff (1977), have opened up a rich field of speculation about the different, but connected, conjunctions 'philosophy and the female' and 'feminism and philosophy'. Through an examination of de Beauvoir's presentation of the female body in *The Second Sex*, I want to look at these conjunctions and to map out the dimensions of some methodological questions that are raised by them.

Le Doeuff's analysis turns on the notion of metaphor. She argues that historically women have been excluded from philosophy as a foil to the quest by philosophy to be a complete, self-enclosed discourse. We have been characterised as negativity, as otherness, as lack, against which the fullness, the centrality, the completeness of philosophy is contrasted. This historical exclusion of women as philosophers finds its internal correlate in the exclusion of the 'female' from the realm of metaphysics. Philosophy is a discourse which defines and produces itself 'through the fact that it represses, excludes and dissolves (or claims to dissolve) another discourse, another form of knowledge'. This 'Other' of philosophy, its undefined, is expressed metaphorically, and the metaphor created for this purpose is the 'female', understood in the philosophical imaginary as ' a power of disorder ... sphinx of dissolution, the depths of the unintelligible, mouthpiece of the underworld gods, an internal enemy who corrupts and perverts without any sign of combat' (Le Doeuff, 1977:6; see Morris, 1981–82). In

SIMONE DE BEAUVOIR

creating itself by virtue of what it excludes, philosophy thus simultaneously creates that 'Other'. The philosophical understanding of the
'female' comes into being with philosophy itself. The 'female' is hence
essential to philosophy as its internal negation, the 'Other' which gives
it being.

For Le Doeuff, the project of feminist analysis is to undo the
operation of this metaphor of the 'female' in philosophical discourse.
Feminist analysis is thus involved in the wider project of undoing
philosophy's traditional self-conception—as rational, self-defining,
self-present, complete. For the deconstruction of the metaphor of the
'female' occurs within the context of an examination of the role of the
imaginary within philosophical discourse. In turn, this involves deconstruction of the whole philosophical enterprise as it has so far existed.
Feminist analysis thus converges with a process already begun in
philosophy, beginning with Marx and continuing in the work of such
thinkers as Foucault, Derrida and Deleuze—an internal crisis brought
about by philosophical questioning of the discourse of rationality in
Western thought.

The question avoided by Le Doeuff's analysis, however, is why *this*
metaphor in particular—that of the female—is used to signify the
'undefined'. In *The Second Sex* Simone de Beauvoir suggests one
possible explanation when she says:

> Women have no grasp on the world of men because their experience does
> not teach them to use logic and technique; inversely, masculine apparatus
> loses its powers at the frontiers of the feminine realm. There is a whole
> region of human experience which the male deliberately ignores because
> he fails to *think* it: this experience woman *lives*. (1972:622)

In other words, the *female* can act as a metaphor signifying the
'undefined' because at a conceptual level philosophy fails to engage
with the life experience of *women*. Philosophical discourse creates a
male philosophical world in which women as philosophical subjects,
that is thinking subjects, are in a sense inconceivable. Philosophy fails
to think the experience of women, either because it constitutes women
as subjects incapable of philosophical or conceptual thought (which is
itself constituted in this process), or more subtly because it claims that
sex is irrelevant to our status as subjects, that philosophy is 'universal'.
It is not just the 'female' as metaphor therefore that philosophy has
created, but at a discursive level, female subjectivity itself.

My analysis of de Beauvoir's presentation of the female body in *The
Second Sex* is in part an attempt to show why it is necessary for
feminist analysis to deconstruct not only the metaphor of the 'female'
in philosophy, but also philosophy's constitution of the female subject.
I hope to suggest therefore that despite the productivity for feminism
of a dialogue with other critiques of philosophy, the specificity of its

questions should not be allowed to disappear.

I also want to discuss the problems inherent in the type of response to philosophy's masculinism exemplified in de Beauvoir's text. She attempts to counter the anti-feminism of philosophy by using certain philosophical concepts to *think* 'woman's experience'. Her text thus works to expand the limits of philosophy while remaining within a specific conceptual problematic. At the same time *The Second Sex* undermines this problematic and shows that it should be superseded. De Beauvoir's text is thus caught between these two impulses. Her account of the female body is symptomatic of this and of the difficulties it creates.

The Second Sex presents itself as an attempt to understand and expose the 'scandal' of woman's situation through a description of women's lived experience. It takes oppression as the given of this description while using the description to reveal the dimensions and the multifarious nature of woman's oppression by man. The text is also however a philosophical text in that de Beauvoir explicitly places her endeavour within the context of a dualistic phenomenology that owes much to Hegel and Sartre, and in which terms such as the following are opposed: subject/object, immanence/transcendence, responsibility/ bad faith, in-itself/for-itself, essential One/inessential Other, species-life/individual. Further, she avows that her description is informed by the phenomenological perspective of Sartre and Merleau-Ponty that 'to be present in the world implies strictly that there exists a body which is at once a material thing in the world, and a point of view towards this world' (1972:39).

For de Beauvoir this interpretation of experiential description through existential phenomenology, and vice versa, results in the claim that woman has been denied the opportunity of becoming the meaning-giving subject of phenomenology, both in terms of her bodily experience and her existence as a cultural-historical individual. Patriarchal oppression robs woman of her subjectivity and turns her into an object, incapable of acting in the world as a free subject. She is seen as, and hence becomes, the inessential Other who never becomes the essential One. Unable to create herself in projects, she never achieves transcendence but is doomed to 'immanence, stagnation ... the brutish life of subjection to given conditions' (1972:29). And, because existence is bodily, what this means is that woman's body 'is not perceived as the radiation of a subjective personality, but as a thing sunk deeply in its own immanence; it is not for such a body to have reference to the rest of the world, it must be the promise of things other than itself; it must end the desire it arouses' (1972:189).

The problem is that in relation to woman's body it is not at all clear what is meant by such a description. Even a very cursory reader of *The*

Second Sex will be disconcerted by the tensions and contradictions in de Beauvoir's account of the female body. Her text in fact creates not one discourse of the female body, but two. In its concern with understanding the female body and its relationship to woman's oppression, de Beauvoir's text ranges from an 'explanation' of female biology through to subjective accounts of what it actually feels like to experience the world as a female body, via detailed historical, cultural and contemporary accounts of the various ways in which women's bodies have been oppressed—from enforced reproduction and bodily mutilation through to myth, fashion, legal and social constraint. The general picture of female bodily experience that emerges is intended both to interpret and substantiate the phenomenological theses. But this interpretation is not transparent.

On the one hand de Beauvoir's account of the female body appears as a description of its social construction and of the construction of 'femininity', a description which discounts the notion that female biology must account at least in part for the oppression of women. In the context of what I shall call this *constructivist* account of the female body, only oppression explains how the female body has come to signify an incapacity to organise and give meaning to experience, and hence how it is that woman has been denied the opportunity of becoming the meaning-creating bodily subject of phenomenology.

Yet throughout the text another discourse of the female body emerges in opposition to this one, and here women's bodies are presented as inherently passive, immanent, fleshly—caught within 'the iron grasp of the species' (1972:63). This oppositional discourse thus seems partly to locate the source of woman's oppression in her *oppressive* body. The female body, it is true, is still perceived as socially constructed, but this construction is built upon the material base of an oppressive female biology. Thus while woman's status as immanent object and inessential Other is ultimately due to patriarchal oppression, this oppression is structured upon the 'fact' that the female body somehow stands between the female human being and her quest for subjectivity and transcendence. What emerges from this is that 'the devaluation of woman represents a necessary stage in the history of humanity' (1972:106–7), to be overcome by the technological transformation of the material base of female biology through such developments as contraception and artificial insemination.

What are we to make of these two accounts, and of a description such as the following, which, in contrasting male and female sexuality and genitalia constantly oscillates between two meanings? It appears simultaneously as a description of how oppressed women experience their bodies—as an account of the construction of the female body— and as a metaphorical description of what it is like to experience the world as a body which is fundamentally and inescapably oppressive:

The sex organ of a man is simple and neat as a finger . . . the feminine sex organ is mysterious even to the woman herself, concealed, mucous and humid, as it is; it bleeds each month, it is often sullied with body fluids, it has a secret and perilous life of its own . . . Feminine sex desire is the soft throbbing of a mollusc . . . man dives upon his prey like the eagle and the hawk; woman lies in wait like the carnivorous plant, the bog, in which insects and children are swallowed. She is absorption, suction, humus, pitch and glue, a passive influx, insinuating and viscous. (1972:406–7)

It is clear that Le Doeuff's analysis of de Beauvoir cannot account for this problem. She argues that de Beauvoir provides an example of how philosophy can cease being anti-feminist by opening itself out to history, by refusing the ideal of being a complete, self-enclosed discourse. She claims that it is because de Beauvoir's existentialism does not form a *system* but is simply a point of view opening out onto the world, that it can dispense with the sexism which, according to Le Doeuff, functions to hold Sartrean existentialism together as a system. But such an account of how the projects of feminism and philosophy can be conjoined glosses over the way in which de Beauvoir's text works against itself, as I have pointed out. The relationship between feminism and philosophy cannot be straightened out so easily.

It seems to me that the way in which *The Second Sex* constantly moves between two meanings of the female body is symptomatic of the way in which de Beauvoir constantly undermines, yet keeps intact, the philosophical framework within which she situates her analysis. In what follows therefore I am not attempting to come down in favour of either account of the female body—both are inadequate. Rather I am attempting to show how the text's *indecision* is the result of an attempt to deconstruct female subjectivity, as it has been constituted by philosophy (for de Beauvoir, to *think* female experience) by using philosophical conceptions and categories—in particular notions of subjectivity—that define themselves in opposition to the feminine.

According to de Beauvoir, at a biological level the lives of both male and female individuals are to a certain extent subject to the dictates of the life of the species. As individual biological organisms they embody the species in so far as their individual lives maintain the species. In this sense they maintain it through creation. But for de Beauvoir there is a crucial difference between man's subjection to the species and woman's. Man's individuality is thoroughly integrated into the life of the species. He senses no contradiction between the maintenance and creation of his own life in projects, and the maintenance and creation of the species-life. Woman's individuality, on the contrary, 'is opposed by the interest of the species; it is as if she were possessed by foreign forces—alienated' (1972:57).

At this same biological level, the genitalia and sexual experiences of the male and female also differ. The penis is animated, a 'tool', the vagina 'an inert receptacle' (1972:54). For the male, although inter-course represents the transcendence of the individual towards the species, it is simultaneously 'an outward relation to the world and others' (1972:54), and a confirmation of his own individuality. For the female, intercourse can only be an 'interior event' (1972:54), a renunciation of her individuality for the benefit of the species. The asymmetry between the single moment in which the male transcends himself towards the species in the ejaculation of sperm, and the lifelong servitude of the female to her offspring accounts for this difference. The result is that

> [f]rom puberty to menopause woman is the theatre of a play that unfolds within her and in which she is not personally concerned. Anglo-Saxons call menstruation 'the curse'; in truth the menstrual cycle is a burden, and a useless one from the point of view of the individual ... Woman, like man, *is* her body; but her body is something other than herself. (1972:60–61).

Now de Beauvoir presents 'the enslavement of the female to the species' (1972:69) *as though* it is a simple question of biological 'fact'. But though some women may recognise aspects of their biological and bodily existence in this 'explanation', there is something distinctly 'odd' about it; it seems to have that oscillating character described earlier. I would argue that this is because de Beauvoir's 'explanation' of female biology is an interpretation of woman's bodily existence in the world that is grounded in Hegelian-inspired notions of subjectivity and rationality—which also underly existential phenomenology. These in their turn are connected with an implicit distinction between production and reproduction, such that for Hegel not only are women precluded from the possibility of attaining true self-conscious rational-ity and subjectivity, but these notions are also defined in opposition to the 'feminine' and ultimately to the female reproductive body.

Hegel argues that engaging in the quest for self-consciousness is what lifts human existence out of the realm of the merely natural and into the realm of the spiritual. It is self-consciousness which enables a natural being to become a spiritual being. Self-consciousness is thus characterised as an attempt to transcend the natural world; it defines itself in opposition to the natural and to itself as a natural being. The attempt to achieve self-consciousness thus signifies the refusal of the individual to identify its interests with the interests both of the species and itself qua species-being. Human self-consciousness stands opposed to the desire for self-preservation. Rather it asserts a value more important than its own life—its own value as self-consciousness, as individual.

In *The Second Sex* de Beauvoir takes up this idea that individuality and rational subjectivity are to be won through a transcendence of the conditions of natural existence. Of particular importance is the transcendence achieved by the servile consciousness through work or labour. The difficulty is however that for Hegel such transcendence is not something women can hope to achieve—at least not in our own right. In the section called 'The Ethical Order' in the *Phenomenology* (1977:266–94), and in the section on 'The Family' in the *Philosophy of Right* (1978:110–22). Hegel makes it clear that women cannot achieve the self-consciousness which the male achieves 'in labour and struggle with the external world and with himself' (1978:114). Women, he says, achieve self-consciousness only in the context of the family and through relations with the male. Thus while male self-consciousness results in a rationality defined in terms of conceptual thought and knowledge of the Universal (Spirit), female self-consciousness achieves a rationality defined in terms of 'knowledge and volition in the form of concrete individuality and feeling' (1978:114).

The reasons for this curtailing of female subjectivity become clear when we re-examine Hegel's life/self-consciousness distinction in the light of de Beauvoir's distinction between species-life and individual, which picks up the subtext of Hegel's dialectic. This rereading will also illuminate de Beauvoir's account of female biology. Reading de Beauvoir it becomes clear that at a metaphorical level Hegel identifies the 'female' with the principle of life and the endless repetitious cycle of life and death; with the natural and the unconscious universal. On the other hand, the individual which consciously asserts itself in opposition to life, the active self-consciousness which transcends mere natural, given existence, is 'male'. At this same level, in so far as the 'female' is identified with the natural world, transcendence of nature is transcendence of the 'female'. Rational subjectivity is transcendence of the 'female'.

How does this metaphorical level relate to women's inability to attain true subjectivity? I think it is through the way in which Hegel's notion of transcendence of the natural invokes a distinction between production and reproduction, in the terms of which reproduction is seen as a merely natural process, requiring nothing on the part of the individual and involving neither creativity nor rationality. Reproduction is immersion in species-being; it is an unreflective process with no specific aim except the unconscious one of perpetuating the species. Production, on the other hand, is seen as an attempt to create a value which does not merely reproduce the given conditions of existence, but transforms them. It is a reflective, rational, man-made process which involves the transformation of nature, the ultimate aim of which is truth, knowledge, self-understanding. In addition, the two terms of this distinction are in a sense in contradiction in that they are seen to occupy two mutually exclusive theoretical spaces.

Through the production/reproduction distinction a connection is made therefore between women and the 'female' principle of life. Our reproductive capacity links women inexorably to the life and death cycle, and so precludes the possibility, both at a theoretical level and at a social level, of women attaining rational subjectivity in our own right. It also means that any productive social labour that women do actually perform cannot bear the same significance that that same labour does for men; it cannot represent the creative externalisation of self that it does for men. However though qua 'female' we signify only reproduction, the dialectical opposition between production and reproduction can be overcome for women through men in the ethical family. Our relations with men lift us out of the merely natural and into the realm of the spiritual. For men of course the production/ reproduction dichotomy is transcended through the containment of the reproductive within the productive.

To a certain extent de Beauvoir's text is an attempt to engage critically with this Hegelian framework in order to then use it to reveal the oppression of woman. Her argument rests on an attempt to transform Hegelian rational subjectivity from a *male* value and a *male* achievment into a *human* value and a *human* achievment. Women, she claims, have been oppressed by being denied the right and the opportunity of attaining what is after all a fundamentally *human* value—rational subjectivity. Female self-consciousness does not only exist de facto through male self-consciousness; it cannot be thought through male experience constituted as 'universal'. If women are indeed incapable of thought, barely subjects, this is because female subjectivity has been constructed in such a way, and because we have been denied the space, both theoretical and physical, for creative self-externalisation: 'Many of the faults for which women are reproached—mediocrity, laziness, frivolity, servility—simply express the fact that their horizon is closed. It is said that woman is sensual, she wallows in immanence; but she has first been shut up in it' (1972:64). Hence the necessity to *think* female experience, in order to transform women into self-determining subjects.

De Beauvoir tries to extend Hegelian subjectivity, to make it a human possibility, by challenging Hegel's assumption that women signify reproduction. This is the meaning and significance of her *constructivist* presentation of the female body. Through this presentation de Beauvoir argues that the meaning of the female body has been overdetermined by woman's reproductive capacity, so that the female body, and hence women, have come to signify reproduction to the exclusion of all other possible meanings. It is this overdetermination that, at both a material/experiential level and at an ideological level, has oppressed women and stifled our subjectivity.

At the level of experiential description de Beauvoir tries to demystify this connection between women and reproduction through detailed accounts of how reproductive overdetermination has mutilated women's lives making, for example, menstruation and maternity crushing burdens rather than just part of what it means to be a female body in the world. She also tries to demystify the connection—and related distinctions such as male/female, rational/irrational, 'man'/nature—through an analysis of male myths about women. Thus she shows, and there are echoes here of Hegel's life/self-consciousness distinction, how, by a curious reversal, woman as the giver of life, as the Mother, also becomes dark, irrational death; and how man, as the rational revolt against death and the female, is transformed into the creator of life.

At a philosophical level de Beauvoir questions this overdetermination by the reproductive, and the consequent repression of women's subjectivity, through the thesis of anti-essentialism. She argues that the female body does not have a fixed, essential meaning—reproduction. Rather it can take on various meanings. These meanings are historically, culturally and socially constructed. Hence, although the female body has come to signify reproduction, and although this meaning has seemed to fix its essence once and for all, making the female body a barrier to subjectivity, this is in fact not the case. The female body need not represent a barrier to subjectivity. We can separate out existence as a female body in the world from the accretion of reproductive signification imposed upon that body. For de Beauvoir, once this nexus between existence and essence is broken, the apparent contradiction between the female body and subjectivity can no longer be sustained, and subjectivity can become a human possibility.

Through the *constructivist* presentation of the female body therefore, de Beauvoir is able to transform subjectivity from a male possibility to a human possibility, and so to argue against the oppression of woman on the grounds that all human beings must be given the right and the opportunity to strive to attain this possibility. Women, she claims, have so far been precluded from subjectivity because we have come to signify only reproduction. However the female body, and women, do not have such a fixed essence, and once this is recognised both reproductive overdetermination and the concomitant curtailing of female subjectivity are revealed as mechanisms of oppression.

There is undoubtedly truth in de Beauvoir's claim that oppression and reproductive overdetermination are linked. However her understanding of both subjectivity and reproduction remains within the Hegelian problematic which presents these two categories as dialectically opposed. Her strategy is to preserve the problematic intact while questioning the necessity of the link between women and reproduction, such that woman signifies nothing but reproduction. The idea that reproduction is unreflective immersion in species-being and that subjectivity involves transcendence of such immersion goes unchallenged however. This is particularly clear in her 'explanation' of female biology, as we have seen.

Lurking beneath the *constructivist* presentation in de Beauvoir's text thus seems to be the idea that in so far as the female body is a reproductive body it is an oppressive body, a body which stands in the way of subjectivity. Challenging the overdetermination of the female body by its reproductive capacity thus does not seem to mean for de Beauvoir allowing a multiplicity of meanings to emerge, one of which will be reproduction. Rather it ends up meaning the denial of the reproductive altogether—not only at the level of signification, but also at a material level. The two presentations of the female body in de Beauvoir's text are thus seen to be in deep complicity. Further, the image de Beauvoir seems to have in mind, by implication, when imagining a female body whose meaning is not overdetermined by reproduction and which is not in contradiction with the quest for subjectivity is in some senses at least an idealised conception of the male body—but with female desires, and so on. But this is not just because the model of subjectivity de Beauvoir adopts is defined in opposition to reproduction; it is defined in opposition to reproduction because it is articulated upon an idealised conception of the male body.

Returning to Hegel, we can now see that subjectivity, as an attempt to transcend the natural, is an attempt to transcend the bodily. The life-and-death struggle can be read partly as an attempt to achieve a value which transcends the merely bodily through a preparedness to risk bodily existence. For Hegel, however, though the risk of the body is an essential step in its eventual transcendence, this risk will not of itself ensure such transcendence; it ends up sacrificing the body to nature. As spiritual beings in nature, human beings must find a way of using our bodies in the quest for a spiritual transcendence of nature. Only in that way will we achieve creative transcendence of the bodily also. For Hegel this can be achieved by harnessing the body to the service of the intellect, or the rational consciousness; it is with his bodily labour that the slave transforms the natural. In putting his body into the service of purposive consciousness in this way the slave checks his own desire and so transcends his bodily attachment to the natural. Further, in doing so, the slave also alters the very meaning of the body; it is no longer a natural body, but has become a spiritual, rational body.

Hegelian subjectivity, which requires a totally self-determining and self-conscious creative 'subject', thus implies a body which is at the service of, and hence controllable by, intellect and will. The body can have no reciprocal and unforeseen effect upon consciousness, but must be entirely subsumed under it; it can have no autonomy of its own.

Underlying Hegel's text is an idealised notion of the male body—a rational body, under the control of the intellect, a body which can transcend its own limitations as body. The female body is clearly inappropriate to such a conception of body, and I think the reasons for this are implicit in Hegel's exclusion of women from the possibility of attaining subjectivity in our own right. As a reproductive body, the female body just cannot be conceived of as totally subservient to consciousness. It has an autonomy of its own which is not controllable by intellect or will. Hence it is difficult to imagine how it could be understood as an 'instrument' of the rational intellect, in the way in which one might understand the male body to be such an instrument. This also explains women's peculiar relationship to the 'female' principle of life. Because the female body is not totally controllable by consciousness it is regarded as 'passive' in relation to nature, as dominated by nature, and therefore as immersed in nature. The male body on the contrary is 'active' because as an instrument of consciousness it acts upon nature to transform it.

When it comes to articulating a different meaning for the female body, de Beauvoir's critique of reproductive overdetermination thus almost inevitably seems to end up as a denial of the reproductive altogether. This is because the kind of subjectivity that de Beauvoir wants women to achieve requires a body that the female body qua reproductive body just cannot be. *The Second Sex* thus often becomes an attempt to grapple with the question of how woman can achieve subjectivity despite her reproductive capacity. Woman's tragedy comes from aspiring, like all human beings, to subjectivity, but being hindered by her biology; for it is that that stands between her and her transcendence. This is particularly clear in de Beauvoir's location of the 'ultimate' source of patriarchal oppression, which occurs in the context of a discussion of hunting:

> The warrior put his life in jeopardy to elevate the prestige of the horde, the clan to which he belonged. And in this he proved dramatically that life is not the supreme value for man, but on the contrary that it should be made to serve ends more important than itself. The worst curse that was laid upon woman was that she should be excluded from these forays. For it is not in giving life but in risking life that man is raised above the animal; that is why superiority has been accorded in humanity not to the sex that brings forth but to that which kills. Here we have the key to the whole mystery. On the biological level a species is maintained only by creating itself anew; but this creation results only in repeating the same life in more individuals. But man assures the repetition of Life while

transcending Life through Existence; by this transcendence he creates values that deprive pure repetition of all value. (1972:95)

Woman's misfortune 'is to have been biologically destined for the repetition of Life, when even in her own view Life does not carry within itself its reasons for being, reasons that are more important than Life itself' (1972:96). Whatever we think of this as anthropology, its philosophical implications for a conception of the female body should by now be clear.

I think this account of de Beauvoir's apparently contradictory presentations of the female body in *The Second Sex* enables us to make sense of many apparent 'oddities' in the text. It explains for instance de Beauvoir's contrasts between the active penis and the passive vagina, and male and female sexuality and biology in general. It also makes sense of her emphasis, as a strategy for liberation, on technological control of women's bodies through contraceptive and gynaecological techniques. Finally it clarifies her attitude towards reproduction and childcare. For de Beauvoir these are not and cannot be individual projects: 'giving birth and suckling are not *activities*, they are natural functions; no project is involved; and that is why woman found in them no reason for a lofty affirmation of her existence—she submitted passively to her biologic fate' (1972:94).

Returning to the question of feminism and philosophy, my analysis of the conceptual relationship between Hegel and de Beauvoir will I hope have shown that it is not enough for a feminist critique of philosophy just to engage with the metaphor of the 'female' in philosophical discourse, and through that, with the issue of how philosophy creates and characterises itself as a discourse. Feminism must also consider the conceptual level at which philosophy so far has been inadequate to understanding women's lived experience. The case of de Beauvoir shows that this is necessary not only if we are to have an adequate understanding of the place women and the 'female' have had within philosophical discourse. It is necessary also if we are going to be self-reflective about feminism's relation to philosophy—about the conditions of possibility of feminist engagement with philosophy—and about the role of feminism within philosophical discourse.

The dichotomised presentation of the female body in *The Second Sex* points to the difficulties of any attempt to counter the constitution/repression of female subjectivity within philosophy by expanding philosophical conceptions to include women. In attempting to do this de Beauvoir's text works against itself. Her critique of the overdetermination of the meaning of the female body by its reproductive capacity points to a need to deconstruct the understanding of both reproduction and subjectivity implicit in the philosophical discourse she is working with. At times the text seems to begin such decon-struction—as sometimes in the *constructivist* presentation of the female body and in remarks to the effect that female sexuality and desire seem to demand altogether different notions of intelligence and subjectivity to those which we have inherited. Within the limitations that the text imposes upon itself however, such deconstruction never even gets off the ground. For de Beauvoir's analysis of oppression, and her strategies for liberation are articulated, as we have seen, from within a masculinist notion of subjectivity. Thus when it comes to articulating new meanings for the female body these end up having to be commensurate with the masculinism of the ideals of subjectivity that de Beauvoir adopts. Hence the reproductive body must be denied.

The central problem of de Beauvoir's approach to philosophy thus seems to be that while her text actually discloses the limits of the conceptual problematic she adopts, it must, at the same time try to contain itself within those limits. This suggests the need for an abandonment of those limits—exploring how and in what ways feminist discourse discloses the limits of philosophy as it has existed and as it now exists. What this involves is the deconstruction of philosophy both as a particular mode of discourse and as a conceptual attempt to order and limit experience, bearing in mind of course that these two aspects of philosophy are not as separable as, for the purposes of my argument in this chapter, I have made them out to be.

Such deconstruction however can only be piecemeal, unsystematic and anti-teleological, connected as it is with a changing order of social practices in relation to women and a changing self-understanding by women of our needs. It must not be conceived as an attempt to peel back layers of falsehood in order to reach some final truth about the fundamental conditions of womanhood, the female body, or what-ever, but as a way of working out theoretical strategies appropriate to particular and changing needs, strategies which will themselves call for their own deconstruction.

But what is the relationship between such feminist deconstructive practice and philosophy? It seems to me that it cannot consider itself outside either philosophy or particular philosophical perspectives. It is not located within philosophy in the same sense as de Beauvoir's text is. It does not try to counter the anti-feminism of philosophy by thinking women's experience philosophically. Nevertheless it is caught within an inevitable paradox of using philosophy to deconstruct philosophy. Such a paradox is obviously one which faces all philo-sophical critiques of philosophy, not just those of a feminist orienta-tion. The nature of the differences between a feminist critique and other critiques, and the particular difficulties that these differences entail, is however beyond the scope of this inquiry.

ANNA YEATMAN

11 Women, domestic life and sociology

Over the last fifteen years or so the social sciences have been placed within the spotlight of feminist concerns and standards of relevance. This has brought fresh life to the current agendas of the social sciences and it has corrected the more obvious androcentric biases within them. While many individual male social scientists remain entirely unregenerate in this regard, officially speaking, by their journals and conferences, the social sciences indicate that women and the gender division of labour are counted now as legitimate, and occasionally as central, topics for investigation and analysis.

The bringing of women within the ambit of social science has had a profound impact in some instances. Within sociology, for example, gender has become a central variable of social analysis alongside class, ethnicity, race and occupation. This has significantly recast the empirical reference points of sociological inquiry, and has made patterns of gender inequality as significant a concern as patterns of class, ethnic or racial inequality. If we turn to history, feminist agendas have combined with the new wave of social history to create a rich and complicated terrain of intersecting histories of family life, family economy, individual life-cycle events and demography. In this context, it has become impossible for us to view 'our' gender division of labour which still endows men with the status of primary 'breadwinner' and women with the status of primary parent ('mother') as anything other than a legacy of the mid- to late nineteenth-century reconstruction of the gender division of labour in terms of what many historians have come to call the nineteenth-century 'cult of domesticity'. Contrary to the innocent belief of some that men and women are, respectively, breadwinners and mothers by nature, the original cult and its legacy are historical artefacts. This insight has been underlined by developments in cultural anthropology which have been immeasurably enriched by a feminist-inspired focus on gender as a critical axis in the cultural construction and symbolic ordering of reality. In turn, this has led us to appreciate how thoroughly a gender division of labour involves a cultural construction of sex difference and thus varies with the particular socio-cultural context in which it is placed.

All of these developments have combined to deepen our insight into human beings as social, historical and cultural beings. We have now a base of rich, comparative data which establishes conclusively that the gender division of labour is historically and culturally variable. It is a socio-cultural construction of biological sex difference which accordingly varies. It is not the raw assertion of biological sex difference as such.

Two very important consequences have followed from this. First, the necessity of a conceptual distinction—first made by Oakley (1972)—between 'sex' and 'gender' has been underlined. The business of social scientists concerns 'gender' not biological sex difference, and the various ways, if at all, gender is socially structured to take the form of a division of labour, that is a division between men and women with regard to the social roles they assume. The second consequence is related to the first. The condition of being a woman can be grasped now as a social condition, which means that women, no less than men, are social beings. With this, the central hindrance to drawing women within the ambit of social science has been overcome. This hindrance resided in the association of women with 'nature' rather than 'society', and in the correlative taking for granted that the proper object of social scientific interest was the activities and concerns of men.

All this amounts to a 'cultural revolution' in social science. Its full implications are not yet felt, nor made explicit. Whether they will be so will depend on feminist social scientists continuing to struggle for the validity and relevance of their agendas, and on their ensuring an accountability of mainstream cultures of social science to those agendas.

We enter now a particular phase of struggle, and it is within this phase that this contribution is to be situated. As most feminists intuit, right now the most fundamental challenge to the ruling paradigms in contemporary soical science comes from requiring them to accommodate the distinctive *world* of women as we see it given our historical type of gender division of labour. This is the world of what we refer to variously as domestic life, family life, or, personal life. It is the world of love relations and of parenting, a world which includes all forms of social interaction which have as their primary reason for being the constitution, by way of social evocation and recognition, of the individual as a unique personality. It is thus a world which functions to express and recognise the personal as distinct from the public aspects of our lives.

Since there is an established history of the modern family within contemporary social history and a well-institutionalised sociology of the family within sociology, it may appear an odd claim to suggest that contemporary social science has some difficulty in accommodating the world of women. The point concerns the nature of this accommodation. Women in their distinctive domestic role and the domain of domestic or personal life are accommodated but at the expense of being located as the lesser part of a dual ordering of social life. The other part concerns the public aspects of our social existence, a world with which men are still more identified than are women.

Accordingly, 'the economy' is placed in the centre of the theoretical space which social science constructs, while 'love' is consigned to the margins if it receives a place at all. A moment's reflection is all it needs to indicate that these respective placements are arbitrary, for how are we to suppose that economic need is more primary than love to our lives.

In other words, the ruling paradigms or theoretical frameworks in social science are flawed by a masculinist bias which is indicated in an arbitrary privileging of the public aspect of social existence. Several things flow from this. First, in so far as women are not drawn into public life via bread riots, economic production or social movements, they, in their domestic world, are marginalised as far as the concerns of mainstream social science go. In this respect, the inclusion of women within the ambit of social science is revealed to be of a superficial nature. Second, within the professional life and career structures of social science, those who choose to work on the domestic aspects of social existence are marginalised in relation to those who work on the public aspects. Since there is a marked tendency for the former to be women and for the latter to be men, the masculinist bias of social science finds expression here in forms of gender segmentation of the social scientific professional labour markets. This, in turn, has implications for who is found to be most relevant to current theoretical definitions of the agenda for social science, and perpetuates the dualistic and gender-coded ordering of that gender.

Third, and returning to the structuring of the social scientific agenda, when the public aspect of social existence is accorded privileged status in that agenda its relationship of mutual dependence to the domestic aspect is obscured. This has the effect of making the public domain falsely appear as self-sustaining, and of encouraging thereby an equation of social life with public life. In this context, it is not just that 'the economy' looms larger in theoretical terms than 'love' but that 'love' disappears altogether from theoretical view. We have, then, a theoretical accounting of social life which proceeds on the basis

159

of *omission* of love relations and domestic life. This has to be a social theory which is not only incomplete but which, if required to insert love relations and domestic life, can do so only by placing them as the second part of a dualistic structuring of social life. Logically, this dualistic approach operates to make these two aspects of social life appear not as mutually dependent but as separate and opposed. It is, accordingly, virtually impossible to bring them together within a logically coherent and consistent account of social life.

Here I want to pursue this line of feminist critique of social science by applying it to the case of sociology understood as a distinctive theoretical enterprise which has its own history. However, before, I turn to that history, it is important to say something of the generic features of sociology as they bear on the issue of inclusion of women, gender and domestic life.

Historically, as the modern division of labour in social science has evolved, it has been the special brief of sociology to offer a theoretical explication of the idea of society. This is an inclusive idea. It has to be explicated in such a way that it subsumes the polity and the economy so that, for example, Talcott Parsons locates the polity and the economy as two subsystems of the social system. This example indicates the implication of this subsumption: when the polity and the economy are included within the idea of society, this inclusion operates by locating the specialised contributions each of these makes to social life taken as a whole.

In this context, the historical significance of Durkheim's first great work *The Division of Labor in Society*, published in 1893, becomes quite clear. This conception of a division of labour in society is the basis of the more sophisticated ideas of the social differentiation of a modern society which are developed later by Talcott Parsons and Niklas Luhmann.

Given the theoretical commitment to an inclusive conception of social life, and with this idea of social differentiation, sociology may be viewed as more vulnerable than economics and politics to the feminist requirement that its agenda incorporate domestic and personal life. In principle, sociology should be able to incorporate domestic and personal life as a particular and specialised branch of the division of labour in a modern, complex society. Since the idea of a division of labour emphasises the mutual *dependence* of specialised subsystems, sociology should be able to incorporate the domestic and personal aspects of social life in such a way as to bring to light the mutual dependence of public and domestic domains.

There is a further implication of this inclusiveness of the idea of society which is its universalism. Human beings are defined as social beings, and all that they do is located in aspects of their social existence. If we find differences between these social beings it is because they occupy different places in the social division of labour, and who goes where in this division of labour depends on what social skills they possess and where those skills belong. The skills are social because they are acquired through processes of learning in specific social interactional contexts. Hence, in principle, an individual actor can play any social role as long as s/he has had access to the right context of learning. This, of course, gives a fluidity to the distribution of actors between the branches of the social division of labour. There is no reason for one's role in life to be fixed, because in principle one can learn new roles if the opportunity to learn them exists. Since actors can change their roles, they have to be accorded an equality which recognises this ability.

This is not all. It turns out to be a small step from the idea of a complex division of labour in society to the idea that a single personality may be internally differentiated. In other words, maturation of an individual personality as a social being is equated with the ability to play a number of different roles and still remain an integral whole. Thus, not only may one occupy socially different roles (first a butcher, then a baker, and so on) but, within the same phase of a social life cycle, an individual actor occupies a number of different contexts and performs plural roles. These may not be differentiated in spatial terms but require always to be differentiated in time so that, for example, an actor can be a husband and a father in the same social space but cannot play both roles in the same unit of time.

That this kind of complexity of a single personality is possible deepens the idea of equality because it establishes credence for the idea of transferability and commensurability of skills. In other words, if the same actor can play a whole range of different skills, in large part this is because s/he is differentially applying the same general range of skills.

The implications of all this for a sociological approach to the differences between men and women are not hard to see. Despite such atavistic tendencies as may exist in individual sociologists to reduce gender difference to the simple assertion of biological sex difference, the *theoretical* tendency is to treat differences between men and women as social role differences and as, therefore, gender differences. If, to use a simplified representation of this role difference, men are workers and women are parents (mothers), in principle it is open to question why this is so, and whether each could play the other's role or would require new learning to do so. Equally, it is open to question whether the same individual could be sufficiently complex in their personality as to play both roles (that is, be both worker *and* parent).

As we know, it is the contemporary feminist agenda which is developing these questions and raising exciting new possibilities for a more flexible and equitable division of labour in society. My point is that the idea of a division of labour in society, which is a distinctively sociological idea, contains these possibilities. It requires only the setting of a feminist agenda to unravel them.

In principle, then, we can say that sociology as a theoretical enterprise offers a welcome to a feminist agenda. However, the actual history of sociology indicates this theoretical friendliness is contradicted and, often overcome, by persisting masculinist bias. If the promise of sociology in respect of the feminist agenda is to be realised, it is important to track and reject this bias. At the same time, this will be to develop and strengthen the general theoretical enterprise that characterises sociology. In the light of what I have argued above to be the current phase of the feminist agenda, I will track this masculinist bias of sociology as it is expressed in failure to incorporate domestic or personal life in how social life is conceived.

I have broken down the history of sociology as an actualised theoretical enterprise into three stages. The first phase is the one sociologists themselves term the 'classical' phase of sociology, the one associated with the great 'founding fathers' of the discipline, Weber, Durkheim, Toennies, Simmel, Mead, etc. The second phase is the 'Parsonian' phase, one which represents the digestion and synthesising of the classical influences in response to mid-twentieth-century issues and developments. This is one I term 'Parsonian' because Talcott Parsons is the towering figure of this phase, in large part because his is the most inclusive theoretical synthesis. The third phase is current and emergent: it is too soon to give it a term, but I will call it 'post-Parsonian'.

In the classical phase of sociology, there is a general tendency to ignore, for theoretical purposes, women and their domestic setting and to assume tacitly that they are subject to a natural form of determination in a way that men and their settings are not. This notwithstanding, the situation is more complex than it indicates, as indeed the generic features of the sociological enterprise would lead us to expect. We can best appreciate this if we take the starting point of classical sociology—the idea of society—and understand how it emerges in contrast with the starting point of liberal political and economic theory. Their starting point is the individual.

Liberal political and economic theory derive society from the individual. Individuality needs to be expressed in a particular way for it to be possible to derive social order and cooperation from it. The minimal condition of this expression is a publicly declared individuality which takes the form of reciprocal recognition. This is contract, which as a series of exchanges between individuals concerns economic theory and, as a generalised contract of reciprocity entered into by all individuals within civil society, concerns classical liberal political theory (the 'Social Contract'). What I want to emphasise is that the individuality which concerns this body of social theory is a publicly manifested and oriented individuality. It is assumed that all that belongs to the individual which is not publicly manifested and declared lies within his private discretion. This private domain lies outside social determination: it is ruled either by the random factor of individual whim or by natural modes of determination of need. It is clear that the terms of liberal political and economic theory consign women and domestic life to this arena of individual private discretion (see Yeatman, 1984a) and thus place them outside civil society.

From the point of view of a theory of society, the central weakness of liberal political and economic theory is that each make the contractually mediated social order dependent on the purely private discretion of individuals since they can choose at will whether to enter or to abide by contractual norms. This is a random factor from which it is impossible to derive any lawful condition (for Parsons' famous analysis of this in the form of the 'utilitarian dilemma' see Parsons, 1968). It is this weakness which classical sociology seeks to address. It does so by substituting society for the individual as its starting point. In so doing, classical sociology focuses on the *shared* components of individuality, and shows that this social identity not only permits but determines the moral and political obligations which individuals assume. Thus, for example, the puritan's inner loneliness and public orientation to impersonal contractual exchange are located by Weber within a Protestant *ethic* (see Weber, 1958), and the freely willed moment of contract is located by Durkheim within a framework of shared beliefs on what proper contracts are, and their place within social interaction (see Durkheim, 1964a: Book I, ch. 7). In short the kind of individuality contract presumes is located by classical sociologists within a shared culture and is thereby given a social determination. This derivation of individuality from society is a direct inversion of the derivation of society from the individual in liberal political and economic theory.

In making individuality subject to social determination, and thus abolishing a domain of private discretion, classical sociology in effect 'deprivatises' the individual. Now, in principle, all that an individual does and thinks and all to whom an individual relates are placed within the sphere of the social. There is, accordingly, no difficulty at all in locating women and domestic life within this sphere. Indeed, since the family is now accorded a central role in the social formation ('socialisation')* of individuality, there is operating a strong theoretical permission for bringing women and domesticity within the theoretical object of sociology. That the classical sociologists so rarely do

---

* Durkheim first uses this term in *The Rules of Sociological Method* (1964b:6).

this in express terms may be attributed to masculinist bias, and the way in which this bias influences their conception of society.

In deprivatising the individual, classical sociology abolishes the public/private division of liberal political and economic theory. This division has the virtue of retaining a clear and distinctive space for the family, though at the serious cost of locating the family as part of the private property of masculine individuals. With the sociological perspective, what distinguishes family or domestic life from public structures of sociality is lost to sight. They all belong to society, a term which in including everything without differentiating between them takes on a high degree of abstraction.

The classical sociological project is caught by the inversion it has effected of the classical liberal starting point. In deprivatising the individual, it abolishes the field of social interaction that makes an individual a particular or unique individual. This makes it virtually impossible for classical sociology to recognise theoretically the sociological distinctiveness of the domestic domain—and of its feminine exponents—since it is in this domain that unique individuality is socially constituted and recognised.

Durkheim's treatment of individuality is a good case in point. He argues that the strictly individual aspect of a concrete individual's consciousness is not a social phenomenon, and that it is antagonistic to the socialised aspects of that individual's consciousness (see Durkheim, 1960). Individual psychology is contrasted with individual sociality, and is identified with 'nature' in contrast to 'society'. The socialised aspect of individual consciousness holds sway only as it effectively constrains the asocial, egoistic and natural aspect of individual consciousness. Of course, logically Durkheim is precluded from showing that this constraint will be always effective, just as the liberal theorists cannot ground individual obligation to uphold the Social Contract and the social order which follows from it.

Given this approach, Durkheim has two options with regard to the family, both of which he follows: he consigns the family in the form of women and domesticity to 'nature', which he does in *Suicide* (1951:270–76) and *The Division of Labor in Society* (1964a:56–61), he assimilates the family as one among other social institutions and agencies of integration and socialisation into the publicly oriented collective conscience, as he does in *Moral Education* (1961) and *Professional Ethics and Civic Morals* (1957). In neither case does domestic or family life become a genuine object for sociological theory, and in general, there is a tacit equation of social life with public life.

The assimilation of the family to an undifferentiated and therefore abstract sociality operates in such a way as to make the family appear the very paragon of sociality. As we have seen, classical sociology's inversion of the liberal starting point sustains the individual/society dichotomy but inverts the value accorded the two terms so that 'society', rather than the 'individual', becomes the valued term. This means that society takes on the signification of 'community', that is, ties which transcend individual interests, which express shared identity and can therefore take the form of communalistic modes of orientation and cooperation. Since the family is seen to epitomise the values of shared identity and communalism, there is a tendency to regard it as, in Toennies' (1963) phrase, 'the embryo' of community (*gemeinschaft*).

This is also the thrust of Cooley's (1962:3–30) idea of 'primary groups', of which the family is the paradigmatic case. Weber's development of Toennies' idea of *gemeinschaft* most clearly illustrates this tendency:

> A social relationship will be called 'communal' (*Vergemeinschaftung*) if and so far as the orientation of social action—whether in the individual case, on the average, or in the pure type—is based on a subjective feeling of the parties, whether affectual or traditional, that they belong together . . . Examples are a religious brotherhood, an erotic relationship, a relation of personal loyalty, a national community, the *esprit des corps* of a military unit. The type case is most conveniently illustrated by the family. But the great majority of social relationships has this characteristic to some degree, while being at the same time to some degree determined by associative factors. (Weber, 1978:40–41)

Here, the family retains no distinctive identity with regard to other communal forms of sociality: conceptually it becomes the same as the national community.

It turns out, however, that 'community' is conceptually set off against contractual associative ties, which are identified with a rational artifice created out of individual reflective choice. In this context, community then appears as less artificial, less reflective and more natural than contractual associations (*gesellschaft*). It then makes sense that family life becomes the prototype of community because it is conflated and confused together with units of kinship, which are thought to be based in natural bonds. This construction of sociality qua community threatens then to undermine the whole conception of society as sui generis, and with that to reactivate the conception of the family as more natural than it is conventional, that is, social. The conception of society as sui generis is secured by now identifying it with rationalised, contractual associations, and thereby subjecting it to the difficulties which beset any liberal, contractual account of society. In this context, the conferral on the family of the privileged status of being the prototype of communal sociality threatens its inclusion within the idea of society.

The classical sociological project elaborates a general and holistic construction of the social at the same time that it reasserts and founders on the individual/society dichotomy. The Parsonian phase of sociology is constituted by the attempt to extend this holistic conception of the social in such a way that the individual is placed squarely and consistently *within* social life. This is simultaneously the elaboration of a holistic conception of the concrete individual: now s/he is no longer divided into two warring parts or selves, each standing in for the values of society and the individual respectively. The individual can become an integral self. The idea of this integral self is the concept of 'personality'.

The task of resituating individuality completely within social life, and of thereby ensuring reconciliation between the two terms of individuality and sociality, logically entails a particular proposition which is extremely promising from the point of view of bringing women and domestic life into sociological focus. The proposition is this: If individuality in all its aspects lies within social life, then society itself must be differentiated into those arenas of social interaction which speak to and express the unique or particularistic aspects of individuality and those which speak to and express the universalistic or public aspects of individuality. I refer to these as domestic and public aspects of social life respectively.

The Parsonian phase, then, promises to make the domestic domain an object for sociological theory, and thereby to sociologically situate what it is women are and do as domestic specialists. Let us now examine how far this promise is realised.

As indicated, this phase is best represented by the work of Talcott Parsons. He explicitly seeks to bring together and to integrate the theoretical accounts of the social system and of the individual personality (see Parsons, 1964:20). He does this through attempting a theoretical synthesis of classical sociology and psychoanalysis. Parsons can be viewed as attempting to work out the holistic idea of personality in his account of the mutual dependence of the family and such public structures of the social system as the occupational system (see Parsons, 1949:chs 5, 9, and Parsons in Parsons and Bales, 1955:ch. 1). These stand for the unique (particularistic) and publicly oriented (universalistic) aspects of personality respectively.

In his account of the modern family Parsons (1955:ch. 1) specifies it as a domain of social interaction for the constitution and expression of unique personality. For the first time we are offered in this a clearly *sociological* conception of the family: the family becomes that sphere of social interaction which functions on behalf of particular or unique personality. Notwithstanding Parsons' own tendency to identify the family with the nuclear family, the import of this socio-functional definition of the family is radical. It is that wherever we find a unit of sociality which functions on behalf of particular personality there we have a family.

What Parsons means by functioning on behalf of personality is quite clear. It means either the function of generating the particular personality—'primary' socialisation—or the function, once the personality is produced, of its continuing maintenance through allowing the unique aspects of personality expression and recognition. Both these functions require a small-scale, intimate social-interactional context, where the orientation of the actors to each other is particularistic and committed. This orientation is a love relation. With Parsons, then, the sociological tradition achieves a theoretical discernment of domestic and personal life as an object for social science. Parsons' achievement is no less because he can presuppose and use the insights of Freud, Cooley, Mead and Piaget. Indeed Parsons' achievement is all the more extraordinary since theorists and commentators after him seem neither to have noticed it nor sought to exploit its implications and insights.

Parsons makes it easy for them. On the one hand, he dresses his theoretical construction of the family in the 'Father Knows Best', 'Feminine Mystique' costume of the day. In short, his tendency to ascribe roles within the family in terms of gender obscures the radical innovation his construction of the family represents. Here it is important to note that Parsons gives a *sociological* account of gender differentiation within the family: in this sense, the roles are not ascribed at all, and any one who can perform the social-functional qualities attached to the role can step into the role. On the other hand, if Parsons' account of primary socialisation is closely examined—and it is in this account that we find the most developed form of his theoretical specification of the family (see Parsons in Parsons and Bales, 1955:ch. 2)—it is not clear that Parsons succeeds in retaining particular personality as a discrete differentiation of the social system. This is evidenced in two ways.

First, in Parsons' account of how the mother originally constitutes the infant as a personality within a system of interaction between mother and infant, there is no concrete theoretical specification of how it is the mother constitutes the infant as a particular or unique unit of agency. Instead, we have a sociologically sophisticated version of a behaviourist theory of conditioning whereby, through the use of sanctions, the mother harnesses the natural-behavioural drives of the infant to a symbolic structure of interaction. Here individual agency is taken for granted, as already residing in a natural given motivation of attraction to gratifications and avoidance of deprivations. Without an account of the social interactional determinations of individual agency, we do not have a sociological account of individual personality, and its place within social life is not theoretically secured. This is the case despite Parsons' rejection of behaviourist readings of Freud (see Parsons, 1964:ch. 4) and his own intention of establishing that 'internalization of the sociocultural environment provides the basis, not merely of one specialized component of the human personality, but of its central core' (Parsons, 1964:80).

Second, there is a general tendency, in Parsons' account of the stages of socialisation, for the maturation of the child as a personality to be located in its socialisation into universalistic structures of public sociality through the father (the representative of public morality), the school and the peer group. In other words, Parsons tends to identify personality proper with its expressions in universalistic, public systems of collective norms, whether these norms be cognitive, moral or expressive. On this account, the personality—if it is adequately socialised—becomes simply an operational unit of 'a common culture' (see Parsons, 1964:ch. 1).

The problem with this is not, as Wrong (1961) puts it, that it involves an 'over-socialized conception of man'. It is that it tends to render residual precisely what it is that makes a personality a particular personality: its concrete specificity, and thus uniqueness, as this is constituted and recognised within a specific context of interaction, the qualitative features of which are determined by the requirements of the mutual recognition of unique personality.

To the extent that Parsons tends to identify the personality with its public expressions the necessity for the family as the social domain of mutual recognition of unique personality becomes lost. In so far as it is presupposed, it tends to be relegated to the pre-verbal stage of infancy. It is, accordingly, not surprising that, even while Parsons declares the family to be a necessary requirement of the maintenance of adult personality, he never provides any theoretical elaboration of the nature of the adult love relation nor even of the adult aspect of the parenting relation. Instead Parsons either takes for granted sexuality and parenting at the adult level or he assumes that the adult personality requires marriage and parenting because these enable it both to recapitulate and, more critically, to contain infantile experience and desire. Particular personality is the primitive foundation of the personality oriented within the common culture, and continuing existence must be secured for it; but, at the same time, it must be effectively corralled and mastered by the properly adult, and public, aspects of the personality. The tendency here to counterpose normative social existence and infantile desire must marginalise the latter, obscure its expression within social life, and give it very doubtful legitimacy as an aspect of social experience.

It appears then that Parsons' contribution of the domestic domain as the site of particular personality to the agenda of sociological theory is more a formal than a substantive achievement. Domestic sociality is admitted, but it is admitted more as a condition than as an inherent feature of sociality, and it is necessary that domestic sociality be regulated effectively and mastered by sociality in its proper and public sense. Domestic sociality is identified with immaturity, a position which does not indicate any genuine appreciation of the place of unique personality in social life. The marginal status of the domestic domain emerges clearly in this formulation (Parsons, in Parsons and Bales, 1955:16): 'the functions of the family in a highly differentiated society are not to be interpreted as functions directly on behalf of society, but on behalf of personality.' The dualism of this construction is clearly evident and must undermine Parsons' insistence both on the social determination of individual personality and on the mutual dependence of the public and domestic aspects of social life.

Parsons develops the promise of classical theory but, ultimately, remains within the basic limits of that framework. A post-Parsonian stage would indicate the transcendence of these limits. There is no doubt that something like this is happening on the contemporary theoretical scene, but at the same time we find more abstract gestures than systematic theorising in the direction of a sociological theory of unique personality and its domestic site. I will deal briefly with this stage, and in selecting what might be taken as representative examples of it indicate that the existing literature does not go very far.

In 'A Sociology of Women' Dorothy Smith not only offers a critique of the existing sociological tradition but specifies the theoretical conditions for the inclusion of women within sociology. She argues (1979:173) that these require us to make 'the everyday world the locus of a sociological problematic'. This is a common resort to be found among contemporary feminist social scientists who insist that sociology—and social science—can deal with women only as they can incorporate everyday experience.

This is not a productive point of departure. The 'everyday world' is *not* the same thing as domestic life which is the distinctive world of women. Were it so presumably symbolic interactionists and ethnomethodologists would have contributed something significant in the direction of the inclusion of women and their world before now. The idea of the everyday world signifies the intersection of macro and micro structures of both public and domestic socialities in the lives of individuals as they enact their various roles and practise daily routines. In this sense, the everyday world—or everyday life—has an undifferentiated aspect. While it is clear that the everyday life of women is not the same thing as the everyday life of men, the concept of everyday life does nothing to clarify and explain this.

We might expect to see indications of a post-classical framework in contributions to a sociology of emotional life. As Hochschild (1976) reminds us few such contributions exist, but one such is Denzin's 'A

Note on Emotionality, Self, and Interaction' (1983). Denzin specifies the formal features of a sociological theory of emotion. He defines emotion as 'self-feeling':

> Self-feelings refer to *any emotion* a person feels, including bodily sensations, sensible feelings, intentional feeling-states, and feelings of self as a moral, sacred or profane object. The feelings that a person feels have a threefold structure: (1) a sense of the feeling in terms of awareness and definition; (2) a sense of the self feeling the feeling; (3) a revealing of the moral and feeling self through this experience. (Denzin, 1983:404)

He adds: 'An emotion that does not in some way have the self or the self-system of the person as its referent seems inconceivable.'

For Denzin, self and emotion are mutually defining terms. They are also undifferentiated general concepts of the kind that 'society' is itself in the classical stage of sociology. Even while they may share the formal features of the repertoire of feelings, the emotional expression of the uniquely oriented (domestically oriented) self is not the same thing as the emotional expression of the collectively oriented (publicly oriented) self. Denzin's approach will not allow us to make or to investigate this distinction.

Finally Nancy Chodorow achieves considerable insight into the domestic domain and its relationship to the formation of individual personality in *The Reproduction of Mothering* (1978). Chodorow is a sociologist and her work owes much to Talcott Parsons, who like Chodorow also draws on the object-relations school of psychoanalytic theory.

Chodorow's theoretical concern is with the reproduction of gendered personality, that is, of masculine and feminine personalities. This leads her to take for granted the idea of personality so far as its status for sociological theory is concerned. Moreover, since her analysis presupposes a gender division of labour, she takes for granted a differentiation of masculine (public) and feminine (domestic) domains. If she directs explicit attention to this inner division of social life it is more to characterise it polemically as a feature of patriarchal, capitalist, industrial society than to investigate it theoretically.

The central point about Chodorow's analysis is that it cannot engage the sociological tradition because her analysis of the social reproduction of gendered personalities in 'mothering' replicates the dualistic structure of sociological theory which has marginalised the domestic domain and all that belongs to it. Her analysis certainly explains why it is that masculine personalities psychologically need to marginalise the domestic domain, but it does not squarely confront the sociological agenda with the necessity for a theory of unique individual personality and of the domestic domain. For this to occur the critique of gender differentiation would have to take the form of retaining the differentiation between public and domestic domains, and thinking away their gendered features.

To conclude then, there is nothing in principle which precludes sociological theory from being developed by the feminist critique. It is time now to say something further of the feminist critique. In the existing context of sociological theory, it is powerful and relevant because of two features belonging to it. The first arises from feminist insistence on the *social* character of domesticity as the distinctive world of women. In short, feminists emphasise the significance of the domestic domain for social life and if they are at risk of marginalising anything it is the public domain, not the domestic domain. Accordingly, even if they themselves have not theoretically specified the sociological characteristics of the domestic domain, feminists will never allow social science in general nor sociology in particular to ignore the domestic domain.

At the same time, and this is the second feature of feminist critique, in placing the domestic domain within the idea of the social, feminists do not thereby conflate public and domestic domains within an abstract sociality. This is because they appreciate that the modern gender division of labour produces two specialised types of personality (masculine, and feminine), each with qualitatively different types of social skills and social orientation. This is a conceptually naive understanding of the internal differentiation of modern social life into public and domestic domains.

The blind spot for feminists, which limits the power of their critique for social science, is their difficulty in analytically distinguishing the gender division of labour, on the one hand, from the differentiation of social life into public and domestic domains, on the other. It is true that these are historically conflated so that 'women' becomes a code name for the domestic domain, and 'men' a code name for the public domain. However, were the social categories of women and men to be deconstituted, that is, if the gender division of labour were to be abolished, the distinction between and mutual requirement of domestic and public aspects of social life would remain. Of course, if gender division is abolished, the differentiation of public and domestic domains must operate and appear very differently from when it is expressed as a gender division. In the former case, the differentiation and the mutual dependence of public and domestic aspects of society are expressed within the same personality, and not as two distinct types of personality. When public and domestic take the form of masculinity and femininity respectively, their expression as separate and opposed types of personality obscures their mutual dependence and the necessity for smoothly ensuring their continuing complementary relationship. In short, public and domestic, when expressed as a gender division of labour, necessarily assume a dualistic and dichotomous appearance, so that stress on one must marginalise and put into question the value of the other.

Feminists too often limit the theoretical promise of their critique by approaching the differentiation of public and domestic domains exclusively in terms of its expression as a gender division of labour. When this occurs the objects of inquiry too readily assume the respective forms of 'men' and 'women'. It cannot be clear what men and women denote in sociological terms if public and domestic are not separate categories of analysis. If men and women are the starting point, the likelihood is that analysis will be driven in the direction of constituting these categories as interest groups engaged in some form of competitive, albeit asymmetrical, power relation. There is nothing wrong with this as far as it goes, but it adds nothing to the extant theoretical agenda of sociology.

This agenda is an especially impoverished one when set against the theoretical promise of the feminist critique that I have sought to identify. As I have argued, in demanding of a theory of society that it incorporate the domestic domain, implicitly this critique is asking that it offer an account of unique personality. In this requirement, the feminist sociological agenda promises to cut the Gordian knot which has beset sociological theory from the outset and caused it to take the form of a contradictory and incoherent theoretical enterprise. This Gordian knot is the society/individual dichotomy which as we saw sociology in an especial fashion inherited from liberal political and economic theory. It would be something remarkable if it turned out that by including the domestic domain in its construction of social life, sociology thereby transcended the individual/society dichotomy.

12 Evidence and silence: *feminism and the limits of history*

Feminism has always engaged with the practice of history. Accounting for the present situation of women involves scrutiny of the past. Interpretations of both ancient and more recent history have underpinned many important works of feminist theory, polemic and literature. The claim that the demise of organic views of nature in favour of mechanical and scientific views facilitated the emergence of a capitalist social order in which women were uniquely subordinated to men pervaded feminist writing from the seventeenth century onwards (Merchant, 1980:157–63). A further goal of feminist interest in women's historical experience has been to establish that patriarchal relations are not natural and inevitable, but contingent and changeable (Davin, 1971:224).

More recently, feminists have engaged with history as a professional discipline. With the major exception of Mary Ritter Beard's *Women as Force in History* in 1946, interventions into academic history only occurred from the late 1960s, inspired by the women's liberation movement. Characteristically, these interventions have usually taken the form of an attempt to write women's history, rather than to revise previous historiographies in feminist terms. That is to say, feminist historians pose women as distinct subjects, not included within the existing terms and varieties of historical writing. Work in the now prolific field of women's history departs in several directions, each presenting different diagnoses of the inadequacies of more 'general' historical work (see Fox-Genovese, 1982:5–24; Daly, 1978:107–175; Smith, 1976:369–83; Matthews, 1984:15–20).

Some practitioners of women's history see their work correcting the unfortunate omission of women by mainstream historians. In writing

173

the experience of women into existing historical knowledge, these historians seek to make it more accurate and more comprehensive. Significantly, they rarely dwell on the omission they set out to correct. Other feminist historians are less confident about the basic tenets of the history discipline. They believe that the overlooking or distortion of evidence concerning women casts doubt on the claim that historical method involves the disinterested research of all available evidence as the basis of a balanced narrative interpretation. Such work aims to expose the patriarchal characteristics of hitherto-accepted varieties of history, while also contributing to our knowledge of women's past experiences.

A further group of feminist historians contends that the very procedures of history are inherently problematic. Even with the best of intentions, investigation of subjects taken to be historically important will yield little information about women, if only because exclusion from activities like politics, diplomacy, war, economic enterprise has marked women's known historical experiences in Western cultures. In their view what must be challenged is precisely the criteria of historical significance that privileges culture over nature, or public over private. A 'woman-centred' history is proposed which takes the prevalent structures and experiences of women's lives at least as seriously as historians have taken those of men's lives. Known sources are re-read, and new sources discovered for historical study of such matters as marriage, divorce and domestic politics, obstetrics, gynaecology, birth control and demography, women's friendships, sexuality and culture.

In such ways feminists working in history have challenged several fundamental tenets of the discipline as it has developed during the past century. Their work challenges the accuracy of previous accounts of the past. Claims about the reliability of the trained professional historian as interpreter of all human historical experience founder under feminist scrutiny. Feminists expose as untenable and indefensible the public sphere/private sphere dichotomy that characterises the work of most historians. And many feminists criticise as inadequate any scholarly approach to evidence from patriarchal cultures that refuses to take account of the effect of power relations based on sex, on the survival, selection or construction of that evidence. What has been done in women's history raises considerable doubt that accepting the discipline of history as presently constituted is a serious option for feminism. This chapter attempts to chart some of the grounds for such doubt, in order to advance some more constructive prospects for an historically grounded feminism. Such an undertaking is premised on the belief that, if only in strategic terms, history matters for feminism.

One could argue that contemporary feminism's need for historical understanding is peculiarly great. Two 'facts' signal this need. The first is that the oppression of women exhibits a longevity organised around a range of cross-culturally similar sites—marriage, kinship, reproduction, sexuality, labour and material resources, political and cultural institutions, knowledge and representation. The second is that in the face of this pervasive oppression, a 'revolution of women' has rarely threatened the course of phallocentric cultures. That is to say, organised and self-conscious feminism appears to have been spasmodic rather than typical or predictable. Instead of erroneous universalising, feminism would be better served by precise understandings of the different circumstances that have made the same basic situations be experienced by masses of women as unendurable oppression in some places and periods, in others less so, or not at all. It simply will not do to think of the centuries and generations of women before the 1950s who 'failed' to analyse the situation of their sex in feminist terms as backward, thoroughly conditioned, or, worse, suffering from 'false consciousness'. We require rather a detailed grasp of options, constraints and gratifications available to the range of different groups of women in past eras and cultures. Only through this perspective will the reasons for the existence of feminism in its present form be clear.

Moreover, such inquiry will not get far if framed by preoccupation with why women of the past did not 'recognise their oppression'. Contrary to the progress rhetoric of twentieth-century Western thought, historical inquiry into such subjects as housework, marriage, childcare, shopping, courtship, prostitution, pornography, local politics, religion, paid work and cultural production provide many instances of deterioration in women's situations by the late twentieth century.

Such a grasp of women's past can only enrich our struggles by revealing what is unique about present circumstances. It can undercut some of the inane smugness of current activists who assume that legal reforms and public debate are the only way forward for women. With struggles about abortion, for instance, it makes a considerable difference to know that termination at any stage in the pregnancy only became a serious felony in the nineteenth century. The content of demands stand to be affected by the knowledge that, less than a century ago, women had a safe variety of abortion methods less expensive than we have at present under medical monopoly. Nor is it without significance to learn that fin de siécle feminists, while primarily concerned to fight male annexation of women's bodies, accorded little priority to working for abortion rights. Many saw abortion serving the interests of a rapacious construction of male sexuality. Understanding such instances in the history of feminist thought may check the process of feminists finding themselves continually 'reinventing the wheel'.

If feminists accept that knowledge of the past matters for these kinds of reasons, then phallocentric characteristics of the discipline of history, as it stands, provide obstacles that impede feminists using history. Equally they deny effective understanding of women's past. As such, these characteristics should be challenged. While history appears to correspond to science, philosophy, psychology and political theory, particularly in so far as the exclusion or 'transcendence' of 'the feminine' and nature has been axiomatic to their constitution as disciplines (Lloyd, 1984:2), the manner in which this phallocentric effect is achieved in historical work seems distinctive in a number of ways. The question of evidence recurs through this survey of tenets of academic history and feminist challenges to them. Underlying many issues in dispute between feminism and the discipline of history is the epistemological question of what can be known and demonstrated by positive historical evidence. For, contrary to the reasonable expectation that history is concerned with the study of the past, the aspiring historian learns from the profession that

> historical study is not the study of the past, but the study of the present traces of the past; if men have said, thought, done or suffered anything of which nothing any longer exists, those things are as if they had never been. The crucial element is the present evidence, not the fact of past existence; and questions for whose answer no material exists are strictly non-questions. (Elton, 1967:20)

By this formulation, the founding fathers of academic history make the discipline prisoner of 'effective discourses'. This might not seem like confinement to those interests confident of ready representation in surviving discourses. Such an approach leads to erroneous interpretations, examined through the example of demographic historiography in the second part of this chapter. Positivist conceptions leave little room for deduction, inference, symptomatic reading or accounting for absences and silences in extant evidence. Instead, they perpetuate the phallocentric preoccupations by which they were designed as methods of knowledge. A central proposition of the third part of this discussion, which uses the case study of recent feminist histories of prostitution, is that without room for these methods of evaluating silence a meaningful women's history cannot be written. Positive evidence, in Elton's sense, is not extant, and probably never existed in literate form for the questions that feminism must put to the past. Feminism cannot be satisfied with the smug exclusion 'it is as if they had never been'. Feminist objectives with regard to history are necessarily distinct, directed by feminism as a political position, just as non-feminist historians demonstrate frequently in their preoccupations, objectives and work the assumptions and methods of phallocentrism as a political position.

OF HISTORIANS AND MEN

The future is dark, the present is burdensome; only the past, dead and finished, bears contemplation. Those who look uoon it have survived it; they are its product and its victors. No wonder, therefore, that men concern themselves with history. The desire to know what went before, the desire to understand the passage down time, these are common human attributes. (Elton, 1967:11)

The history of the discipline over the last century has been one of professional expansion, based in universities, and concerned with conflicts around marxism, the role explicit theory and politics play in historical work, and the dispersal of a mainstream discipline into varieties or specialisations—economic, labour, social, socialist, urban, colonial and popular histories (see Barraclough, 1972:15–19; Munz, 1979:13–22). Professionalisation has meant, at least initially, a denigration of older, popular practices of history, oral traditions and so forth, as the 'babble of blurred reminiscences and fanciful inter-pretation' (McLennan, 1981:100). Further, the strongly anti-socialist preoccupations of most prominent nineteenth–and twentieth-century historians resulted in their denunciation of instrumental or strategic questioning of the past as 'suspect' and 'dangerous' (Elton, 1967:52). When E.H. Carr, historian of the Russian Revolution, asserted in his *What is History?* that a function of history is to increase man's mastery over society of the present, the profession reacted sharply in defence of history studied for its own sake, against the imposition of external theories. Theoretical and political commitments were held to reduce the historian to propagandist, and the past to quarry, mined for evidence in support of these commitments.

Against these 'stultifying' effects of theory, David Thomson writes

The historical attitude, by definition, is hostile to system moulding ... This need not lead to the nihilistic view that the past is a tale of sound and fury signifying nothing. But it does mean a constant emphasis on the uniqueness of situations, the individuality of men, the novelty of each situation that arises ... In the last resort, of course, it looks like common sense. (Thomson, 1969:105)

No less than marxism, feminism is opposed by professional histo-rians as an ahistorical grid of abstraction and prescription, threatening the integrity of the historical evidence (Pascoe, 1979:116). Women's history has joined the sub-disciplinary specialisations, sometimes having a dialogue with the mainstream, most often not. The extent to which exponents of women's history challenge the credibility of that mainstream tends to remain implicit. From a feminist perspective, it is worthwhile making the scope of the challenge explicit.

It is apposite to indicate the extent to which mainstream historians are as inscribed within theoretical commitments as any marxist or feminist. Marxists have demonstrated the degree to which 'objective', 'scholarly' historians have been little more than propagandists for political liberalism, social democratic consensus, or fascism, uncritical perpetuators of empiricism and positivism. Rather less recognised, however, has been the ways in which the working assumptions and methods of both mainstream and marxist historians have been fully committed to the theoretical and political position of phallocentrism. The agenda and values of most history, whether of the Right or the Left, serve to promote masculinism, thereby distorting the experiences and agency of women.

Historians' commitment to an unexamined public/private split, typical of Western notions of male rationality, produces a number of patriarchal effects in historical work. Symptomatically enough, published history was dominated by works of political, diplomatic and military history, and studies of great men and great ideas, until fairly recently. Women's lack of formal participation usually meant that the question of patriarchal bias or omitting women did not arise. For these historians, it was not they but their objects of study which excluded women. Even so, evidence about women at times cluttered their notepads. E.H. Carr showed the manly virtues of the historian in distinguishing matters of public importance: 'Stalin is said to have behaved cruelly and callously to his second wife; but as an historian of Soviet affairs, I do not feel myself much concerned. A more serious question arises over the question of moral judgements on public actions' (Carr, 1961:75). Carr further disparaged the role of personal relations in historical interpretation, taking as his example Antony and Cleopatra's relationship and the Battle of Actium:

> It is unnecessarily discourteous to Cleopatra's beauty to suggest that Antony's infatuation has no cause. The connection between female beauty and male infatuation is one of the most regular sequences of cause and effect—interrupting and so to speak clashing with the sequence with which the historian is primarily concerned to investigate. (Carr, 1961:98–99)

That is to say, the historian should be concerned with *larger* matters of public concern, a preoccupation shared by professionals in other disciplines, and predicated on the repudiation of the 'feminine, the maternal' (Benjamin, 1980:306). This privileging of public matters has contributed to the maintenance of positivist, empiricist approaches of historical evidence.

Since the mainstream historian of public matters may find more or less ample evidence, it has been possible for the history profession to perpetuate the fiction that the good historian sits before the facts with little in the way of assumptions, and the facts speak to him. No historian is entitled to know his conclusions, wrote Elton, before he has got there by specific study of the evidence. This is a view shared by some prominent left-wing historians, such as E.P. Thompson (1983:47–48), who advises historians never to begin with projects too rigidly formulated because the material takes over and determines the outcome. Such positivist approaches retard scrutiny of surviving evidence in epistemological terms as well as in terms of the context in which it was produced. What aspects of given historical situations might we expect to generate records? How primary are various primary sources as evidence for particular hypotheses? (Blainey, 1979:97). What would we expect extant sources to record, and represent, and what are they most likely to omit or distort? These questions are critical for understanding evidence and its role in historical argument. Conversely they bear critically on historical interpretation where evidence is scanty or non-existent.

In addition to the public/private split which excludes the experience of women as communicable, and which retards the critical epistemological scrutiny of evidence that would be required to render that experience visible, mainstream history proposes a model of the supposedly universal historian that is phallocentric in effect. The history manuals convey a strong portrait of the historian as a man, and a man of remarkable qualities. He is a fearless free thinker, 'ready to challenge even the best established conventional wisdom, provided adequate facts and logical arguments can be mobilised against it' (Thomson, 1969:35). He is detective, judge and jury in something the trade calls 'the court of history' (McLennan, 1981:127); as such, he is obliged to consider every kind of evidence for and against his own hypotheses, checked only by his conscience and his academic peers (Thomson, 1969:42). While he acknowledges the problems of subjectivity and bias, his shrewd common sense, discrimination and intuitive historical understanding will deliver as objective an account as possible (Carr, 1961:123). He instinctively knows the 'right' question to put to the evidence (Elton, 1967:32). He is a man whose life is enriched by deeper insights into human behaviour than professionals in other fields—insights bequeathed by a discipline whose study is 'gritty, tough, challenging and mentally strenuous', imbued with 'persistent reflection and thoughtful questioning' (Thomson, 1969:101). This man of history is a love object of historians; that his virtues comprise a list of Western masculine qualities is not taken to be relevant in appraising the 'rightness' of the questions he asks; his justice and his instincts are posed as universal, rather than partial and mediated by the lived experience of a male body in a patriarchal culture (Gatens, 1983:149). This man of history does not find the question of a likely in-built masculine bias in most surviving evidence to be one of the 'right' questions. If it were, then most of what the discipline offers as 'general' histories might have to be re-evaluated, and certainly retitled, 'A Short History of Men in Australia', 'The Making of the English Male Working Class' and so forth. It would, of course, only be 'common sense'.

Left-wing and younger historians of various kinds have struggled to make a legitimate place for socialist theories particularly, and for more adequate conceptual frameworks generally, in historical work. They have thereby raised broad epistemological questions about the nature of historical knowledge. In an attempt to convey the historical experience of ordinary people, and the processes of class formation, class-consciousness and changing social conditions in different modes of production, socialist scholars have explored a large range of subjects, including work, the household, kinship, population patterns, fertility and birth control, diet, public health, poor relief, urbanisation, industrialisation, religion, magic and popular culture (see McLennan, 1981:98–118) that necessarily include the history of women. More than 'mainstream' historians, then, left-wing and social historians have been embarrassed by the continuing patriarchal bias of most labour, popular and socialist history. Women have figured as an assumed part of the unified working class; even where conflict between the sexes is apparent separate inquiry is rarely undertaken by these historians.

The challenge that feminism poses to left-wing historiography is of more intense character than its challenge to mainstream work, where the charges involve omission, biased selection or trivialisation, and pretended objectivity. Many left-wing commentators concede that feminist history represents a profound critique of the characteristic conduct, methods and personnel of the history profession (McLennan, 1981:119). Moreover, to pose sex differences and sexual power as variables integral to each mode of production and culture does not necessarily clash with marxist historical preoccupations (Rubin, 1975:75). This is the form of feminist intervention into history-writing applauded and eagerly accepted by socialist historians, offering as it does a more accurate account of the past. The struggle to intersect theoretical analyses of class with those of sex, capitalism with that of patriarchy, is vigorously pursued by socialist historians (Zaretsky, 1976; Weeks, 1981). Much greater hostility confronts feminist historians whose work gives little credence to marxist notions of periodisation, cause and effect, modes of production and class struggle. Feminists who claim theoretical as well as political autonomy, often employing the concept of patriarchy, have encountered trenchant criticism from marxist historians and theorists (see Allen, 1983). The latter take such feminist approaches to threaten marxism's claim to universalism, and scientific truth. The nature of these responses however, exposes the clear limits of socialist historians' acceptance of feminist history: it is tolerated so long as its actual function is descriptive, serving to buttress the privileged socialist schema. Histories of menstruation are ridiculed as 'soft', and 'not political' when compared to the histories of workers' struggles (Judt, 1979:88–89). Marxist historians employ notions of 'the political' that are traditionally patriarchal. Effectively they embrace a public/private split that is no less impoverishingly sexist than that discussed with regard to mainstream historians. Feminism challenges precisely these prevailing definitions of 'the political', as well as criteria of historical significance and change. Despite the advances made by left-wing and social history during the past fifteen years, the refusal to allocate centrality and autonomy to the analysis of sex difference and sexual power nonetheless classes this history with earlier and other historiographies as patriarchal. An inescapable fact is that women existed and exerted agency in the past. The sex-blindness of partriarchal historiographies, whether of the Right or Left, leads to lamentable omissions, distortions and inaccuracies, or simply poor judgment in historical interpretations. As Daniels has argued, the writing of women's historical experience will never be just a matter of putting women back, as if they somehow slipped out. The entire basis and procedures of the discipline have been inadequate to the task; and the history written can be an entirely different account of the past only because the consideration of gender becomes central (Daniels, 1977:xiii).

History is too important to feminism to leave to patriarchal methodologies, whether Right or Left. An examination of some aspects of histories of demographic change in Western countries 1875–1925 illustrates the extent to which acceptance of patriarchal approaches to evidence and argument is not an option for feminism.

EVIDENCE

Official statistical sources, even with all their problems in comprehensiveness, show considerable alterations in life expectancy, causes and distribution of death, birthrates, family sizes, illegitimacy, infant and maternal mortality, during the late nineteenth and early twentieth centuries in Britain, Australia, New Zealand and the United States. Historians have provided various explanations, depending on their theoretical and political commitments, whether stated or not. Work on declining birthrates, family sizes and the rising and falling rates of illegitimacy, infant and maternal mortality 1875–1925 demonstrates the contrast between historians who realise that these trends concern women's bodies and social relations, and those who overlook this focus.

Many historians attribute the decline of the mid-Victorian family of from ten or more, to the interwar rate of one or two, solely in terms of the use of barrier forms of contraception by husbands/couples, motivated by material aspirations (Banks, 1964). This decline was mirrored for a time in the fact that fewer women were confined than previously, and then in the fact that most women gave birth fewer times in their lifetimes in any year, hence a lowering of the gross birthrate in most Western countries. In the event of contraceptive failure, abortion is thought to have provided a second line of defence (McLaren, 1977:78–79). The rising rates of illegitimacy and infant mortality in the late nineteenth century are often attributed to the vulnerability of urban women, no longer able to draw on traditional, rural community support and pressure on the man to marry. The decline in these rates the first two decades of the twentieth century in England and in Australia is attributed by some historians to an increased use of artificial contraception, and by others to an outbreak of Edwardian chastity (H. Smith, 1978:300). Finally, mainstream historians are puzzled to find that maternal mortality increased from the late nineteenth century and that it continued until the introduction of sulphonamides in 1936. They take this to be odd because during the same period doctors substantially succeeded in excluding midwives and quacks from obstetric and gynaecological care, and also pioneered new procedures such as curettage, which should have reduced deaths from septicaemia caused by uteral retention of placental matter.

Explanation of declining birthrates, family sizes and illegitimacy in terms of contraception rests mainly on the evidence of advertisement and the technical availability of devices and preparations during the period. It would be unwise to discount the role of barrier methods of contraception, but many other factors must have limited its efficacy. While it is true that working-class families were larger than middle-class families, the trends of decline were manifested across all classes and regions in, for instance, Britain, Australia and the United States. Barrier methods, particularly condoms, were expensive, and required consistently high levels of male cooperation and motivation. Even if the working class generally gave such expense some priority, a faulty theory of ovulation (nominating around the menstrual period as the fertile stage and the middle of the cycle as infertile) would have worked against contraception. The currently held theory of mid-cycle ovulation was not established until 1928 (Weeks, 1981:148).

Feminist historians specifically investigating abortion consistently find that it was the first and main form of birth control used by women living in working-class areas (Knight, 1977:57). Further, as access to surgical abortion increased with the introduction of curettage, and family sizes steadily declined, so too did the rate of illegitimacy and infant mortality. As for the rising maternal mortality rate, closer scrutiny of returns and archival sources shows that the increase was not in the area of deaths consequent upon childbirth, but rather in the category 'accidents of pregnancy'. This designation included, as well as 'spontaneous miscarriages', cases of death from induced miscarriage and surgical curettage where the circumstances did not provide sufficient evidence to enable an indictment to be made for criminal abortion. In other words, the increased maternal mortality rate so puzzling to mainstream historians looks more like a crucial indicator of the increased resort to surgical abortion by women in Western industrial cultures. In view of the severe constraints entailed by the use of barrier contraception, it seems clear that to ignore the history of abortion is effectively to ignore the agency of women in momentous demographic changes that concerned their bodies and material circumstances. That so much demographic history is so Aristotelian, treating women's bodies as the inert matter on which dynamic economic and social forces operate, shows historians' reluctance to accept that women would play an active role in determining family size (McLaren, 1977:248). Criminal abortion remains seriously underresearched in both crime history and social histories of medicine. Since large-scale positive evidence of this family formation practice would be unlikely to exist, and only be created in the event of tragedy, for most historians it is as if it had never been; the role of abortion in demographic transition remains a 'non-question'.

The capacity to impose the 'right' questions, to make astute guesses or pursue sound intuitions about historical evidence seems to be critically influenced by the world view and the theoretical position (however much unacknowledged) that the historian brings to bear. At some level these depend on the individual's experience, a considerable proportion of which will differ by membership in various cultural groupings. Race, religion, age, region, class and education are all recognised as factors that may vary, enrich and detract from the capacity to reconstruct and interpret historical situations with insight. Examination of published work demonstrates that gender, however, seems to be less acknowledged as relevant.

Even feminist historical research, however, can be bedevilled by using methodologies erected by the men of 'common sense'. A significant body of women's history offers reason for concern for feminists. For all the unprecedented advances in understanding the past already achieved, feminist history may be retarded by this adherence to positivism in relation to what counts as evidence. This proposition will now be explored with regard to the history of prostitution.

SILENCE

Significantly, we know most about those social groups or institutions which kept and left written records. This leads to the sardonic reflection that only immense ignorance makes the study and writing of history possible. (Thomson, 1969:18)

Thomson's reflection, it could be argued, is not just sardonic in view of the immense ignorance that passes for general history; it is indisputable that extant evidence contains more of the opinions, desires and activities of the powerful (mostly powerful men) than any rounded representation.of past social reality. This is not a limitation that has pressed as greatly upon men eminent in the history profession as might be expected; otherwise more attention would be found in historiographical and methodological writing to questions of 'reading' evidence, modes of inference and deduction, accounting for presences and absences in extant sources. To account for the silence of those who have not registered themselves in historical discourses—the silence of women, the colonised, the peasantry, the proletariat, children, the institutionalised, all effectively the non-discursive (Foucault, 1977)—is to cast into sharp relief the evidence of extant, or effective discourses, in a way that precludes empiricist presumptions. Any such account would require theorising, irrespective of whether one is a feminist, a marxist, a liberal, a social democrat, a black separatist, a social determinist, or whatever.

On the basis of current experience, a feminist historian is likely to suppose, for instance, that the extent of rape and wife battering has been obscured in remaining evidence by underreporting, hesitant policing and levels of community condonation. She will not find the lack of evidence surprising, and probably would search the limited evidence with different questions (such as what led these particular instances to result in outside interventions, creating records thereby; and what kinds of instances of rape or violence seem never to have led to action). She would not infer that silence, or lack of evidence, or low arrest rates indicates conclusively that women from the mid-nineteenth century, for instance, had little to fear from men. But this is precisely the far-fetched though empiricist conclusion offered by various crime historians (Philips, 1978:142; Zehr, 1977:134–36). It is based on an unacknowledged functionalist theory of policing. That is, police enforce the rule of law impartially upon the community. The police statistics, then, will provide a mirror-image of crime patterns, even if a large dark figure of undetected offences makes them incomplete. This is an ahistorical theory of policing, lamentable enough when found in the work of criminologists. It is inexcusable in historical work; and it has even further retarded the accounting for silences in extant evidence on crimes and illicit practices that by definition involved women as complainant or offender.

The subject of prostitution provides a useful instance of prevalent and conflicting approaches to evidence and silence in women's history.

A privotal symbol of woman's estate and the subject of intense analysis by fin de siécle feminists, the theme of prostitution recurs through histories of women's work, poverty and welfare, class relations, sexuality, public health, crime and policing, leisure and popular culture. Of all the work touching this subject, that by feminist historians has radically shifted the terrain from much earlier work, which had a voyeuristic and moralistic tendency, often based on male memoir sources. Nonetheless, approaches to the questions of evidence and silence in some recent feminist works on prostitution differ widely. In contrast to earlier work, recent studies examine prostitution as a remunerative option for women at 'street level' as it were, with attention to conditions and organisations of trade, supply and demand and occupational hazards (see Finnegan, 1979; Walkowitz, 1980; Goldman, 1981; Rosen, 1983; Daniels, 1984; Bennett and Perkins, 1985). Of necessity, police are central to generating evidence about prostitution, since they were the initial—and often the only—agency engaged in identifying prostitutes as 'public women'. Other evidence about prostitution comes to exist from particular incidents, public outcries, venereal disease, organised crime scandals, or allegations of public corruption. Records originating in such incidents generally omitted or minimised several of the key historical features of prostitution. These include the prevalence of endemic male violence against prostitutes that forced them to obtain the services and hazards of pimps; the interaction of enforcement agents and criminal interests in the regulation and extortion of the lucrative market in prostitution; and finally the question of clients and the character of male sexuality entailed by the demand for prostitution—that is, the erotic implications of the male 'right' to purchase sexual mastery, without reciprocal desire (Pateman, 1983a:563). Police, politicians and ministers of state obviously do not leave documents attesting to their part in exempting the beneficiaries of prostitution from prosecution in return for payment.

It is therefore mindless to follow Elton in saying 'it is as if they had never been'. The inference of routine relations of corruption here is surely reasonable, and, on the balance of alternative explanations, not very speculative. Evidence created on those prosecuted for prostitution, brothel-keeping, or living on the earnings of prostitution suggests that they were only a selective sample from among those working as and living on prostitutes (Allen, 1984:201). Yet some feminist historians tend to take such evidence at face value. Surprisingly often, these scholars use police files, or registers from philanthropic institutions, as reliable or representative indicators of the social characteristics of the prostitution workforce, rather than as sources that reveal police or philanthropic selection (Finnegan, 1979:69–82; Walkowitz, 1980: 16–31). This is most problematic with regard to policing, since it reveals no reflection about the stakes police in different regions and periods have had in the construction and regulation of the prostitute workforces. In other words, police are taken as a constant, and are not subjected to historical scrutiny.

For example, Walkowitz uses police and philanthropic evidence to deny the prevalence of child prostitution and white slavery in the late-Victorian period. The police claim requires close scrutiny in any case, especially in the light of diverse grounds to presume the contrary (see sources in Rosen, 1983). However, the larger issue remains: what kind of scrutiny would feminists need to accept historical denials of the widespread existence of child prostitution, as Walkowitz does? (Walkowitz, 1980:17). What interests might be served by denying the prevalence of child prostitution? Can a feminist reader afford to presume that all aspects of Victorian child prostitution would survive in the form of literate evidence? As with rape or domestic violence, can lack of alternative evidence justify our believing the police claim that child prostitution was rare? In their advocacy of unpopular campaigns directed against men's sexual abuses of young women and children, late-nineteenth-century feminists disputed such police claims.

It is unfortunate that some recent interpretations of such feminist campaigns regarding prostitution and male sexuality are both empiricist and ahistorical. Late-nineteenth-century feminists have been blamed for an alleged legislative crackdown on all forms of non-marital sexuality during this period (Weeks, 1981:92). This crackdown included the criminalisation of male homosexuality, raising of the age of consent, and the imposition of serious penalties for men living from the earnings of prostitutes soliciting in public. These measures are categorised together with other forms of 'sexual repression', and laid at the door of feminists, who are characterised as puritanical fanatics (Walkowitz, 1983:434).

To dispute that feminists were responsible for the state suppression of prostitution is not to say that feminists had no influence or impact on their political and cultural milieu. On the contrary, politicians of the period showed a very clear understanding of feminist objectives, particularly the critique of male sexuality, that underpinned the women's movement. A crucial response to feminism by masculine legislatures, regardless of party or faction, was to oppose demands for women's suffrage. Libertarian elements in all parties articulated the threat to male interests that they perceived in the electorate that would be constituted by the female sex (Jeffreys, 1982:644).

If apparently repressive laws were passed affecting the organisation of prostitutes, we must suppose that a cluster of influential interest groups, apart from feminists, came to coincide in the interests served by these measures. To blame feminists of the past is to ignore the extent to which the history of organised crime and its penetration of political and legal systems across the twentieth century does much to explain the current organisation of prostitution and pornography. This displacement of 'blame' is symptomatic of the deep and unresolved conflict, both within and outside the women's liberation movement, over libertarianism and conflicting theories of male sexuality. With this rather extraordinary model of the past, feminists currently active in campaigns against pornography, legalisation of prostitution, paedophilia and sadomasochism are warned by history. Such feminists are frequently characterised by libertarians as puritanical, as opposed to sexual expression, or else as confining female sexuality to a nurturing 'vanilla' mode.

It is vitally important to current and future debate within the women's movement that a distorted representation of the history of feminism, based on such positivist or empiricist conflations, does not prevail. As feminists, we must be more perceptive about the significance of the silences and specific strategies of our ancestors.

The historical sources available for the study of prostitution are uneven and often unhelpful; but, from context to context, there are similarities in the nineteenth- and twentieth-century periods examined in these different women's history texts. Different conclusions by feminist historians researching these comparable sources seem best explained by the degree to which the approach to evidence departs from those of non-feminist historical methods. On a topic such as prostitution, a 'straight' reading of 'the facts' as they are represented in surviving literate sources not only fails to disclose much about the questions feminists must put to the past. Such a reading actually distorts and misses the inferences that can be drawn from the history of prostitution on the basis of what *is* disclosed in the existing evidence.

In this brief survey I have contended that the professional discipline of history is axiomatically phallocentric. Despite differences between Right- and Left-wing historians over their tolerance of 'theory', especially marxism, and their empiricist approaches to evidence, both exhibit a commitment to phallocentric assumptions and masculinist approaches to interpretations of the past. This is not a contingent or provisional feature of the discipline, amenable to some simple reform of content or approach.

Feminist historians have engaged in historical debates, contributed greatly to the knowledge of the past, and ruptured existing interpretations of most topics examined—with something of a Midas touch. This was demonstrated by reference to the changes in Western demography, 1875–1925. Yet the standard procedures and assumptions of the discipline, those which have so firmly excluded, distorted or trivialised women's historical experience, remain substantially intact. Even where feminists have criticised the content and approach, these systems have not been useful to feminist understandings of the past—as demonstrated in some feminist histories of prostitution. The uncritical reproduction of positivist and empiricist methods and modes of interpretation developed by phallocentric theorists can represent only a certain masculine vision of the past, severely limiting the value this work has for feminists interested in understanding the past.

Furthermore, it seems likely that alternative approaches used by feminists—the re-scrutiny of evidence which aims to locate the silences or non-discursive domain against which such evidence is framed—has not and will not produce the kinds of work professional historians will regard as valid history. Hence it is likely that the phallocentric nature of the discipline can remain intact, despite the radical and logical character of the current feminist critique. The question then must be whether it matters *for feminism* if feminist critique does not have the effect of altering the professional discipline of history. It may be of great consequence for the discipline of history, especially for those historians who recognise the extent of the malady and the degree to which universalistic claims have been challenged by feminist history. It is not clear that the assertion that feminism matters to history carries any imperative for feminism. This would be to assume that feminism bears some obligation to do the theoretical and methodological housework, to nurse the patient back to health, to play philosophical mother to the historical child.

To reject these obligations to the discipline of history is not to say that feminism does not have a vital interest in history and historical understanding. Against the claims of the profession, this chapter has argued that the discipline of history and historical understanding are neither contiguous nor synonymous. Feminism seeks a knowledge and understanding of the past; the discipline of history is a poor servant in this quest. The implication of this argument is that the future of feminism lies outside the known boundaries of Western thought.

This may at first glance appear a frightening prospect. It implies that the tradition has, or could, include women's historical experience; that we are already inside it and can choose to remain within or stand outside. This is an illusion. Phallocentric disciplines like history are constituted on the exclusion of women—literally, professionally, conceptually, methodologically and epistemologically. Concern about women's marginalisation through institutional, disciplinary or inter-disciplinary separation are located firmly within this illusion, the fear of incoherence and loss. It is only when we realise that we lose nothing in recognising and acknowledging our position outside traditional academic disciplines, that we find where our strength lies. The source of this strength is, paradoxically, that we have no choices. For feminists there is no choice but to start and continue on from this position, most of the time separate and external to traditional knowledges. Our historical silence is then merely an effect. It is the beginning, not the end of our history.

ELIZABETH GROSS

13 Conclusion
What is feminist theory?

> If we continue to speak this sameness, if we speak to each other as men
> have spoken for centuries, as they have taught us to speak, we will fail
> each other. Again ... words will pass through our bodies, above our
> heads, disappear, make us disappear. (Irigaray, 1980:69)

In the sixties, feminists began to question various images, representations, ideas and presumptions traditional theories developed
about women and the feminine. To begin with, feminists directed their
theoretical attention to patriarchal discourses, those which were either
openly hostile to and aggressive about women and the feminine, or
those which had nothing at all to say about women. Feminists seemed
largely preoccupied with the inclusion of women in those spheres from
which they had been excluded, that is, with creating representations
which would enable women to be regarded as men's *equals*. Instead of
being ignored by and excluded from theory, women were to be
included as possible objects of investigation. Issues of direct relevance
to women's lives—the family, sexuality, the 'private' or domestic
sphere, interpersonal relations—were to be included, in some instances for the first time, as a relevant and worthy object of intellectual concern. Generally, feminists continued to rely on the methods,
techniques, concepts and frameworks of traditional patriarchal
theories, especially in leftist or radical form, using them to develop
accounts of women's oppression. Some of the relevant names circulat-
ing in feminist discourses at the time included Marx, Reich, Marcuse,
Mcluhan, Laing, Cooper, Sartre, Fanon, Masters and Johnson.
Women used these texts in their attempts to include women as the
equals of men in the sphere of theoretical analysis, developing out of

various theories of (class or race) oppression by modifying and adjusting their details in order to account for women's specific oppression.

Among the relevant features or characteristics describing this phase in the development of feminist theory could be the following:

1.   Women and the feminine become worthwhile objects of theory and research. Having been neglected, or denied value in patriarchal terms, women become focal points of empirical and theoretical investigation.

2.   Women and the feminine, as excluded or neglected objects in traditional theoretical terms, are now conceptualised as men's equals—as the same as men in relevant socio-economic and intellectual terms.

3.   While elements or components of patriarchal discourses may be criticised, questions about their more basic framework and assumptions, whether ontological, epistemological or political, remain unasked.

4.   While remaining critical toward the attitude of patriarchal discourses to the position of women, feminist theory is largely concerned with 'women's issues', those which directly affect women's lives, leaving other, 'broader' or more 'public' issues uncriticised.

5.   Patriarchal discourses were subjected to an either/or decision: either they were considered thoroughly infiltrated with patriarchal values and thus need to be rejected; or they are capable of 'rectification' so that women can now be included. Patriarchal discourses, in other words, were either rejected outright or were more or less wholeheartedly accepted (with 'minor adjustments').

However, within a short period it became clear that the aim of including women as men's equals within patriarchal theory contained a number of problems not anticipated at the outset. Perhaps most strikingly, it became increasingly clear that it was not possible simply to include women in those theories where they had previously been excluded, for this exclusion forms a fundamental structuring principle and key presumption of patriarchal discourses. Many patriarchal discourses were *incapable* of being broadened or extended to include women without major upheavals and transformations. There was no space within the confines of these discourses to accommodate women's inclusion and equal participation. Moreover, even if women were incorporated into patriarchal discourses, at best they could only be regarded as variations of a basic humanity. The project of women's equal inclusion meant that only women's *sameness to men*, only women's *humanity* and not their *womanliness* could be discussed. Further, while women could now be included as the objects of theoretical speculation, their positions as the subjects or producers of knowledge was not raised. In other words, in adopting the role of the (male) subjects of knowledge, women began to assume the role of surrogate men.

As subjects of knowledge, women were faced with a dilemma. They could either remain detached from the 'objects' of their theoretical investigations (where these objects are women or femininity), in which case women may be considered to retain their 'objectivity' and 'neutrality'; or women could maintain a closeness to and identification with their 'objects'. In the first case, such women, while gaining the approval of their male colleagues and possibly some position of respect within academic communities, must nevertheless disavow their own positions as women. In the second case, by their self-inclusion within the category of objects investigated, many women lose the detachment needed to be considered 'scientific' or 'objective', resulting, perhaps, in ridicule or some form of academic secondariness. Yet such women, through the risks they thus take in questioning the most general assumptions and *givens* of intellectual inquiry, retain some possibility of maintaining identities as women. In the long run this may have led to questioning the use and value of the distinction between subject and object, transforming the very grounds of current debate.

In abandoning such attempts to include women where theory excluded them, many feminists came to realise that the project of women's inclusion as men's equals could not succeed (see chapter 6). This was because it was not simply the range and scope of objects that required transformation: more profoundly, and threateningly, the very questions posed and the methods used to answer them, basic assumptions about methodology, criteria of validity and merit, all needed to be seriously questioned. The political, ontological and epistemological commitments underlying patriarchal discourses, as well as their theoretical contents required re-evaluation from feminist perspectives, as it became increasingly clear that women could only be included in patriarchal texts as deviant or duplicate men: the a priori assumptions of sameness or interchangeability, sexual neutrality or indifference, the complete neglect of women's specificities and differences, could not be accommodated in traditional theoretical terms. The whole social, political, scientific and metaphysical underpinning of patriarchal theoretical systems needed to be shaken up.

While problematic and ultimately impossible, the aspiration towards an equality between men and women was nevertheless politically and historically necessary. Without such attempts, women could not question the naturalness or seeming inevitability of women's second-class status as citizens, subjects, sexual beings etc. This aim of equality served as a political, and perhaps as an experiential, prerequisite to the more far-reaching struggles directed towards female *autonomy*—that is, to women's right to political, social, economic and intellectual self-determination. This seems probably the most striking shift in feminist politics since its revival in the sixties.

This basic shift from a politics of equality to a politics of autonomy may have created an uneasy tension within feminist circles, for these two commitments are not necessarily compatible. Autonomy implies the right to see oneself in whatever terms one chooses—which may imply an integration or alliance with other groups and individuals or may not. Equality, on the other hand, implies a measurement according to a given standard (cf. Thornton, Thompson, Gatens). Equality is the equivalence of two (or more) terms, one of which takes the role of norm or model in unquestionable ways. Autonomy, by contrast, implies the right to accept or reject such norms or standards according to their apppropriateness to one's self-definition. Struggles for equality—so convincingly criticised in a number of the essays in this book—imply an acceptance of given standards and a conformity to their expectations and requirements. Struggles for autonomy, on the other hand, imply the right to reject such standards and create new ones.

Feminists concerned with questions surrounding women's autonomy and self-determination are, ironically, no less concerned with the work of male or masculinist theory than their equality-oriented counterparts, although the male proper names have changed significantly over the twenty-year period of feminism's existence as a self-consciously political intervention into theory. The names of Freud, Lacan, Nietzsche, Derrida, Deleuze, Althusser, Foucault in France, and Richard Rorty. Anthony Wilden, Frederic Jameson, Stephen Heath, Terry Eagleton, Paul de Man etc. in England and North America constitute just some of the 'names' with which contemporary feminist theory has engaged. But what has dramatically changed is the feminist attitude towards and use of patriarchal discourses. Instead of these discourses and their methods and assumptions providing uncriticised tools and frameworks by which women could be analysed as objects, now these discourses become the objects of critical feminist scrutiny. Such discourses and methods are now *tactically used* without necessarily retaining general commitment to their frameworks and presumptions. Feminists do not seem so eager to slot women into pre-existing patriarchal categories and theoretical spaces; instead, it is women's lives, and experiences, that provide criteria by which patriarchal texts can be judged. Basic, unspoken assumptions of patriarchal theories, the ways in which they develop and gain precedence, their use of criteria and methods of inclusion and exclusion are all beginning to be analysed from feminist perspectives (for example, Harding and Hintikka; Miles and Finn). Women asserted themselves not as objects but as subjects of knowledge with particular perspectives and points of view often systematically different from men's. Such perspectives or viewpoints are not simply 'subjective' in the sense of individual, personal or idiosyncratic positions—'subjectivity' being seen as an *interference* with the 'objective' procedures of knowledge in just the same way that men's theoretical productions are a function of their lived positions in the world. The production of discourse is, for the first time, being examined as a process of *sexual division* and exclusion (cf. chapter 4).

Feminists of autonomy can be contrasted with feminists committed to struggles of equality on at least the following points:

1. Women become both the subjects as well as the objects of knowledge; but, in occupying the position of subject, feminists do not continue to produce knowledge as if they were men, as if knowledge were sexually indifferent. Women's femininity is asserted as a theoretical undertaking, with a number of consequences, among them:

2. In assuming the positions of knower or subject, the methods, procedures, presumptions and techniques of theory are all put into question.

3. Feminists develop perspectives not just *on* or *about* women and 'women's issues' but about *any* object at all—including other theories, systems of representation etc., etc.

4. Feminists don't simply assert the either/or alternative, based on 'expelling unsound' or patriarchal elements or wholesale adoption of theoretical viewpoints. Instead, while attempting to 'work through' patriarchal texts, understanding how they work and how they exert their dominances, feminists attempt to use what they can of these theories—often against themselves! No longer simply condemning or accepting certain discourses, now they are analysed, examined and questioned—actively engaged with and challenged in their operations.

5. Feminist theory challenged both the content and the frameworks of discourses, disciplines and institutions, attempting to present alternatives or develop them where they did not yet exist.

These interventions and interrogations may have produced one of the most subversive challenges to patriarchal theory that this century, or epoch, has seen: 'It is a major historical event which holds the promise of enabling a more complete challenge to domination than has yet been possible before' (Finn and Miles, 1982:10).

In the diverse disciplines constituting the social sciences and humanities, in which most feminist, theorists received their training, many matured from a position akin to apprenticeship (where women learned the skills of prevailing (masculine) forms of scholarship and research) to a position of relative self-determination (where women are able to use the techniques and skills they have acquired against the very disciplines in which they were trained). These disciplines, and the specific texts and practices associated with them, have become the objects of feminist analysis and criticism. Theory, rather than 'Woman' is now the terrain of contestation between feminists and non- or anti-feminists.

Feminist struggles for autonomy, self-determination and a viable place which women can occupy as women in the theoretical and socio-political universe—as can be seen from the diverse yet interconnected essays presented here—have developed into a two-pronged or dual-faceted form. On the one hand, feminist theory has radically questioned and attempted to undermine the presumptions, methods and frameworks of phallocentric or patriarchal discourses and disciplines. On the other hand, feminist theory has simultaneously attempted to explore and develop alternatives to these phallocentric systems, bringing into being new, hitherto unarticulated, feminine perspectives on the world. In other words, today feminist theory is involved in both an *anti-sexist* project, which involves challenging and deconstructing phallocentric discourses; and in a positive project of constructing and developing alternative models, methods, procedures, discourses etc.

The anti-sexist project clearly implies a thorough knowledge of and familiarity with prevailing theoretical paradigms and their histories. Such an endeavour means working with, understanding and reflecting on those theoretical systems which comprise women's history and their contemporary situation, and participating in women's oppression. Yet anti-sexism is largely negative and reactive, aiming to challenge what currently exists, what is presently dominant and responsible for women's phallocentric position in theoretical representation. Such a critical, reactive project is necessary if feminist theory is to avoid the intellectual perils of abstraction, idealisation or irrelevance. It risks projecting an ideal or utopian future for women which is unanchored in or unrelated to what exists here and now. It risks a series of commitments it may wish, on reflection, to reject. It risks repeating problems of the past without recognising them as problems or learning from them. The critical, anti-sexist project is directed against the methods, assumptions and procedures by which patriarchal discourses reduce women to a necessary dependence on men as well as against more insidious, structural expressions of misogyny, which, rather than making sexist pronouncements about women instead present perspectives on the world from a masculine point of view as if such a position were sexually neutral.

If, however, feminist theory remains *simply* reactive, *merely* a critique, paradoxically it affirms the very paradigms it seeks to contest. It remains on the very grounds it wishes to question and transform. To criticise prevailing theoretical systems *without posing viable alternatives* is to affirm such theoretical systems as necessary. Although feminist theory must retain a familiarity with these systems, it must also establish a theoretical distance from too close an adherence to them. If feminist theory does not extend beyond the terms of anti-sexism, it remains bound up with a politics of sameness or equality even while criticising it. The limited but strategically necessary aim of destabilising and dismantling patriarchal discourses is only the first stage or prerequisite for a more encompassing and threatening challenge to patriarchal domination—the struggle for autonomy, implying struggles for the right to different paradigms, theoretical tools, and possibly even a reconceptualisation of the entire system of knowledges and acceptable theoretical methods.

Coupled with the anti-sexist project, feminism must thus also be involved in the positive task of experimenting with and creating alternatives to patriarchal theoretical norms. Feminist theory can no longer be content with adapting patriarchal theories so that they are capable of analysing woman—which in itself is a phallocentric endeavour, for it reduces women to theories and categories appropriate for and developed from masculine points of view. The positive components question and displace the very foundations upon which traditional theories are based.

It cannot be specified in advance what an autonomous feminist theory would involve, for this contradicts the very idea of autonomy, the right to choose and define the world for oneself. In their diversity and multiplicity, women claim the right to define their own aims and goals. Although it cannot be specified using one or many models, feminist theory can nevertheless be outlined negatively, for it seems clear that there are a number of theoretical assumptions it would not wish to reproduce. It cannot be regarded, for example, as the reverse or opposite of patriarchal texts, transforming their objects but not their underlying assumptions. On the contrary, it attempts to move beyond them, their frameworks and their limits.

In other words, feminist theory cannot be accurately regarded as a *competing* or rival account, diverging from patriarchal texts over what counts as true. It is not a true discourse, nor a mere objective or scientific account. It could be appropriately seen, rather, as a *strategy*, a local, specific, concrete, intervention with definite political, even if provisional, aims and goals. In the 1980s, feminist theory no longer seems to seek the status of unchangeable, trans-historical and trans-geographic truth in its hypotheses and propositions. Rather, it seeks effective forms of intervention into systems of power in order to subvert them and replace them with others more preferable. Strategy implies a recognition of the current situation, in both its general, structural features (macrolithic power alignments), and its specific, detailed, regionalised forms (microlithic power investments). It needs to know the spaces and strategies of its adversaries in order to undermine their positions within an overall system. It must thus be aware of the kinds of counterstrategy or tactics used by phallocentric discourses to deploy in order to seek the points of vulnerability. All forms of strategy, in short, involve recognising what *is* in order to move on to what *should* be. Strategy always involves short-term aims, seen as necessary for the achievement of longer term ideals, which themselves are capable of being modified and transformed during the processes of struggle. As a form of strategy, feminist theory needs to use whatever means are available to it, whether these are 'patriarchal" or not. Phallocentric insights, concepts and theoretical tools are evaluated in terms of their usefulness, their functioning in particular contexts, rather than in terms of an ideal but impossible purity. As strategy, it is necessarily implicated in the systems it wishes to challenge. Aspirations to a theoretical purity, a position 'untainted' by patriarchal impingements, that is, forms of theoretical separatism where patriarchal terms and practices are rejected, seem naive. They are unable to struggle with, or thus move beyond the patriarchal terms that return to haunt them. In order to challenge and move beyond patriarchal models, feminists must be able to use whatever means are at hand, including those of the very systems it challenges.

As a series of strategic interventions into patriarchal texts, feminist theory does not simply aim to reveal what is 'wrong' with, or false about, patriarchal theories—to replacing one 'truth' with another. It aims to render patriarchal systems, methods and presumptions unable to function, unable to retain their dominance and power. It aims to make clear how such a dominance has been possible; and to make it no longer viable. Since feminist theory lacks the means to directly confront a sophisticated patriarchal theoretical regime in creating alternatives, feminists have had to resort to forms of intellectual guerilla warfare, striking out at the points of patriarchy's greatest weakness, its blindspots (see Irigaray, 1985a: Part I). The grounds and terrain upon which patriarchy develops its arguments reveals their partial and partisan instead of universal or representative position. Patriarchal intellectual systems are unlikely to allow such attempts at political subversion to proceed uncontested. In fact, it is clear that traditional discourses and the positions they support have developed a series of counter-strategies and tactical response to the incursions of feminism, and indeed, women, into its fields of operation. These range from more or less personal or petty tactics to more serious, far-ranging threats—from personal ridicule, ignorance, stereotyping, to forms of counterattack including wilful misrepresentation, being refused access to professional status and/or a livelihood or having one's work co-opted or neutralised. Such counterattacks are by no means mutually exclusive and are exercised with greater or lesser strength according to the degree of threat feminist theories and objections pose. Without at least some awareness of the range and ferocity of these counterattacks, feminism may be unable to effect the wide-ranging subversions it seeks. It need not be committed to patriarchal discourses and their values, yet without understanding them in detail, feminists will be unable to move beyond them.

In summary, feminist theory involves, first, a recognition of the overt and covert forms of misogyny in which discourses participate. This means developing the skills of recognising what makes these discourses patriarchal—including their explicit pronouncements about men and women, and their respective values, as well as the capacity to see how such theories divide up the world according to masculine interests. Second, it involves an ability to recognise patriarchal discourses in terms of their absences, gaps, lacunae, around the question of women and the feminine, understanding how these silences function to structure and make patriarchal discourses possible. Third, feminist theory must be capable of articulating the role that these silences and masculinist representations play in the suppression of femininity, and of affirming the possibility of other, alternative, perspectives, making patriarchal texts unable to assert their hegemony; and fourth, it must develop viable methods for superseding phallocentric systems of representation even if this means relying on patriarchal methods, using them as a starting point for new directions in theoretical research. By its very existence, such forms of feminist theory demonstrate that patriarchal discourses are *not* neutral, universal or unquestionable models, but are the effects of the specific (political) positions occupied by men.

On the basis of the essays gathered together in this collection, and works by a number of other feminists within social and political theory (see the bibliography), feminist theory can be provisionally located at the interface of the negative, anti-sexist project and a more positive, speculative, project. It is the refusal of a number of central values, concepts and operations necessary for the functioning of patriarchal theory, and an affirmation of the alternatives to these given forms of discourse. Among the central concepts and values questioned by feminist theory is a core of assumptions shared by most, if not all of the social sciences. In particular, it has seriously questioned patriarchal adherences to the following theoretical commitments:

1. Commitment to a singular or universal concept of truth and methods for verifying (or falsifying) truth. Few theories aspiring to the status of scientific objectivity and truth, conventionally understood, accept their own historicity and the effects that context, environment and particular circumstances have on the production and evaluation

of theory. In particular, such theoretical aspirations cannot acknowledge the costs (the silences, exclusions and invalidations) on which they are founded: in seeking the status of truth, they seek a position beyond history and outside power.

2. Its commitments to objectivity, observer-neutrality and the context-independence as unquestioned theoretical values. These are closely related to the overevaluation of science and truth as models for knowledge. Objectivity is considered as a form of interchangeability or substitutability of observers or experimenters, as a check against individual bias. This ideal of interchangeability is based on the assumption of a similarity of viewpoint and position between observers—who must be 'appropriately trained'. This assumption is necessarily blind to the different structural positions men and women occupy, their different degrees of access to suitable training, and their (possibly) different relations to their disciplines. The neutrality and universality of many patriarchal discourses presumed in the social sciences is thus sex-blind—unable to acknowledge the different social positions of men and women in presuming a neutral, interchangeable subject.

3. The commitment to a universal subject of knowledge, a subject presumed to have certain qualities and features: the ability to separate *him*self from feelings, emotions, passions, personal interests and motives, socio-economic and political factors, the past, one's aspirations for the future etc. This subject of knowledge is capable of achieving a distance from the object known, thus being able to reflect on it. It is, however, a subject incapable of accepting its own limits, its materiality and historicity, its immersion in socio-economic and political values. The subject is conceived as disembodied, rational sexually indifferent subject—a mind unlocated in space, time or constitutive interrelations with others (a status normally only attributed to angels! cf. Irigaray, 1984).

4. The commitment to a fixed, static truth, an immutable, given reality, a guaranteed knowledge of Being and access to Reason. Such an ahistorical view cannot account for the variability and historical nature of what counts as true except in terms of a greater and greater access to and knowledge of the truth, that is, except in terms of historical views being *false* views. It refuses to endorse the possibility of a 'politics of truth', of the political investments in truth (cf. Foucault, 1976; 1978). Truth, as a correspondence or veridical reflection of reality, is a *perspectiveless* knowledge, a knowledge without a point of view—or, what amounts to the same thing, a truth claiming a universal perspective.

5. The commitment to the intertranslatability of concepts, terms, truths, propositions and discourses. As embodied in a propositional form, knowledge 'is not regarded as dependent on its particular modes

of formulation, but on the underlying thoughts it is presumed to express. Language is considered a vehicle for the communication of pre-existent thoughts or ideas. It is seen merely as a medium, a dispensable tool for the transmission of thought, rather than being seen as thought's necessary condition. In denying the materiality of language, prevailing discourses can avoid recognising their dependence on and debt to tropes, figures of speech, images, metaphors etc. evoking the feminine, women or maternity. Patriarchal discourses ignore the complicity of discursive systems with oppressive social structures, and the dependence of discourses on particular positions established by particular modes of language.

There are, of course, many positive features that can be briefly sketched out in general ways which do not pre-empt women's various attempts at self-determination. Included among them are:

1.   Intellectual commitments, not to truth, objectivity and neutrality, but to theoretical positions openly acknowledged as observer and context-specific. Rather than deny its spatio-temporal conditions and limits, feminist theory accepts and affirms them, for they are its raison d'étre. Following Nietzsche, it seems prepared to avow its own perspectivism, its specific position of enunciation, its being written from a particular point of view, with specific aims and goals.

2.   In acknowledging its conditions of production, feminist theory seems prepared to question the value of the criteria of objectivity and scientificity so rigidly and imperialistically accepted by intellectual orthodoxies. This is not, however, an admission of any 'subjective bias'. The very distinction between objective (knowledge) and subjective (opinion) is put into question. Feminists seem prepared to accept that the knower always occupies a position, spatially, temporally, sexually and politically. This is a corollary of its perspectivism. It is neither subjective nor objective, neither absolute nor relative. These alternatives, for one thing, cannot explain the productive investments of power in the production of knowledges. This does not, however, mean that feminist theory used no criteria of evaluation or self-reflection. Rather, its norms of judgment are developed from *inter-subjective*, shared effects and functions; and in terms of a discourse's *intertexual* functions, its capacity to either undermine or affirm various dominant systems and structures.

3.   Instead of presuming a space or gulf between the rational, knowing subject and the object known, feminist theory acknowledges the contiguity between them. Prevailing views of the rational subject posit a subject artificially and arbitrarily separated from its context. This creates a distance required for its separation from the emotions, passions, bodily interferences, relations with others and the socio-

political world. Feminist theory seems openly prepared to accept the constitutive interrelations of the subject, its social position and its mediated relation to the object. For feminists (in so far as they uphold such a notion) the rational subject is *not* free of personal, social and political interests, but is necessarily implicated in them. Theories are seen as sexualised, as occupying a position in relation to the qualities and values associated with the two sexes, or the attributes of masculinity and femininity. But to claim a sexualisation of discourses and knowledges is not to equate the discourse's position with that of its author or producer; there is no (direct) correspondence between feminine or feminist texts and female authors, or between phallocentric texts and male authors. The sexual 'position of the text' can only be discerned contextually and in terms of the position which the speaking subject, (the implicit or explicit 'I' of the text), speaks from; the kind of subject (implicitly) presumed as the subject *spoken to* (or audience), and the kind of subject *spoken about* (or object). As well as the range of various subjects posited in any or all texts, the text's position also depends on the *kind of relations* asserted between these different subjects (cf. Benveniste, 1961:chs 19–20). In the case of feminist theory, the subject, object and audience are not dichotomously divided into mutually exclusive and mutually exhaustive categories (subject/object, knower-master/ignorant-disciple, teacher/pupil, self/other etc. cf. Jay) but may be defined more in terms of continuities and/or differences. The speaking subject, the subject spoken to and the subject spoken about may be equated; but in any case, there is a constitutive interrelatedness presumed between all three terms. This means, for example and to take a concrete case, that men do not speak with greater objectivity about women's oppression, as some male academics recently asserted with great sincerity. Men too are necessarily implicated in and part of women's oppression. It is of course clear that their relations to such oppression must be very different from women's. In short, particular interests are served by every theoretical position and in any textual or discursive system. The politics or 'power' of the text (cf. Foucault, 1972) cannot, however, be automatically read off from what the text overtly *says*, but, more frequently, from *how* it says it, what is invoked, and what is thus effected. Feminist theory has the merit over prevailing discursive systems of being able not only to accept but to actively affirm its own political position(s) and aspirations, to accept that, far from being objective in the sense of 'disinterested' and 'unmotivated', it is highly motivated by the goals and strategies involved in creating an autonomy for women. Such motivation or purposiveness, however, does not invalidate feminist theory, but is its acknowledged function, its rationale;

4. Because it refuses to accept the pre-given values of truth,

objectivity, universality, neutrality and an abstract reason, feminist theory—along with some contemporary male theorists—is not committed to or motivated by these values. It sees itself in terms of a critical and constructive strategy. It is neither abstraction, blueprint nor handbook for action, nor a distanced form of reflection. These views, for one thing, imply a theory outside or beyond practice. In questioning the dichotomous conceptualisation of the relation between theory and practice, feminist theory considers itself both a 'theoretical practice'—a practice at the level of theory itself, a practice bound up with yet critical of the institutional frameworks within which the production of theoretical discourses usually occurs, a practice involving writing, reading, teaching, learning, assessment, and numerous other rituals and procedures; as well, it is a 'practical theory'—a theory openly seen as a part of practice, a tool or tactic playing a major part in the subversive, often dangerous assault on one particular site of the functioning of patriarchal power relations—the sphere of knowledge, which provides patriarchy with rationalisations and justifications for its ever-expanding control. Feminist theory is an interweaving of strands that are simultaneously theoretical and practical. It is a site where dominant discourses, subjugated discourses, voices hitherto silenced or excluded (cf. Allen, Thiele), forms of coercion and control as well as concerted forms of resistance are able to be worked through in relation to each other. It is a threshhold for the intervention of theories within concrete practices, and the restructuring of theory by the imperatives of experience and practice, a kind of hinge or doorway between the two domains. In aiming at a destruction of misogynistic theory and its fundamental assumptions and at establishing a positive influence on day-to-day and structural interactions between the sexes, it is neither a prelude to practice, nor a reflection on practice because it is already a form of practice within a specific region of patriarchy's operations.

5.   Feminist theory, similarly, cannot be conceived in terms of the categories of rationality or irrationality. Since at least the seventeenth century, if not long before, reason has been understood in dichotomous terms, being characterised oppositionally and gaining its internal coherence only by the exclusion of its 'others'—the passions, the body, the emotions, nature, faith, materiality, dreaming, experience, perception, madness or many other terms (cf. Jay; Lloyd, 1984; Irigaray, 1984). In questioning this binary mode of categorisation, feminists demonstrated that reason is a concept associated with the norms and values of masculinity, and its opposites, or 'others', with femininity. Feminist theory today is not simply interested in reversing the values of rational/irrational or in affirming what has been hierarchically subordinated, but more significantly, in questioning the very structure of binary categories. In short, feminist theory seeks to

transform and extend the concept of reason so that instead of excluding concepts like experience, the body, history, etc. these are included within it or acknowledged as necessary for reason to function. In taking women's experiences and lives as a starting point for the development of theory, feminism attempts to develop alternatives to the rigid, hierarchical and exclusive concept of reason. It seeks a rationality not divided from experience, from oppression, from particularity or specificity; a reason, on the contrary, that includes them is a rationality not beyond or above experience but based upon it.

6. In challenging phallocentrism, feminist theory must also challenge the evasion of history and materiality so marked in theoretical traditions in the West. In conceiving of itself as a rational, private, individual activity and struggle towards truth and knowledge, a pure, intellectual activity, it must also deny its status as a historical and political product. Predominant theoretical traditions refuse to accept their dependence on the materiality of writing, on practices involved in training, producing, publishing and promoting certain methods, viewpoints and representatives, on struggles for authority and domination. In opposition to these prevailing theoretical ideals, feminist theory openly acknowledges its own materiality as the materiality of language (language being seen as a weapon of political struggle, domination and resistance), of desire (desire as the will to achieve certain arrangements of potentially satisfying 'objects'—the desire for an identity, a sexuality and a recognised place in culture being the most clear-cut and uncontentious among feminists) and of power (power not just as a force visible in the acts, events and processes within political and public life, but also as a series of tactical alignments between institutions, knowledges, practices involved with the control and supervision of individuals and groups); in more particular terms, the alignments of male socio-economic domination with the forms of learning, training, knowledge, and theory.

7. In rejecting leading models of intellectual inquiry (among them, the requirements of formal logic, the structuring of concepts according to binary oppositional structures, the use of grammar and syntax for creating singular, clear, unambiguous, precise modes of articulation and many other assumed textual values), and its acceptance of the idea of its materiality as theory, feminist theory is involved in continuing explorations of and experimentation with new forms of writing, new methods of analysis, new positions of enunciation, new kinds of discourse.

No one method, form of writing, speaking position, mode of argument can act as representative, model or ideal for feminist theory. Instead of attempting to establish a new theoretical norm, feminist theory seeks a new *discursive space*, a space where women can write, read and think *as women*. This space will encourage a proliferation of voices, instead of a hierarchical structuring of them, a plurality of perspectives and interests instead of the monopoly of the one—new kinds of questions and different kinds of answer. No one form would be privileged as *the* truth, the correct interpretation, the right method; rather, knowledges, methods, interpretations can be judged and used according to their appropriateness to a given context, a specific strategy and particular effects.

Feminist theory is capable of locating itself historically, materially, enunciatively and politically in relation to patriarchal structures. During its development over the last 25 years it has emerged as a capacity to look at women in new, hitherto unexplored ways by refusing to reduce and explain women's specificity to terms that are inherently masculine; it has developed the ability to look at any object from the point of view of perspectives and interests of women, of understanding and going beyond phallocentrism in developing different kinds of theory and practice. This description may sound like an idealised or utopian version of what a self-conscious and politically committed, active and informed theoretical practice should involve. Perhaps. It is not yet clear how far along this utopian path feminist discourses have come. But as the essays published here testify, feminist theory is in the process of developing along these diverse trajectories. It is in the process of reassessing the theoretical heritage it needs to supersede in order to claim a future for itself. This future may initiate a new theoretical epoch, one capable of accepting the full implications of acknowledging sexual difference. Theory in the future would be seen as sexual, textual, political and historical production. Although this may threaten those who adhere to the values of phallocentrism, it may open up hitherto unimagined sites, sources and tools for theoretical exploration. An autonomous femininity may introduce, for the first time in our recorded history, the possibility of dialogue with an 'alien voice', the voice of woman.

> Sexual difference would constitute the horizon of worlds of a still unknown fecundity ... Fecundity of birth and regenerescence for amorous partners, but still production of a new epoch of thought, art, poetry, language ... Creation of a new *poietics*. (Irigaray, 1984:1)

Bibliography

Adams, P. and J. Minson (1978) 'The subject of feminism' *m/f* 2, pp. 43–61

Allen, J. (1982) 'Octavius Beale Re-considered: Infanticide, Babyfarming and Abortion in New South Wales 1880–1939' in Sydney Labour History Group (ed.) *What Rough Beast?: The State and Social Order in Australian History* Sydney: Allen & Unwin

—— (1983) 'Marxism and the Man Question: Some Implications of the Patriarchy Debate' in J. Allen and P. Patton (eds) *Beyond Marxism* Sydney: Intervention Publications, pp. 99–102

—— (1984) 'The Making of a Prostitute Proletariat in Twentieth Century New South Wales' in Daniels (ed.) *So Much Hard Work*

Alther, L. (1975) *Kinflicks* Knopf/Random House

Althusser L. (1969) *For Marx* Harmondsworth: Penguin

—— (1971) *Lenin and Philosophy and Other Essays* London: New Left Books

Annas, J. (1976) 'Plato's Republic and Feminism' *Philosophy* 51, pp. 307–321

—— (1977) 'Mill and the Subjection of Women *Philosophy* 52, pp. 179–94

Banks, J.A. and O. Banks (1964) *Feminism and Family Planning in Victorian England* Liverpool: Liverpool University Press

Barker-Benfield, B. (1972) 'The Spermatic Economy: A Nineteenth Century View of Sexuality' *Feminist Studies* 1, 1, pp. 45–74

Barraclough, G. (1972) *Main Trends in History* New York: Longmans

Bateson, G. (1972) *Steps to an Ecology of Mind* New York: Pantheon Books

Beitz, G. (1980) 'Tacit Consent and Property Rights' *Political Theory* 8, 4, pp. 487–502

Benjamin, J. (1977) 'Authority and the family revisited' *New German Critique* 13, pp. 35–57

—— (1980) 'The bonds of love: rational violence and erotic domination' in Eisenstein and Jardine *The Future of Difference*

205

Benveniste, E. (1961) *Problems in General Linguistics* Miami: University of Miami Press

Blainey, G. (1979) 'Antidotes to History' in J. A. Moses (ed.) *Historical Discipline and Culture in Australia* St Lucia: University of Queensland Press

Boals, K. (1975) 'The Politics of Male–Female Relations' *Signs* 1, 1, pp. 161–74

Braidotti, R. (1982) 'Femmes et philosophie, questions à suivre' *La Revue d'en Face* 13

—— (1983) 'Pour un feminisme critique' *Les Cahiers du Grif* 28

Brennan, T. and C. Pateman (1979) ' "Mere Auxiliaries to the Commonwealth": Women and the Origins of Liberalism' *Political Studies* 27, 2, pp. 183–200

Bridenthal, R. (1982) 'The View from a Room of Her Own' in B. Thorne and M. Yalom *Rethinking the Family: Some Feminist Questions* New York: Longmans

Brookes, B. (1983) 'The Illegal Operation: Abortion 1919–39' in London Feminist History Group (ed.) *The Sexual Dynamics of History* London: Pluto Press

Brownmiller, S. (1975) *Against Our Will* Harmondsworth: Penguin

Cacciari, M. (1976) *Krisis—saggio sulla crisi del pensiero negativo* Milan: Feltrinelli

Canguilhem, G. (1966) *Le normal et le pathologique* Paris: PUF

Carr, E.H. (1961) *What Is History?* Harmondsworth: Penguin

Carroll, L. (1972) *Alice in Wonderland and Through the Looking-Glass* ed. M. Gardner, Harmondsworth: Penguin

Charvet, J. (1982) *Feminism* London: Dent

Chodorow, N. (1978) *The Reproduction of Mothering: Psychoanalysis and the Sociology of Gender* Berkeley: University of California Press

Cixous, H. (1979) 'Rethinking Difference: An Interview' in G. Stambolian and E. Marks (eds) *Homosexualities in French Literature: Cultural Contexts/Critical Texts* Ithaca, NY: Cornell University Press

—— (1980) 'The Laugh of the Medusa' in Marks and Courtivron (eds) *New French Feminisms*

—— (1981) 'Castration or Decapitation' *Signs* 7, 1, pp. 41–55

Cixous, H. and C. Clement (1975) *La jeune née* Paris:UGE

Clark, L.M. and L. Lange (eds) (1979) *The Sexism of Social and Political Theory: Women and Reproduction from Plato to Nietzsche* Toronto: University of Toronto Press

Collin, F. (1974) 'Nouveau feminisme, nouvelle société ou l'avènement de l'autre' *La Revue Nouvelle* 1, pp. 61–68

—— (1978) 'Au Revoir' *Les Cahiers du Grif* 23–24, pp. 5–23

Cooley, C. H. (1962) *Social Organization: a Study of the Larger Mind* New York: Schocken

Daly, M. (1978) *Gyn/Ecology: The Metaethics of Radical Feminism* Boston: Beacon Press

Daniels, K. (1977) Introduction to K. Daniels, M. Murnane and A. Picot *Women in Australia: An Annotated Guide to Records* vol. 1, Canberra: AGPS

—— (ed.) (1984) *So Much Hard Work: Women and Prostitution in Australian History* Melbourne: Fontana

Davin, A. (1972) 'Women in History' in M. Wandor (ed.) *The Body Politic: Women's Liberation in Britain 1969–1972* London: Stage 1

d'Eaubonne, F. (1980) 'Feminism or Death' in Marks and de Courtivron (eds) *New French Feminisms*

de Beauvoir, S. (1975) *The Second Sex* Harmondsworth: Penguin

Deleuze, G. (1962) *Nietzsche et la philosophie* Paris: PUF

—— (1968) *Spinoza* Paris: Minuit

—— (1969) *Logique du sens* Paris: Minuit

Denzin, N.K. (1983) 'A Note on Emotionality, Self, and Interaction' *American Journal of Sociology* 89, pp. 402–410

Derrida, J. (1972) *Marges* Paris: Minuit

—— (1976) *Of Grammatology* Baltimore: Johns Hopkins University Press

—— (1978a) *Éperons* Paris: Flammarion

—— (1978b) *Writing and Difference* London: Routledge & Kegan Paul

—— (1979) *Spurs: Nietzsche's Styles* Chicago: University of Chicago Press

—— (1981a) *Dissemination* Chicago: University of Chicago Press

—— (1981b) *Positions* London: Athlone Press

Descartes, R. (1970) *Philosophical Works* vol. 1, transl. E.S. Haldane and G.R.T. Ross, London: Cambridge University Press

Deutsch, H. (1945) *The Psychology of Women* New York: Grune & Stratton

Dinnerstein, D. (1976) *The Rocking of the Cradle and the Ruling of the World* London: Souvenir Press

—— (1977) *The Mermaid and the Minotaur* New York: Harper & Row

Dubois, E. and L. Gordon (1983) 'Seeking Ecstasy on the Battlefield: Danger and Pleasure in Nineteenth-Century Feminist Thought' *Feminist Studies 9*, 1, pp. 1–26

Durkheim, E. (1951) *Suicide* New York: Free Press

—— (1957) *Professional Ethics and Civic Morals* London: Routledge & Kegan Paul

—— (1960) 'The Dualism of Human Nature' in K.H. Wolff *Emile Durkheim, 1858–1917* Columbus: Ohio State University Press

—— (1961) *Moral Education* New York: Free Press

—— (1964a) *The Division of Labor in Society* New York: Free Press

—— (1964b) *The Rules of Sociological Method* New York: Free Press

Ehrenreich, B. and D. English (1979) *For Her Own Good: 150 Years of the Experts' Advice to Women* London: Pluto Press

Eisenstein, H. and A. Jardine (1980) *The Future of Difference* Boston: G.K. Hall and Barnard Women's College

Eisenstein, Z.R. (1981) *The Radical Future of Liberal Feminism* New York: Longman; reprint (1986) Boston: Northeastern Univ. Press

Elshtain, J. (1981) *Public Man, Private Woman: Women in Social and Political Thought* Princeton, NJ: Princeton University Press

Elton, G.R. (1967) *The Practice of History* Melbourne: Fontana

Faderman, L. (1981) *Surpassing the Love of Men* New York: William Morrow & Co.

Feyerabend, P.K. (1975) *Against Method* London: New Left Books

Finn, G. and A. Miles (eds) (1982) *Feminism in Canada: From Pressure to Politics* Montreal: Black Rose Books

Finnegan, F. (1979) *Poverty and Prostitution: A Study of Victorian Prostitutes in York* Cambridge: Cambridge University Press

Finzi Ghisi, V. (ed.) (1978) *Crisi del sapere e nuova razionalita* Bari: De Donato

Firestone, S. (1970) *The Dialectic of Sex: The Case for Feminist Revolution* New York: Bantam Books

Flax, J. (1980) 'Mother–Daughter Relationships: psychodynamics, politics and philosophy' in Eisenstein and Jardine (eds) *The Future of Difference*
—— (1983) 'Political Philosophy and the Patriarchal Unconscious: A Psychoanalytic Perspective on Epistemology and Metaphysics' in Harding and Hintikka (eds) *Discovering Reality*

Foreman, A. (1977) *Femininity as Alienation* London: Philo Press

Foucault, M. (1972) *The Archaeology of Knowledge* New York: Harper & Row
—— (1976) *Discipline and Punish* New York: Pantheon Books
—— (1976) *L'Histoire de la sexualité* vol. 1, Paris: Gallimard
—— (1984a) *L'Histoire de la sexualité* vol. 2, Paris: Gallimard
—— (1984b) *L'Histoire de la sexualité* vol. 3, Paris: Gallimard
—— (1978) *The History of Sexuality* vol. 1, New York: Pantheon Books

Fox-Genovese, E. (1982) 'Placing Women's History in History' *New Left Review* 133, May–June, pp. 5–24

Freud, S. (1900) *The Interpretation of Dreams* Standard Edition vol. 5, ed. S.F. Strachey. London: Hogarth Press
—— (1905) 'Three Essays on the Theory of sexuality' Standard Edition vol. 7
—— (1925) 'Some Psychical Consequences of the anatomical differences between the sexes' in SE vol. 19
—— (1930) 'Civilisation and its Discontents' in SE vol. 21
—— (1932) 'Femininity' in New Introductory Lectures to Psychoanalysis in SE vol. 21

Gadamer, H. -G. (1976) 'Hegel's Dialectic of Self-consciousness' in *Hegel's Dialectic: Five Hermeneutical Studies* transl. P.C. Smith, New Haven and London: Yale University Press, pp. 54–74

Gallop, J. (1982) *Feminism and Psychoanalysis: The Daughter's Seduction* London: Macmillan

Garrison, D. (1981) 'Karen Horney and Feminism' *Signs* 6, 4, pp. 681–90

Gatens, M. (1983) 'A Critique of the Sex/Gender Distinction' in J. Allen and P. Patton (eds) *Beyond Marxism? Interventions After Marx* Sydney: Intervention Publications, pp. 143–63
—— (forthcoming) 'Rousseau and Wollstonecraft: Nature vs Reason' *Australasian Journal of Philosophy* Special Issue: Women and Philosophy

Goldman, M.S. (1981) *Gold-Diggers and Silverminers: Prostitution and Society on the Comstock Lode* Ann Arbor: University of Michigan Press

Gordon, C. (1980) *Power/Knowledge* New York: Pantheon Books

Gordon, L. (1982) 'Why Nineteenth Century Feminists Did Not Support "Birth Control" and Twentieth Century Feminists Do: Feminism, Reproduction and the Family' in B. Thorne and M. Yalom (eds) *Rethinking the Family: Feminist Questions* New York: Longmans

Goreau, A. (1985) *The Whole Duty of a Woman: Female Writers in Seventeenth Century England* New York: Dial Press

Gould, C. (1980) 'Philosophy of Liberation and the Liberation of Philosophy' in Gould and Wartofsky (eds) *Women and Philosophy*

Gould, C. and M.W. Wartofsky (eds) (1976) *Women and Philosophy:*

Toward a Theory of Liberation New York: Capricorn Press

Gould, M. (1980) 'Review Essay: The New Sociology' *Signs* 5, pp. 459–68

Gross, E. (1982) 'Women and Writing: The Work of Kristeva in Perspective' *Refractory Girl Writes* 23, pp. 28–36

—— (1983) The Body of Woman: Psychoanalysis and Foucault, unpublished paper

Habermas, J. (1979) *Communication and the Evolution of Society* transl. Thomas McCarthy, London: Heinemann

Harding, S. and M. Hintikka (1983) *Discovering Reality: Feminist Perspectives on Epistemology, Metaphysics, Methodology and Philosophy of Science* New York: Reidel

Hartsock, N. (1982) Prologue to a Feminist Critique of War and Politics, paper presented to 12th World Congress, International Political Science Association, Rio de Janeiro, Brazil, 1982 (forthcoming in Judith Stiehm (ed.) *Women Look at the Political World of Men* New York: Transnational Publishers); reprint (1985) Boston: Northeastern Univ. Press

—— (1983) *Money, Sex, and Power: Toward a Feminist Historical Materialism* New York: Longman

Hatfield, E.J. Traupmann and G.W. Walster (1979) 'Equity and Extramarital Sex' in Mark Cook and Glenn Wilson (eds) *Love and Attraction* Oxford: Pergamon Press

Heath, S. (1978) 'Difference' *Screen* 19, 3, pp. 51–113

—— (1982) *The Sexual Fix* London: Macmillan

Hegel, G.W.F. (1977) *Phenomenology of Spirit* transl. A.V. Miller, Oxford: Clarendon Press

—— (1978) *Philosophy of Right* transl. T.M. Knox, Oxford and New York: Oxford University Press

Hicks N. (1978) *'This Sin and Scandal': Australia's Population Debate 1891–1911* Canberra: Australian National University Press

Hobbes, T. (1968) *Leviathan* ed. C.B. Macpherson, Harmondsworth: Penguin

Hochschild, A.R. (1976) 'The Sociology of Feelings and Emotion: Selected Possibilities' in M. Millman and R.M. Kanter *Another Voice: Feminist Perspectives on Social Life and Social Science* New York: Octagon

Horney, K. (1927) 'The Flight From Womanhood: the Masculinity Complex in Women, as viewed by men and women' *International Journal of Psychoanalysis* 7, pp. 320–27

Houghton, W. (1978) *The Victorian Frame of Mind 1830–1870* New Haven: Yale University Press

Hughes, P. (1979) 'The Reality vs the Ideal: J.S. Mill's treatment of Women, Workers and Private Property' *Canadian Journal of Political Science* 12, 3, pp. 523–42

Huilgol, G. (1979) 'Psychodynamics of Nayar Family Life: the Matrilineal Puzzle Re-examined' *Women's Sociological Bulletin* 1, 3, pp. 2–14

Huston, T. and R. Cate (1979) 'Social Exchange in Intimate Relationships' in M. Cook and G. Wilson (eds) *Love and Attraction* Oxford: Pergamon Press

Irigaray, L. (1974) *Speculum de l'autre femme* Paris: Minuit

—— (1977a) *Ce Sexe qui n'en est pas un* Paris: Minuit

—— (1977b) 'Women's Exile' *Ideology and Consciousness* 1, pp. 62–77

—— (1978) 'That Sex Which is Not One' in P. Foss and M. Morris (eds) *Language, Sexuality and Subversion* Sydney: Feral Publications

—— (1980) 'When Our Two Lips Speak Together' *Signs* 6, 1, pp. 69–79.
—— (1981a) 'And One Doesn't Stir Without the Other' *Signs* 7, 1, pp. 60–67
—— (1981b) *Le Corps-à-corps avec la mère* Montreal: La Pleine Lune
—— (1981c) 'This Sex Which is Not One' in Marks and de Courtivron *New French Feminisms*
—— (1984) *L'Ethique de la différence sexuelle* Paris: Minuit
—— (1985a) *Speculum of the Other Woman* Ithaca, NY: Cornell University Press
—— (1985b) *This Sex Which is Not One* Ithaca, NY: Cornell University Press
Jameson, G. (1981) *The Political Unconscious: Narrative as a Social Symbolic Act* London: Methuen
Janeway, E. (1980) 'Who is Sylvia? On the Loss of Sexual Paradigms' *Signs* 5, 4, pp. 576–82
Jardine, A. (1982) 'Gynesis' *Diacritics* 12, pp. 54–65
Jay, N. (1981) 'Gender and Dichotomy' *Feminist Studies* 7, 1, pp. 38–56
Jeffreys, S. (1982) 'Women's Campaigns Around Sexuality 1880–1914' in E. Sarah (ed.) *Re-assessments of 'First Wave' Feminism*, special issue of *Women's Studies International Forum* 5, 6, Oxford: Pergamon Press
—— (1983) 'Sex Reform and Anti-feminism' in London Feminist History Group (ed.) *The Sexual Dynamics of History* London: Pluto Press
Judt, A. (1979) 'A Clown in Regal Purple: Social History and the Historians' *History Workshop* 7, Spring, pp. 64–93
Kant, E. (1952) *Critique of Judgment* Part I, Book II, Analytic of the Sublime, section 28, transl. J.C. Meredith. Oxford: Oxford University Press, pp. 112–13
Kearns, D. (1983) 'A Theory of Justice and Love: Rawls on the Family' *Politics* 18, 2, pp. 36–42
Knight, P. (1977) 'Women and Abortion in Victorian and Edwardian England' *History Workshop* 4, Autumn, pp. 57–68
Koedt, A., E. Levine and A. Rapone (1973) *Radical Feminism* New York: Quadrangle Press
Kollantai, A. (1972) *Love and the New Moralism* Bristol: Fallingwall Press
Kristeva, J. (1973) 'Unes femmes' *Les Cahiers du Grif* 7, pp. 22–27
—— (1976) 'Signifying Practice and Mode of Production *Edinburgh Review* 1, pp. 64–77
—— (1977) *Polylogues* Paris: Seuil
—— (1980) *Desire in Language* New York: Columbia University Press
—— (1981) 'Women's Time' *Signs* 7, 1, pp. 13–20
—— (1982) *The Powers of Horror. An Essay on Abjection* New York: Columbia University Press
—— (1984) *The Revolution in Poetic Language* New York: Columbia University Press
Krueger, B. (1983) *We Won't Play Nature to Your Culture* London: Institute of the Contemporary Arts
Lacan, J. (1966) *Écrits* Paris: Seuil
—— (1978a) *Écrits. A Selection* London: Tavistock
—— (1978b) *The Four Fundamental Concepts of Psychoanalysis* Oxford: Blackwells
—— (1982) *Feminine Sexuality. Jacques Lacan and the École Freudienne* eds J. Mitchell and J. Ross, London: Macmillan

Lasch, C. (1977) *Haven in a Heartless World: The Family Besieged* New York: Basic Books

Le Doeuff, M. (1977) 'Women and Philosophy' *Radical Philosophy* 17, Summer, pp. 2–11

—— (1979) 'Operative Philosophy: Simone de Beauvoir and Existentialism' *Ideology and Consciousness* 6, Autumn, pp. 47–57

—— (1980) *Recherches sur l'imaginaire philosophique* Paris: Payot

—— (1981–82) 'Pierre Roussel's Chiasmas' *Ideology and Consciousness* 9, pp. 39–70

Le Guin, U. (1975) *Left Hand of Darkness* St Albans, Hertfordshire: Panther

Leach, W. (1980) *True Love and Perfect Union: The Feminist Reform of Sex and Society* New York: Basic Books

Lekachman, R. (1975) 'On Economic Equality' *Signs* 1, 1, pp. 93–102

Levine, L. (1984) 'The Limits of Feminism' *Social Analysis* 15, pp. 11–19

Lloyd, G. (1979) 'The Man of Reason' *Metaphilosophy* 1

—— (1983a) 'Masters, Slaves and Others' *Radical Philosophy* 34, Summer, pp. 2–9

—— (1983b) 'Public Reason and Private Passion' *Politics* 18, 1, pp. 27–35

—— (1983c) 'Rousseau on Reason, Nature and Women' *Metaphilosophy* 14, 3–4, pp. 308–326

—— (1984) *The Man of Reason: 'Male' and 'Female' in Western Philosophy* London: Methuen

Locke, J. (1976) *Two Treatises of Government* ed. P. Laslett, Cambridge: Cambridge University Press

Lonzi, M. (1974) *Sputiamo su Hegel* Milan: Rivolta Femminile

—— (1977) *E già politica* Milan: Rivolta Femminile

Lukacs, G. (1971) *History and Class Consciousness* London: Martin Press

Lyotard, J.F. (1978) 'One of the things at stake in women's struggle' *Sub-stance* 20, pp. 9–19.

—— (1979) *La condition post-moderne* Paris: Minuit

McCormack, T. (1981) 'Good Theory or Just Theory?: Towards a Feminist Philosophy of Social Science' *Women's Studies International Quarterly* 4, 1, pp. 1–12

McLaren, A. (1977) 'Women's Work and the Regulation of Family Size' *History Workshop* 4, Autumn, pp. 70–79

—— (1978) *Birth Control in Nineteenth Century England* London: Croom Helm

McLennan, G. (1981) *Marxism and the Methodologies of History* London: Verso and New Left Books

McMillan, C. (1982) *Women, Reason and Nature: Some Philosophical Problems with Feminism* Oxford: Blackwell

Maine, H.S. (1963) *Ancient Law* Boston: Beacon Press

March, A. (1982) 'Female Invisibility in Androcentric Sociological Theory' *Insurgent Sociologist* 11, 2, pp. 99–107

Marini, M. (1978) 'Scandaleusement autre' *Critique* 373, pp. 603–622

Marks, E. and I. de Courtivron (1981) *New French Feminisms* Brighton: Harvester Press

Martin, R. (1980) 'Hobbes and the Doctrine of Natural Rights: The Place of Consent in his Political Philosophy' *Western Political Quarterly* 33, 3, pp. 380–92

Marx, K. (1954) *Capital* vol. 1, Moscow: Foreign Languages Publishing House
—— (1970) *The German Ideology* London: Lawrence & Wishart
Marx, K. and F. Engels (1978a) *German Ideology* in R.C. Tucker (ed.) *The Marx–Engels Reader* New York: W.W. Norton & Co.
—— (1978b) *Communist Manifesto* in Tucker (ed.) *The Marx–Engels Reader*
Matthews, J.J. (1984) *Good and Mad Women* Sydney: Allen & Unwin
Mead, M. (1962) *Male and Female: A Study of the Sexes in a Changing World* Harmondsworth: Penguin
Melandri, L. (1977) *L'infamia originaria* Milan: L'Erba Voglio
Merchant, C. (1980) *The Death of Nature: Women and the Scientific Revolution* San Francisco: Harper & Row
Midgley, M. and J. Hughes (1983) *Women's Choices: Philosophical Problems Facing Feminism* London: Weidenfeld & Nicolson
Mill, J.S. (1972) *Utilitarianism, On Liberty and Considerations on Representative Government* London: J.M. Dent & Sons
—— (1977 (1835)) 'Rationale of Representation' in J.M. Robson (ed.) *Essays on Politics and Society* Toronto: University of Toronto Press
—— (1980) (1869)) *The Subjection of Women* Illinois: AHM Publishing
Mill, J.S. and H.T. Mill (1970) *Essays on Sex Equality* ed. A. Rossi, Chicago: The University of Chicago Press
Miller, P. and M. Fowlkes (1980) 'Social and Behavioural Constructions of Female Sexuality' *Signs* 5, 4, pp. 785–90
Millett, K. (1970) *Sexual Politics* New York: Virago Press
—— (1974) *Flying* New York: Paladin Press
Mills, P.J. (1979) 'Hegel and "The Woman Question": Recognition and Intersubjectivity' in Clark and Lange *The Sexism of Social and Political Theory*
Mitchell, J. (1974) *Psychoanalysis and Feminism* London: Allen Lane
Mitchell, J. and J. Rose (1982) *Feminine Sexuality* London: Macmillan
Moller-Okin, S. (1979a) 'Rousseau's Natural Woman' *Journal of Politics* 41, pp. 393–416
—— (1979b) *Woman in Western Political Thought* Princeton: Princeton University Press
—— (1980) *Woman in Western Political Thought* London: Virago Press
—— (1984) Justice and Gender, paper presented at the Annual Meeting of the American Political Science Association, Washington, DC
Montrelay, M. (1977) *L'Ombre et le nom* Paris: Minuit
Morris, M. (1979) 'The Pirate's Fiancée' in M. Morris and P. Patton (eds) *M. Foucault: Power, Truth, Strategy* Sydney: Feral Publications
—— (1981–82) 'Operative Reasoning: Michele Le Doeuff, philosophy and feminism' *Ideology and Consciousness* 9, pp. 71–101
—— (forthcoming) 'Identity Anecdotes' in *Camera Obscura*
Munz, P. (1979) 'Cast a Cold Eye' in J.A. Moses (ed.) *Historical Disciplines and Culture in Australia* St Lucia: University of Queensland Press
Nicholson, L. (1981) '"The Personal is Political": an analysis in retrospect' *Social Theory and Practice* 7, 1, pp. 96–100
—— (1983) 'Women, Morality and History' *Social Research* 50, pp. 514–37
Nin, A. (1976) 'Eroticism in Women' in *In Favour of the Sensitive Man and*

Other Essays London: Harcourt Brace

Oakley, A. (1972) *Sex, Gender and Society* London: Temple Smith

O'Brien, M. (1981) *The Politics of Reproduction* London: Routledge & Kegan Paul

Offen, K. (1985) 'Toward An Historical Definition of Feminism: the Contribution of France', Working Paper No. 22, Center for Research on Women, Stanford University

Owens, C. (1983) 'The discourse of others—feminists and post-modernism' in H. Foster (ed.) *The Anti-Aesthetic* Washington, DC: Bay Press

Parsons, T. (1949) *Essays in Sociological Theory* rev. edn, New York: Free Press

—— (1951) *The Social System* New York: Free Press

—— (1964) *Social Structure and Personality* New York: Free Press

—— (1968) *The Structure of Social Action* New York: Free Press

Parsons, T. and R.F. Bales (1955) *Family, Socialization and the Interaction Process* New York: Free Press

Pascoe, R. (1979) *The Manufacture of Australian History* Melbourne: Oxford University Press

Pateman, C. (1980a) 'Women and Consent' *Political Theory* 8, 2, pp. 149–68

—— (1980b) ' "The Disorder of Women": Women, Love and the Sense of Justice' *Ethics* 91, pp. 20–34

—— (1983a) 'Defending Prostitution: Charges Against Ericsson' *Ethics* 93, April

—— (1983b) 'Feminist Critiques of the Public/Private Dichotomy' in S. Benn and G. Gaus (eds) *Public and Private in Social Life* Canberra and London: Croom Helm

—— (1983c) The Impact of Feminism on Political Theory, paper presented to Section 44, 53rd ANZAAS Congress, Perth

—— (1984) The Fraternal Social Contract: Some Observations on Patriarchy, paper presented at the Annual Meeting of the American Political Science Association Washington, DC

Pengelly, B. (1981) Durkheim's *Suicide*: Social life without women, unpublished paper, Murdoch University

Perkins, R. and G. Bennett (1985) *Being a Prostitute: Prostitute Women and Prostitute Men* Sydney: Allen & Unwin

Person, E. (1980) 'Sexuality as the mainstay of identity: psychoanalytic perspectives' in C.R. Stimpson and E. Person *Women, Sex and Sexuality* Chicago: University of Chicago Press

Philips, D. (1978) *Crime and Authority in Victorian England* London: Croom Helm

Pitkin, H.F. (1984) *Fortune is a Women: Gender and Politics in the Thought of Niccolo Machiavelli* Berkeley: University of California Press

Plato (1970) *The Complete Texts of Great Dialogues of Plato* transl. W.H.D. Rouse, New York: New American Library

—— (1974) *The Republic* Harmondsworth: Penguin

Rawls, J. (1972) *A Theory of Justice* Oxford: Clarendon Press

Rella, F. (1978) *Il mito dell'altro* Milan: Feltrinelli

Rich, A. (1976) *Of Woman Born* New York: Norton & Co.

—— (1978) 'Natural Resources' in *Dream of a Common Language* New

York: Norton & Co.
—— (1979) *On Lies, Secrets and Silence* New York: Norton & Co.
Richards, J.R. (1982) *The Sceptical Feminist: A Philosophical Enquiry* Harmondsworth: Penguin
Rorty, R. (1980) *Philosophy and the Mirror of Nature* Oxford: Blackwell
Rose, J. (1983) 'Feminity and its discontent' *Feminist Review* 14, pp. 5–21
Rosen, R. (1983) *The Lost Sisterhood: Prostitution in America 1900–1918* Baltimore: Johns Hopkins University Press
Rousseau, J.J. (1911) *Emile* transl. B. Foxley, London: J.M. Dent & Sons
Rovatti, P.A. (1979) 'Dai bisogni alle nuova razionalita' *Aut-Aut* 170–71, pp. 2–26
Rubin, G. (1975) 'The Traffic in Women: Notes Toward a Political Economy of Sex' in Rayne Reiter (ed.) *Toward An Anthropology of Women* New York: Monthly Review Press
Ruddick, S. (1982) 'Maternal Thinking' *Feminist Studies* 6, 2, pp. 342–69
—— (1983) 'Drafting Women in the Interests of Peace' *Signs* 8, 3, pp. 471–89
Salleh, K. (1984) 'Contribution to the Critique of Political Epistemology' *Thesis Eleven* 8, pp. 23–43
Sartre, J.P. (1964) *Saint Genet: Actor and Martyr* New York: Plume Books
—— (1977) *Being and Nothingness* London: Methuen
Simms, M. (1981) 'Political Science, Women and Feminism' *Politics* 16, 2, pp. 318–24
Singer, P. (1981) *The Expanding Circle: Ethics and Sociobiology* New York: Farrar, Straus & Giroux
Smith, D. (1979) 'A Sociology for Women' in J.A. Sherman and E.T. Beck (eds) *The Prism of Sex: Essays in the Sociology of Knowledge* Madison: University of Wisconsin Press
Smith, F.B. (1979) *The People's Health 1830–1910* London: Croom Helm
Smith, H. (1976) 'Feminism and the Methodologies of Women's History' in B.A. Carroll (ed.) *Liberating Women's History* Urbana: University of Illinois Press
Snitow, A., C. Stansell and S. Thompson (eds) (1983) *Powers of Desire* New York: Monthly Review Press
Solanas, V. (1969) 'The S.C.U.M. Manifesto' in B. Roszack and T. Roszack (eds) *Masculine/Feminine* New York: Harper & Row
Spender, D. (1980) *Man Made Language* London: Routledge & Kegan Paul
—— (1982) *Women of Ideas (and What Men Have Done to Them)* London: Routledge & Kegan Paul
Starrett, B. (1976) *I Dream in Female* San Francisco: Cassandra Publications
Tavris, C. and C. Offir (1977) *The Longest War: Sex Differences in Perspective* New York: Harcourt Brace
Tax, M. (1973) 'Woman and her Mind' in A. Koedt, E. Levine and A. Rapone (eds) *Radical Feminism New York:* Quadrangle Press
Tenenbaum, S. (1982) 'Women through the Prism of Political Thought' *Polity* 15, pp. 90–102
Thompson, E.P. (1983) interview, 'E.P. Thompson' in Mid-Atlantic Radical Historians Association (ed.) *Visions of History* New York: Pantheon Books
Thompson, J. (1983) 'Women and the High Priests of Reason' *Radical Philosophy* 34, pp. 10–14

Thomson, D. (1969) *The Aims of History* London: Thames & Hudson

Ti-Grace Atkinson (1975) *L'odyssée d'une amazone* Paris: Des Femmes

Toennies, F. (1963) *Community and Society: Gemeinschaft and Gesellschaft* New York: Harper Torch Books

Trebilcot, J. (1984) *Mothering: Essays in Feminist Theory* Totowa, NJ: Rowan & Allenheld

Vetterling-Braggin, M., F. Elliston and J. English (eds) (1978) *Feminism and Philosophy* New York: Littlefield, Adams & Co.

Vicinus, M. (1982) 'Sexuality and Power' *Feminist Studies* 8, 1, pp. 136–42

Walkowitz, J.R. (1980) *Prostitution and Victorian Society: Women, Class and the State* Cambridge: Cambridge University Press

—— (1983) 'Male Vice and Female Virtue: Feminism and the Politics of Prostitution in Nineteenth Century Britain' in Snitow, Stansell and Thompson (eds) *Powers of Desire*

Ward, E. (1984) *Father–Daughter Rape* London: Virago Press

Watson, L. (1984) An Aboriginal Perspective on Australian Feminism, paper presented at 4th Women and Labour Conference, Brisbane

Weber, M. (1958) *The Protestant Ethic and the Spirit of Capitalism* New York: Scribner's

—— (1978) *Economy and Society* vol. 1, Berkeley: University of California Press

Webley, I. (1984) The Challenge of Ethnicity to Feminist Thought, paper presented at 4th Women and Labour Conference, Brisbane

Weeks, J. (1981) *Sex, Politics and Society: The Regulation of Sexuality Since 1800* London: Longmans

Wilden, A. (1972) *System and Structure: Essays in Communication and Exchange* London: Tavistock

—— (1981) *Speech and Language in Psychoanalysis* Baltimore: Johns Hopkins University Press

Wollstonecraft, M. (1967) *A Vindication of the Rights of Woman* New York: Norton & Co.

—— (1975) *A Vindication of the Rights of Woman* Harmondsworth: Penguin

Woolf, V. (1928) *A Room of One's Own* Harmondsworth: Penguin

—— (1938) *Three Guineas* Harmondsworth: Penguin

Wrong, D. (1961) 'The Over-Socialized Conception of Man' *American Sociological Review* 26, pp. 183–92

Yeatman, A. (1984a) 'Despotism and Civil Society: the Limits of Patriarchal Citizenship' in J.H. Stiehm (ed.) *Women's Views of the Political World of Men* New York: Transnational

—— (1984b) 'Introduction: Gender and Social Life' *Social Analysis* 15, pp. 3–11

—— (1984c) 'Gender and the Differentiation of Social Life into Public and Domestic Domains' *Social Analysis* 15, pp. 32–50

Zaretsky, E. (1976) *Capitalism, the Family and Personal Life* London: Pluto Press

—— (1981) review of William Leach *True Love and Perfect Union: The Feminist Reform of Sex and Society Signs* 7, 1, pp. 230–33

Zehr, H. (1977) *Crime and the Development of Modern Society* London: Croom Helm